TALES FROM BEHIND THE CHAIR

Steve Molloy

2QT (Publishing) Ltd

First Edition published 2014 by
2QT Limited (Publishing)
Lancaster, Lancashire LA2 8RE

Publisher Disclaimer:
The events in this memoir are described according to the Author's
recollection, recognition and understanding of the events and
individuals mentioned, and are in no way intended to mislead or
offend. As such the Publisher does not hold any responsibility for
any inaccuracies, views or opinions expressed by the author. Every
effort has been made to acknowledge and gain any permission from
organisations and persons mentioned in this book. Any enquiries
should be directed to the author.

Cover image of Preston Bus Station © Steve Molloy
Illustrations: Chris O'Flaherty
Illustrations © Steve Molloy

Printed by in Great Britain by Lightning Source UK

A CIP catalogue record for this book is available
from the British Library

ISBN 978-1-910077-19-1

Dedication

For my Grandchildren,
Victoria, Callum, & Phoebe Mae
And whoever comes along thereafter!

Pops not only is daft, he can write as well!

Contents

Contents continued/...

Biography

Steve Molloy was born at a very early age in a rural village in Lancashire to a loving family. Although he didn't miss a day of his schooling life he was found wanting when it came to exams. He left school in 1969 to become an apprentice hairdresser where upon he gave his life to cutting hair and serving the public. He now lives on the outskirts of Preston, the town he grew up in, learning his trade and where all the tales and his life experiences stem from.

Married to Jean for over 35 years, he is a proud father of two daughters and granddad (pops) to three grandchildren (at present).

In 1977 the business opened a new salon in a massive, and what is now the iconic bus station in Preston. It was at the time, considered a gamble to open a hairdresser's in a bus station, however it still thrives today after 35 years!

Outside of cutting hair Steve has been a football referee in local amateur football for over 35 years, and has, over the last 19 years, also climbed every 'Wainwright' summit in the Lake District. He also tries very hard to master the art of golf.

Acknowledgements

The bloke that wrote this book is the same person that cuts hair, listens to people all day long, and talks all sorts of stuff to anybody that wants their haircut. The same bloke wrote every word to every tale in this entire book because that was what he wanted to do. A project, a labour of love, a challenge to complete, although my timing to finish the project went well out of the window.

When I started, I didn't really know whether I would finish it and if I did finish it when that would be. I had tales written all over the place, exercise books, scrap paper, toilet paper, you couldn't open the computer without a chapter confronting you at every click of this damn mouse. The tales were saved on hard drives, pen drives, memory sticks, floppy discs, yes floppy discs; the book goes that far back! Because I wasn't a writer and I didn't know what the hell I was doing, I would either save the chapter and not put a name to the work or I would save the work and use the same name for everything. Confused... I was. After over eight years my ink started to dry up in my John Bull Printing Set and I figured it was time to draw a line under this literal assignment. Up to then I hadn't needed anybodies assistance it was all my own work but having over 90,000 words written down in some sort of disarray, reality dawned; I had gone as far as I could. I needed help. That help came from my true friend Paul Livesey who I am much indebted to for his literacy skills and experience of the English language, not to mention his patience for not strangling the author.

When some sort of organisation had been achieved I thought the pages to this book I had pictured in my mind needed something special to break the monotony of just plain print. That is where another good friend of the family came to put that special touch to my book. Give Chris O'Flaherty a pencil and paper and plenty of beer and with his ideas he has lit the blue touch paper with some outstanding artwork. Thanks Chris. It's my round in the Black Bull.

The jigsaw was coming together piece by piece and I then went out looking for a publisher. I met with many but my publisher I chose has helped me through the maze, thank you Catherine and your team at 2QT.

The front cover had to grab the reader; obviously it had to have a chair somewhere on the cover but I thought it would look the part with the iconic bus station in the background. Thanks to Steve O for pushing my trusted chair around the bus station looking for a front cover. We got some strange looks!

Believe it or not my family haven't read this book yet! They have encouraged me over the years, they have heard many of the tales but no doubt when they do read it I could have some explaining to do. Thanks to Jean and all my family for all your help and support, you have made me the man I am today… skint!

The book is about the public and everyday lives. Thanks to the 'big boss man' for choosing my job to deal with the public.

Steve Molloy writing a book? Can he write?

He wasn't clever at school, and when he left school he only finished up as a barber; he would do well to write his own name let alone write a book. If he's ever finished a book he would have done it with coloured pencils.

I think our Peter has more chance of becoming a chef than our Stephen becoming a hairdresser.

Run a business? No bloody chance - and he will never finish that book he's writing!

Just a few of the comments that I have heard during a lifetime of learning to grow up.

From the beginning I learned never to grow up, to do my best at whatever I enjoy doing, and to appreciate time with loved ones.

Preface

"HAIRCUT SIR.?"

On Tuesday 9th September 1969, I entered the wonderful and unexpected world of hairdressing. This job, career, occupation, profession, vocation has filled my working life with so much more pleasure, enjoyment and satisfaction than I could ever have anticipated. This roller-coaster ride of enjoyment and heartache, the desire to satisfy, the achievement of making a person you have never met and may never meet again look smart, stylish, clean and tidy gives me immense fulfilment; it did more than forty years ago and it still does to this very day. When anyone is dealing with the public, they should never expect the expected, but in no profession is this truer than in hairdressing. I take you, the reader, on this unpredictable voyage as I'm stood in very close proximity to my ever-faithful chair.

About this book

I cut hair and I don't profess to be a writer. I have written this book with my own slant on life. For many readers who know me, I have worded the book in such a way that hopefully you can imagine my voice telling you the stories as if you were sitting in my chair. If it doesn't come across that way then, ladies, just pretend it is Brad Pitt narrating the tales.

The book follows two paths: the odd chapters follow my life in hairdressing - choosing hairdressing as a career, my apprenticeship, the circumstances behind my two-hour ungainly haircut, an interruption in the business, and my own unparalleled cock-ups. The even chapters contain the many tales that have happened in my business or relate to customers or associates I have encountered along the way. The tales in this book are all genuine; I have either witnessed what happened or I am quite convinced that the people who told their amazing stories were telling the truth. I have to admit I may have put details of two or three tales together so as to protect certain people from total ridicule. All the names, and some relevant details, have been changed to avoid embarrassment and broken windows in my salon. I suppose I could have called everybody Bob or Fred, but that would have diluted the tales somewhat.

At the start of each chapter there's a quote or expression (I like quotes), and at the end of each chapter there's a joke that tickled me. All hairdressers hear loads of jokes, and a hairdressing book written by a hairdresser wouldn't be complete without one or two. This book could be a close companion whilst you are sitting on the throne in the little boys' room.

I have purposely made the chapters short so that boredom doesn't set in and your legs don't go numb whilst sitting in the little boys' room doing what many of my customers do best. For me to read a book is quite an occasion but for me to write a book is incredible; providing he is still alive, I can't wait to tell my English teacher I wrote and completed a book without the help of coloured crayons.

It could be said that I tried and I failed when it comes to writing, but if something in this book makes you smile then, for me, I have achieved the goal I set out to accomplish.

I really do hope you enjoy reading ... *Tales from Behind the Chair.*

Steve.

"The best present you can give to your children is your time."

Chapter 1 - the early years

A well shorn Stephen Molloy
Aged 15, 1968.

Winter 1968

So tonight I have to rush home from school on me bike, have me tea quickly 'cause me dad is taking me for me haircut. Hope there's no long queue like last time, all night waiting, sat staring at all the other people waiting for their haircut, and me dad telling me to sit still, it'll be my go soon. More blokes with their kids walk in and I think, 'I'll be home before them.' The barber looks a really old man, he won't see eighty again. Tall, and he appears to stoop from his shoulders. He wears this grubby white overall buttoned over one shoulder, with a load of scissors and combs poking out of his breast pocket. A big black chair is situated in front of a large mirror, which is mucky from all the mis-aimed spraying from the smelly concoctions in all shapes and sizes of bottles.

There's only three more then it's my go. Not long now, although it seems a long time listening to that dreadful music. It's better when them noisy clippers clatter - at least it drowns the sound of Freddie and the Dreamers. Them grubby magazines have seen better days; who would want to read *National Geographic* or *Time* magazine? There's no *Playboy* or *Fiesta* mags to be seen, probably a good job really as me dad would give me a clout if I so much as glanced at one. Me next, but that could take ages, as the barber starts rabbiting on about football: Alex Dawson, Jimmy Greaves and Preston North End.

At long last it's my turn. I jump on this big chair with a warm seat and the barber pumps up the chair so my feet are dangling off the floor. "Short back and sides," my dad tells the barber. 'And sit still,' he tells me in his 'you will do as you're told' voice. I sit perfectly still and watch intently through the murky mirror at the barber's every move. I am not spoken to, as he thinks I don't know who Alex Dawson is, so his only communication with me is 'head down', 'head up' and 'sit still'. Them clippers don't half rattle round your ears. Snip, snip, and my fringe has now found a new home on the barber's floor, and that's me done.

I climb down from the big chair, knowing what a shorn sheep feels like. All that fuss, wait over an hour to sit still for five minutes, itch all the way home and look like all the other shorn sheep in the pen.

'Molloy... Stephen Molloy, are you with us?'

'Yer, yes sir,' I answer, not really knowing what the question was. I was on another planet, reminiscing about my earlier years after I remembered I had to go for a haircut that night.

'Right, Fourth Years, it's that time of year. Yes, it's decision time. No doubt you've all talked it over with your parents and you know which direction you want to take by the end of term this summer. All of you wanting to continue at school and go into the fifth year will meet in the Grand Hall at 1pm today. The rest of you will meet in Room 7, Mr Lloyd's room, also at 1pm. All clear…? Class dismissed.'

It is 9.45am and I have just over three hours to make a decision that could affect my whole working life.

If I continue at school, can I keep up ~~accerd academemackally ackademically~~? I mean really, I'm not that clever. If I leave school, what do I do? More to the point, what can I do?

Another year at school? The thought of it didn't scare me; in fact, I enjoyed school. The 9am to 3.30pm was good, I got on with all - well, most of - the teachers, got involved with most activities, although in the school play I was a tree, and standing on stage painted an awful brown with green leaves stuck to my body wasn't my idea of fun. Cricket - Second Team captain; scored a few goals for the football team; chess club - I was barred because I couldn't understand the difference between a castle and a bishop. And I held the privileged position of joint school bank manager with my mate Les; it was privileged because we missed lessons on Wednesday afternoons to cash up. If you have a go at every activity that's on offer, at least you can say you had a go. My biggest problem was the bits between the activities … those bloody lessons!

History was always a mystery. Why does anybody want to know why King Canute whipped the waves? Maths - what the hell were cosines and logarithms? I have never used them in cutting anybody's hair to this day. If the French spoke English, then there would be none of this masculine and feminine grammar jargon. English: *I before E except after C* … who the hell remembers that from school?

There should be lessons in common sense: if you drop it then pick it up; if it's cold outside then put yer coat on.

How about lessons in filling in forms? All your adult life you fill in forms for everything - passports, credit cards, car rental, insurance - they are part of everyday life. How about lessons in growing up, respecting other people, handling money, the correct way to handle alcohol, how to deal with falling in love, and the wonderful wake-up call when you have your own children.

I say this now as I have gone through the tunnel of ignorance and appeared at the other end a better person for it. I am sure that if at the age of fifteen the youngsters of today and tomorrow had just a small insight into what is to come, then they might be prepared for some of the mysteries of life.

Sorry, that's me just going off on one. You will find I do that quite often.

My years at school had not been much to write home about as far as academic qualifications were concerned. Although I had a very happy time, mainly due to a caring and strong family, the words 'clever' and 'intelligent' were never found in my pencil case, and 'university' was never in my vocabulary. To be fair, I was brought up quite strictly compared with today's standards, and I learned from a very early age to respect my parents or get a clout. I did as I was told: I always put on clean underpants before I went out just in case I was knocked down by a bus! (*The shame that would have been brought on our house if Stephen had had an accident, been taken to hospital and had skiddies on his underpants!*) I always ate all my crusts so one day I would have curly hair (*what good them bloody crusts did me - I was bald before me curls arrived*), and in junior school I always bought a picture of a little black baby from a wee small book to help poverty in a far away place.

School life started at the infants' in a tiny village in Lancashire. This quaint, picturesque village gave me a wonderful start to life, although because I was born there I didn't appreciate the surroundings - it just felt like home. I have many fond memories of a life I just took for granted. There was no hatred (every lad was your mate and all the girls were cissies), no racial tension due mainly to the fact that you rarely saw any non-white people, the sun shone in summer, it got cold and snowed in winter, and the word 'stress' hadn't been heard of.

School was a breeze most of the time; playing in sand and painting with those silly powder paints was fun, except when my mate Billy, who sat next to me, sneezed. I went home looking like I'd contracted yellow fever with spots.

As the work got harder, I found school was not all it was cracked up to be. Arithmetic was about counting with shells, boring as I thought, so I came up with the idea that if I *borrowed* a few shells every lesson, then I wouldn't have to do any more counting because there wouldn't be enough shells left to count... Oops!

I wasn't the brightest shell on the beach.

The times tables were becoming harder by the week as we learned higher numbers. When we got to eight, it was time for new measures. We all used to sing the tables parrot fashion in groups, 'Two times one is two, two times two is four,' and so on. With the arrival of eights, this was way above my head, so as the rest of the group sang the words I mimed and hummed the tune!

Every Christmas, parents would bring all sorts of food parcels for the annual Christmas Party, a major 'Jacob's Join' feast. Meat pies, paste butties, jellies of all colours, biscuits, all brought in the same brown paper bag. You can imagine the sight of butties squashed with strawberry jelly. The teachers had the unenviable task of making the long table covered in crepe paper look appetising for all the starving kids. There were no paper plates and plastic knives and forks, so you brought your own cutlery with strips of Elastoplast with your name inscribed in ballpoint pen for identification purposes. Father Christmas always arrived at the end of the party with presents for us all; we all knew it was Mr Davies from the Post Office but nobody would say in case you didn't get a present.

With my birthday being 13th August, the intake for the higher school was borderline, and I bet my mate Peter that I was going up to BIG school like him. He lost, I won. Where would I have been with another year of education at that tiny infants' school? Probably a heart surgeon or a helicopter pilot, but as common sense tells us: 'If there is nowt in th'ead to begin with then yel get nowt out of th'ead at th'end.'

I suppose I would have learned the words to those dreaded tables, although only up to twelve. The times tables stopped at twelve times twelve is one hundred and forty four.

Leaving infants' school to join junior school usually means going into the next building on the same site. In such a tiny village, we had to uproot and move half a mile to the east, not a great distance away but a vast change in a young lad's life. The school was very ancient by today's standards, with three classrooms for approximately one hundred children varying in age from eight to eleven. Wood-varnished tongue and groove flooring, large blackboards and coloured chalks; there wasn't a computer in sight. The 'mod cons' consisted of a large manual duplicator. This was used for all letters home and also the dreaded school report every year end. Your report comprised one sheet of A4 paper with all the subjects written down on the left side, a column for your exam mark, a column with position in class, a space for teacher's remarks and a tear-off strip at the bottom of the sheet for your parents to return after they had read the report, all written in purple that smelt of methylated spirit.

I had one teacher for all subjects; his remarks read 'Stephen's 100% attendance is a wonderful achievement. It would be in his interest to bring his brain with him on a more regular basis.'

'Just do your best. That's all you can do,' was always Mum's answer when exams came round. A clever woman, my mum - she knew Einstein didn't have his tea at our house. My target was to beat the school bully. On returning home with the report, I was pleased to say that: 'I am not bottom of the class, I am next to bottom, but I am next to top in fighting,' to which she replied: 'Let's fill in that return slip before your dad sees it'.

Looking back, I suppose I was very lucky when it came to being off school through illness; I was rarely ill. I remember having to go through the pain of a few injections for polio; years later the pain was withdrawn and we were given the vaccine on a sugar lump. Another visitor to our school was this huge lady nurse that seemed to take pleasure in ferreting through our hair. This lady must have trained with the Gestapo, as the words 'gentle' and 'caring' were definitely not in her vocabulary. If you were sent home with a letter, you were one of the chosen few on whom 'Nitty Nora' had detected some uninvited visitors.

Nothing like that today. No 'Nitty Nora' in schools today, and parents are very naive when it comes to head lice, so they take them to the hairdresser's. The hairdresser informs the parent, the parent is devastated, and the hairdresser loses a customer because they are too embarrassed to return to the same shop. Read on and you can have a real good scratch, as there are more head lice tales to be told!

If the whole class had been in school all week with no absences, we were allowed home an hour early on Friday afternoon. Something that regularly messed up our early Friday finish was that there was always somebody in the class who was having their tonsils out. What the heck were tonsils? The kids came back to school a week later and didn't look any different, but they had had their tonsils out. What were they, what had they had out? Being mates with some of the bigger boys in the school, we finally found out that when you had your tonsils out it could affect the voice. The bigger boys swore us to secrecy and told us that tonsils were the little 'nuts' under your willy and they took them out if you got a sore throat. When asked about girls' tonsils, we were told that theirs were inside so that's why you couldn't see them. I never had a sore throat till I left school, and still I wonder why I wasn't good in biology!

Living two miles away from school meant school dinners were mandatory. Meals consisted of mashed potato with something else and a pudding. Steamed pudding and custard were always favourites, but who the hell thought up that stupid concoction of semolina and jam or tapioca (we all called it frogspawn) and raisins? Keep drinking the water lad - it won't taste so bad then!

We had a large playing field next to the school yard. That's where I found that there was life after numbers and poetry, which were well down the batting order in my world. Sport played a big part in my life, and at the tender age of nine I went on to play and score for the school football team playing at a school near Chorley. We won 3-0.

Playing football in the rain was no problem, playing cricket in summer was enjoyable, even girly rounders was acceptable and running was cool, but who came up with the daft idea of country dancing when it was too wet? Bloody stupid, if you ask me. First you listen to that dreadful music, and then you have to find a girl partner; how bad is that? Then you have to hold their hand, now that is sick… And all because it's raining. We don't melt, and if we did it would be better than holding hands with a girl!

At the age of ten I sat the compulsory eleven-plus exams and, to nobody's surprise, I failed miserably. This exam was to sort out the 'wheat from the chaff'; in my case there wasn't even a harvest that year. Natural progression was to follow in my brother's footsteps and attend The Bishop Rawstorne Secondary School.

Big brother Peter went to this school and all my mates were going, so in hindsight it was a good job I cocked-up the exam. The local grammar schools were for the clever people, and anyway it was too far for me to travel on my bike.

I had just turned eleven years old, when September 1965 saw me make the major step from junior school to senior school. After being a large fish in a small pond, I was now a minnow in a huge ocean, and found it tough. Bishop Rawstorne School stood 250 yards away from my old school but it might as well have been on another planet - a massive establishment with a maze of many classrooms, hundreds of pupils and numerous teachers. Nobody said it was going to be easy; it was scary, it was terrifying but little did I know that this school was to give me the scaffolding on which to build a better, stronger person. Academically I was well down the train - probably very near the guard's van - but the next five years helped me to grow up and face the world and its many challenges.

My dad taught me irony:
Keep crying and I'll give you something to cry for!

My mum taught me about contortionism:
Will you look at the dirt on the back of your neck?

"The most important thing a father can do for his children is to love their mother."

Chapter 2 - Those precious little children

"That wasn't a fart lad.
In my game you call that a blow dry"

One of the good things about many gentlemen's hairdressing salons, including mine, is that we work on a 'walk in' basis, so appointments are not required. For me it works on two counts: firstly, my customers are happy to turn up at their leisure, sit and wait, or call back at a later time; secondly, my day is always a mystery waiting to unfold. I never know what the day will bring; I am in the dark when I enter the salon in the morning. For this reason alone my job is a bit special. With most jobs you know what you will be doing when you go into work that day: I will be cutting hair but I haven't a clue whose hair. Whether it be an old man, a policeman, an awkward individual, an actor performing at the local theatre or a screaming, fidgety child with sticky fingers and a smelly nappy, it's all in a day's work. Not knowing who is coming through your door is a bonus, as you are prepared for any eventuality. If they knew they were going to face a full day of appointments for the likes of mummy's teeny-weenie soldier, daddy's soccer-mad superstar or granny's spoilt little wonder boy, the suicide rate amongst hairdressers would escalate rapidly.

Cutting children's hair can be a good, bad or nightmare experience for both the recipient and the poor devil with the scissors, who has to use every last bit of skill, patience and persistence to accomplish the desired effect. Upset and bad feeling can be the cost of a child's haircut. When paying for any professional service, the major cost is the professional's time. A small amount may be for products used and business overheads, but mainly you are paying for time. That said, when you have spent ages cutting the hair of an uncontrollable little rebel, then you've really earned your money! To charge for the full time spent working would be off the scale, so we compromise on the bill, only to be told: 'That's quite expensive for a little lad.'

A colleague of mine used to say, 'When you can buy cheaper sausages for the kids at the butcher's, that's when I will do cheaper haircuts for kids!'

In general, most of the children are good fun and on many occasions they deliver the best lines of humour to help pass the day. Because of their age and innocence, children say it as they see it; they don't wrap anything up. It is purely black and white.

Little Ryan had come for his haircut in such a good mood, as grandad was taking him for a burger if he sat still and didn't talk the barber's head off; those were his instructions, as he had past history on previous visits. He climbed aboard my big chair, dressed in his football kit, still wearing his football boots and goalkeeper's gloves.

'Bet I know what you have been doing at school today,' I said to Ryan.

'Go on, guess.'

'I bet you've been playing football and I bet you were the goalkeeper.'

'How do you know that?' he asked.

I smiled.

'I am the bestest goalkeeper in our school, me is,' Ryan told me. 'Today we had a proper footie match and I had twenty shots kicked at me and I saved nineteen of 'em.'

'You must be a good keeper, Ryan. What was the score?' I asked.

'We made a draw - five each.'

You may see Ryan in years to come playing professional football, but I don't think he will make a mathematician.

Garth always had a lot to say for himself and I struggled to get a word in edgeways on numerous occasions. So when the peace was shattered by him and his mum, I knew I was in for some classic entertainment.

'Have you been a good lad for your mum, Garth?' I ask, knowing that he would come back with some priceless banter.

'Me mam's got herself pregnant again,' says Garth.

Now Garth is aged about seven, and I am rapidly searching for a reply to ease the embarrassment without making eye contact with mum.

'So you'll be having a new baby at your house for Christmas?' I say, trying my best to lighten the predicament.

'Fink so. Not bothered really. I'm geddin' a computer, so I won't have much time anyhow.'

'It would be nice to have a brother or sister at your house for Christmas,' I say encouragingly.

'Muuuuum, it won't be a girl, will it?'

'A tiny sister would be nice for you to look after, wouldn't it?' I say.

'Mum said she wasn't having any more babies. She said she had had enough with me and now she is having another. She is not having any more, because her feller has buggered off.'

'Big Mouth,' shouts his mum.

I quickly finish the haircut and keep all opinions to myself. Garth has now got a little brother that he thinks the world of.

Another 'little man with big mouth' occasion happened on a very busy Saturday morning when my usual calm exterior dissolved thanks to a little blighter aged seven. I don't think I deserved to be humiliated, humbled and embarrassed the way that I was. If kids see it, they say it. If they see gel on my shelf, they want some; if they see combs for sale, they want one.

I remember many years ago, when we were looking to buy a house, the wife and I took our children with us to visit a property. During the inspection of the bathroom, on spying the bidet, my little girl Emma asked the agent why there were two toilets. The agent bypassed the question as if he hadn't heard it. She asked again ever so politely: 'Why two toilets?' He told her that one wasn't a toilet; it was a bidet. She enquired: 'What is it for?' By now the agent was a little embarrassed, so I helped him out by saying it was for mum to wash her feet in. Emma was happy; case closed.

You have probably got the idea by now that, with the inquisitive kids, there is an invisible connecting rod that controls the mouth once the eyes have recognised an image.

Meanwhile, back to being humbled by 'junior rent-a-mouth'. Unfortunately, with this noisy, curious, meddling little mummy's treasure there was an invisible connecting rod from his nose that also controlled his mouth. Now it wasn't my fault that the Indian curry the previous evening had given me wind. I thought I was doing fine controlling my bottom burps, as nobody had said anything and nobody had fainted.

At one juncture, Junior had made a small murmur of disapproval, but I told him to put his head down and keep still. I thought this had worked, as I had almost finished the haircut, when from nowhere he shouted, 'Muuuuum, you'll never guess. Barber's just farted.'

Not only did all my customers hear his announcement, but I think the centre of Preston was made very much aware of where my Friday evening had been spent and what I had eaten.

There are very few places to hide on the salon floor, and there isn't much you can say once the world knows you have broken wind.

Nits are always a cause for concern and are more common on children than on adults. They are thought to be a disease that everybody else's kids contracts but never your own. If your child has them (*what shame*), then they must have been caught from the dirty kids at school. There are many myths about nits (or, to use the correct terminology, head lice) and one error is thinking they only infest dirty hair. Head lice will make contact with, and set up home in, any hair, clean or grubby, usually by head contact with other people with the infestation.

I have dealt with many cases of this annoying pest and, although it is not life-threatening, it is wise to eradicate it as soon as possible, if only for Mum's sanity. I feel as a professional I must inform a child's parent or guardian that unwanted squatters are in residence.

Common sense prevails. I don't shout out that the person has got nits or I'll be knocked down by the stampede of customers leaving my salon. I quietly inform the person concerned about my findings and give them some literature about how to eradicate the infestation - which I did when a young lady brought in a little lad for his haircut. The only disturbing issue was that as I was explaining that her son had contracted head lice, she told me she knew he had got them and had had them for over a month. She actually brought him for his haircut and knew he had head lice! Aren't some people thoughtful? You can stop scratching now.

Tales of such thoughtless people are few and far between, and to offset them there are many tales that show the better side of people. This particular day, the lad and dad combination were on their way home after young Robert had had a hard day at school, and decided to call for their haircuts. I was happily cutting Robert's hair and dad was having his haircut with Gary, my co-worker.

Robert was seven years old and a really grand lad; a little shy, he spoke only when spoken to. Throughout the haircut, he sat still and didn't say a word. Just as I was about to finish the haircut, he mumbled something that I failed to hear, so I asked him, 'What was that you were saying?'

'I am going to heaven one day,' Robert said quietly.

A little puzzled and wondering where this was leading, I asked, 'Where are you going, Robert?'

'I am going to heaven one day.'

Both his dad and I were a little mystified. Where on earth did that come from?

'So when will you be going to heaven, Robert?' I asked.

'It will be a long time off, but me dad will be going a lot sooner than me, 'cause he is a lot older than me. He's twenty-seven.'

What a classic line to a nice innocent tale. It transpires that on that particular day Robert had been doing scripture stories at school and the teacher had told them that one day, when they grew old, they would go to heaven; I think it was Robert's own conclusion that it would be dad's turn before his. After all, he was a very old twenty-seven.

All hairdressers have their own ways of dealing with children. If one attempt fails, then there are many more tricks in the box. I find a soft tone of voice and slow delicate movements often work. The less the hairdresser gets worked up, the less the child and parents get hot and bothered. Imagine it from the child's point of view: you sit on a big chair; then an unknown person covers you with what looks like a big table cloth; you are told to sit still whilst this person comes at you with a pair of scissors about which you have been told since you were big enough to stand up and open the cupboard drawer 'naughty, not to touch scissors, cut, hurt'; and then these clever parents expect you to sit still while the scissors go whizzing round your head.

On many occasions it is the adults that cause the aggravation. Many years ago, I had a youngster who had a big problem with having his hair cut. He was genuinely petrified. All my efforts were lost on this lad; he would shake uncontrollably with fear. He always came along with his grandad. The grandad stood no messing; he was there for one reason, and the quicker I could do the young lad's haircut, the sooner they could leave. Over many haircuts, I tried to find out the reason behind his fear. A quiet word from me often helped the situation, although his grandad didn't like me talking to the lad because it took up more time.

This particular day, no talking from me could help the situation, the lad was really upset. But I did solve the problem.

His grandad came over and said, 'Now stop it, lad, or you know what you'll get.'

As grandad spoke, I stood back. The youngster started crying, then - wallop - his grandad smacked him across the back of his head.

Now I was brought up understanding the value of respect, so I knew what a smack felt like, but that was because I probably needed it. This lad was in a state and had not done anything wrong. Many years ago I suppose it was the done thing, but even at my young age as an apprentice I could see that it was not helping the situation. I asked grandad not to smack him, as it wouldn't help the lad. And it definitely didn't help me, because suddenly the floodgates opened and it was man-the-lifeboat time. The youngster had also turned on the wee-wee machine, and I needed to find the mop bucket once again.

The young lad kept coming to our salon for his haircut for many years, but after that episode he would arrive with his mother. The haircut wasn't the fear factor: it was his grandad and the threats of what could happen every time he visited the hairdresser's. To this day I still see that young lad, who has grown up and now has his own family. He takes a very different approach when his children have their own hair cut.

My apprenticeship was way back in the early 70s and, although that is many years ago, it doesn't seem to me that my job has changed too much. I learned to cut hair to a very high standard and I still do that today. That said, since then the changes in my working day have been immense, some good and some not too good. People's views are different: thankfully it is now frowned upon to smack children around the head; children as young as five now give the instructions for their haircut; parents allow children to take days off school solely to get their hair cut; and children are seen and *also* heard. But we have to move with the times.

Way back in the 70s I can't really say that a crèche had been thought of. I suppose children were left with family and friends, but probably the first unregistered crèche in my home town was in our hairdressing establishment.

As an apprentice, you learned to cut human hair on children; when mum left her child to nip to the shop, the apprentice had his chance to practise what he had learned. This particular lady had twin boys aged about five, and thought it a good idea to nip out shopping whilst she left her little treasures in our capable hands - only she left them for four hours. By the time she arrived back I had cut both lads' hair and completed the training course in 'nanny competence for young men'. I had to keep them amused, as I was the apprentice. We had a large upstairs salon with about twelve rooms, and so we played hide and seek. I lost one of the twins, then the other went AWOL, then they thought it highly amusing to wash the salon sweeping brush in the client shampoo sink.

On her return to collect the boys, the mother admitted she had forgotten about them and had gone home expecting them to be there with their dad. For my babysitting duties and all my trouble she left me a whole shilling (5p) tip.

Anthony was six and the youngest of a family of seven. He was the only boy, and his female siblings took turns to mother their cute little brother. On this busy Saturday, he had been for his haircut with his dad. An hour later his dad came back asking if we had seen Anthony, as he had gone missing. We couldn't help but as the day went by our concern increased as dad kept calling to see if we had any news. The police were called and a full-scale search of the town centre developed, but to no avail.

His dad rang us just as we were about to close at 5pm to say the boy had arrived home, six hours after he had left the salon. At the tender age of six, he told his parents he had got lost but found his way home; at the age of fourteen, he admitted he purposely hid from his dad so that, when he was found, they would give him sympathy and he would be allowed a huge ice cream.

On that particular day after he lost his dad, he had spent ages looking for him. He then walked the streets of Preston until he found a road he knew. He followed that road until he recognised another, then followed that road until he eventually got home. His dad took him on a drive the following day to find the route he had used to get home; the boy had walked 5.3 miles at the age of six, on his own, looking for his way home. The journey by bus is 1.5 miles.

Many years have passed and he is married with his own children, and he still likes ice cream!

A small boy got parted from his grandad whilst in the local shopping centre and started to cry. A uniformed policeman found the boy wandering about and asked him why he was crying.

'I've lost my grandad,' he said with tears rolling down his little face.

The policeman asked, 'What's he like?'

The little boy stopped crying, hesitated for a moment, then replied, 'Beer, whiskey and ladies with big tits.'

"In a world where you can be anything ... be yourself."

Chapter 3 - The learning curve starts here

'Stephen Philip Molloy,' said this balding teacher wearing a master's gown.

'Yes, sir?' I spoke with a clear but timid voice.

'1B in Room 7 with Mr Dolby.'

1B was about the best I could have hoped for under the circumstances… seeing that there was no 1C. We were told that pupils were put into classes according to their ability from the eleven-plus exam we had sat the previous year; 'As you find your footing as the year progresses, you will be moved to a more appropriate class.' So 1B in my first year progressed to the appropriate class - 4B - in my fourth year. Not much progress, but I was very consistent. But back to 1B…

'Class, please leave quietly. Go to your form rooms to meet your new form teacher who will give you your timetable for the new term.'

A timetable? What was a timetable?

At the age of eleven you are introduced to the world of organisation for the first time in your life. Assembled in Room 7, we were informed by Mr Dolby: 'Your timetable tells you where you should be, at what time and with whom. Get this right and it is plain sailing for the rest of your life.'

Never a truer word spoken: the learning curve starts here.

Sport was a big part of learning the ropes at this new school and, after a few months, I had made many new friends and impressed a few of the teachers. I was picked to play for the school football team against the local St Mary's School in Leyland. The whole family were pleased for me, and my dad said he would give me a shilling (5p) for every goal I scored. We returned unsuccessful, with our tails trailing somewhere down below.

'How did you go on?' asked Dad.

'We did OK,' said I, a little apprehensively.

'How many did you score?'

'One,' I replied very sheepishly.

'So I owe you a shilling? What was the score?'

'15–0.'

'Good result. Your team scored 15, but you only scored one. You could have done better than that, couldn't you?'

'No. We lost 15–0. I scored at the wrong end.'

I never did get my shilling.

Cross-country running was for the masochists in the school. In my eyes, running along roads, over fields and through rivers can only be classed as a spectator sport. Every year the annual event was held for the whole school to see who would represent us for the county championships. After three miles I was holding my own about half-way up the field, then the wheels fell off and I was looking behind me in case somebody handed me the red tail-light for the last competitor.

With a mile to go, things took a turn for the better. I knew the area and I knew the course ... the good runners didn't and went the wrong way. I came in ninth out of the whole school and there was no cheating. A stewards' inquiry thought differently and we had to do it again the next week. Don't think country dancing was that bad after all.

On the academic side I plodded along with loads of interest but few results to show for it.

I still remember to this day the Galileo Principle, the speed of light and the speed of sound, the height of Blackpool Tower, the reproductive organs of a hen, don't use a chisel for a screwdriver, and don't draw pictures with that stupid charcoal and wipe your face - some things do stick!

One term we were introduced to a new student geography teacher just out from college, wet behind the ears and ideal for the B class. This small chubby man in his early twenties, with idiotic large spectacles, waltzed into the class with a weird sense of humour and a warped mind. He would have been more at home on the stage as Widow Twankey than teaching us. In his clear northern but distinctly posh accent, he laid down the law to us all about what he taught and what he expected from us. He got it in no uncertain terms.

We found out who was the boss very quickly. On one occasion this lad Andy was talking during lesson.

'You boy, was that you talking?'

'No sir,' said Andy.

'Yes it was. Now bring your school bag with you to the front of the class.'

The puzzled and bemused lad lethargically arrived at the front of the class.

'Stand up straight, boy, arms out straight in front of you.'

With this command, he placed the lad's bag on top of his arms and then continued with the lesson. No problem for a young fit tough guy with a measly bag on his arms. After three minutes, arms and bag begin to waver. Mrs Twankey never looked round but just bellowed, 'Keep them arms up, you stupid boy,' then continued with the lesson. He got attention and respect immediately but, as I said, he was a weird man.

Years later this same man appeared on television in a television advert. When I first saw it, I nearly choked on my chips. Nobody would believe that the funny bespectacled man was my ex-schoolteacher from years back. He later starred in a top soap programme, appearing every week for many years on television. The character he portrayed was a wacky, stupid and senseless young man, and from what I remember of the bloke he didn't have to act much. To this day, he still looks like Widow Twankey.

Squeaky clean or whiter than white I was not. Corporal punishment was still used regularly, and I have to say I was in total agreement with it then as I am today. With discipline you gain respect; with respect you learn self-discipline. (*There he goes again!*) I had many close calls with discipline, when my navy blue blazer was regularly peppered with white chalk from the board-duster, and the only time any females required my company was the numerous times 'see me' was written in red ink all over my text books.

On one occasion my posterior was positively tendered. The girls did cookery; the boys did woodwork, taught by Mr Mason, or 'Chiseller' as we called him. On this particular occasion we were all working conscientiously, as you do, minding our own business, when Chiseller went into the small wood-store with one lad looking for a length of wood. One of the boneheads in the class that I can't name, as we were all sworn to secrecy, locked the storeroom door. Big laugh, loads of fun and a very big mistake. As the knocking on the door got louder, Chiseller shouted, 'Right lads, one of you must open this door immediately.'

At that moment the school bell went; it was break time. Everybody froze, wondering what the outcome would be. I still find it hard to believe, but we all left the woodwork room and went for break. A nervous fifteen minutes later and we had the same dilemma, but this was now turning into a major kidnap. We all knew who had locked the door but nobody was prepared to split on him. Eventually one brave lad crept up to the door and unlocked it, then ran back to his workbench.

Out walked the teacher and the lone pupil.

'Right lads, I will ask this question only once. Who locked the door?'

Nobody said a word. Silence filled the room.

'Right lads, line up in groups of six,' Chiseller instructed.

We all lined up in groups of six, not knowing what was to come, but something told us it wasn't going to be pleasant.

'First six, stand side by side and face the window.'

They nervously did as instructed. I was on the third sitting, or should that read 'third hitting'? Out of the storeroom appeared Chiseller with an eight-foot-long plank of wood, three inches wide and half an inch thick. He then straightened the line to perfection.

'Bend over.'

Crack, all six walloped at one go.

'Next six.'

All six rushed to be next to Chiseller, as the poor sod at the far end was the unlucky recipient that caught the full force of the plank.

I never sat down for a week. It couldn't, and it shouldn't, happen in this day and age, but I still recall the pain of that plank. We all had every respect for Chiseller after that painful experience.

'What are you going to do? Come with us to the Grand Hall and stay on next year, or are you going to leave?' Les asked. He was concerned about my indecisiveness over my future but was hoping I would stay on another year, because I brought the ball to school to play footie with at break time.

'Don't know yet,' I said, still unsure where my future lay.

'We're going now. Are you coming?' asked Les.

'I'll see you in the Grand Hall. You go, save us a place.'

It was fast approaching 1pm and I hadn't a clue what my future would hold. My parents were putting no pressure on me, but encouraged me to train for a career. 'Once you've got a trade, you can always sweep the streets afterwards, but you've always got something to fall back on.' Mother's favourite saying.

She also told my brother the same, so when he left school he went to college and trained in catering.

I could work on a farm, as there were plenty in the village, or as a labourer at Leyland Motors, as many of my school colleagues were going to do. How about a trainee bank assistant who hummed his eight times table... I don't think so!

One-thirty pm and the school bell sounded. I had two options and I didn't take either, as I was outside playing footie with my ball.

'Where were you?' Les was still puzzled; to be honest, so was I. A fifteen-year-old lad with no idea what he was going to do when he left school.

Mum: 'It's true what they say ... children brighten up a home.'
Dad: 'That's because they never turn the bloody lights out!'

"When your mum is mad at your dad, don't let her brush your hair."

Chapter 4 - Those precious little children get bigger

Doing this job for so many years has given me an insight into how families live their lives. We all have different priorities and goals. What is important to one family could be well down the batting order for another family. With my job, I have seen children grow up through all those important stages of life, developing through wisdom and good care from their parents.

I had cut David's hair since he was a two-year-old and, after much water under the bridge, little David is now Daddy David to little Craig, who has just turned three. Craig would usually sit on his dad's knee for his haircut, but today Craig is having a bad day at his own little office and would surely get thrown out due to his high-decibel rendering of the word 'Noooooooooo'. We eventually calm him down and find out he wants to sit on the big chair like his daddy. I install the child's seat that straddles the chair arms and he is happy. We have achieved a smile, and the tears are wiped away.

'This chair that you are sitting in is ever so special, because many years ago, I used to sit in this same chair,' his dad tells him to help pacify him.

'And that is a long time ago,' I chip in mischievously.

'And you will never guess - all those years ago it was this man that cut my hair for me,' dad says. 'He really is an old man,' he adds, with the sort of smile you usually see on someone doing a lap of honour at Wembley Stadium.

Tales like that make me realise I have been doing this job for ages. They also make me realise I not only cut hair but am part of people's lives and have been for many a year - and that, I can assure you, is something very special.

Most lads when they reach the age of fifteen are well aware of hairstyles and fashion, and know exactly what they want from their hairdresser. This particular young lad of about fifteen has other ideas; his priorities are certainly not fashion.

'Yes sir, how would you like me to cut your hair?' I ask, as is the norm.

'I would like two haircuts, please,' he says.

'Go on then, give us a clue,' I say, puzzled.

'I don't know how you can do it, but I would like it to look like I am fourteen this afternoon and eighteen tonight, please.'

He had fairly long hair, so I had something to work with. The younger style was shaped with a side parting brushed back to make him look a schoolboy, and then with added gel I created a roughed-up style that gave him an older-looking appearance.

'How does that look? Does it produce the required effect?' I enquire, with a great deal of self-satisfaction.

'Brilliant, I'll go home now and get the gel out ready for tonight.'

'So what is the big deal about looking a young fourteen-year-old this afternoon and then changing to an adult tonight?' I ask.

'Well, this afternoon I am going to the footie match and I want to pay child entry, and tonight I'm going to the pictures with my girlfriend, and we want to watch an adult movie. I tried last week and they would only let my girlfriend in. They wouldn't let me in; they said I wasn't old enough.'

My magic worked, as he got to watch both. Add another one to the satisfied customer list.

It was probably the mid-80s when we saw the most rapid and radical changes in male hairstyles, especially for the eleven-to-sixteen-year-old lads. Over the years, schools have had to set certain standards as to what can be allowed with young lads' hair. Tidy and modern, not too long, about collar length at the back and over the ears was permissible, but definitely not too short, no skinhead haircuts. I remember many years ago receiving a letter from a school headmaster instructing me and my staff to: 'Use a common sense approach when attending to pupils from my school. Very short hair will not be tolerated, and any long hair styled haircuts will have to be approved by me,' the letter read.

Fortunately for this lad it wasn't his headmaster that had written to me.

'Can you leave it long on the top and sides and under-cut it really short on the back and sides, so the top hair goes over the short hair?'

This haircut went against all I had been taught. The hair is long on the top of the head, the hair is clipper-cut to about ¼ inch on the back and sides and with the long hair falling over the short hair, a symmetric line is cut all around the head about an inch above the ear. As well as an undercut it is called a mushroom cut, or a wedge haircut. An awful haircut, but I don't have to like it; I cut hair and people pay for the service!

This lad was sixteen and in his last year at school. It was the week before Christmas and he was making a fashion statement to all his mates. This style became very popular years later with kids at school, but this lad was way ahead of the times; he was up front in the fashion stakes and his family were happy to back him with the money for his clothes.

'It will look strange, it will look silly, and it will be very unconventional. What will your parents say about you coming home with a haircut like that?' I asked, making sure there would be no repercussions from his odd request.

'No problem, they're happy if I'm happy,' he told me.

'What about school? Will they allow it?'

'It's Christmas. What can they say?' he answered, with bullish confidence.

I did the haircut to the young lad's specification and satisfaction. A thick line symmetrical around the head looked stupid, but he was very happy. I am paid to achieve the style specified by the customer.

Next day, the lad came back with his mate. Immediately I assumed the lad had been sent back to have the haircut changed to look more sensible. Either his dad didn't like it or his school was not very happy.

'I suppose I'd better put it back to normal. Who didn't like it?' I asked, not expecting the answer I received.

'It's not me who wants it cutting, it's my mate. When I went back to school today they SUSPENDED me from school till after Christmas. So if my mate gets his done, he will get suspended too and we can have a longer holiday.'

'What about your parents? Will they be OK with this new style and getting suspended from school?'

'I can handle them,' the lad said, brimming with confidence.

So for the second day running I did another oddball haircut to satisfy my customer.

Next day the second lad came back.

'So what happened? Did you get suspended like your mate?' I asked.

'Yes, but when I got home me dad went ballistic and me mam started crying, so I have to have it done properly,' he told me.

'So you thought you could handle your parents?' I said.

The young lad had now lost his cocky attitude and was looking quite forlorn as he replied, with an embarrassed grin, 'I lost, they won... this time.'

Right from the early years, mum and dad accompany their little treasure for the haircut experience. Whether it be happy or hell, it is another chapter in the life of a child. It is usually when lads go to senior school that parents allow them to go for a haircut on their own, usually without any instructions for the hairdresser. In most cases, you recognise the youngsters and know what to do.

This youngster, aged about eleven, was new. A very polite, small lad, he arrived after school with longish hair.

'How would you like me to cut your hair?' I ask.

'I want to keep it as long as possible please, hardly anything cutting off; I only want you and me to know I have had my haircut,' he says.

'So I understand you're trying to grow it and you just need me to take the ends off,' I say, just to confirm matters.

'Yes please, if that's possible.'

I am taken by the lad's polite attitude, and he appears to be a lot older than he looks. After I have taken very little length off and slightly thinned his hair, he leaves my establishment not looking much different from when he arrived - but a happy chappie nonetheless.

Next day after school the youngster comes back.

'Well, was it not short enough?' I ask, knowing the answer.

'You know when I said could you cut my hair so only you and me had to know I'd had my haircut? Well, could you cut it so you, me and my dad know I've had it cut, because he says it didn't look as if I had anything off, and seeing he was paying, he wants his money's worth.'

I am only too happy to comply with his dad's request.

It's Friday afternoon and the salon is busy. This lad of about seventeen speaks to me as if he is my best mate. 'How yer doing, Steve? It's been a bit since I've been in here. Do yer remember me? Rob. I used to come with me dad when I was at school years ago,' he tells me.

'No, sorry I can't say I do,' I reply, keen to get cracking on the haircut.

'Me dad still comes here. You'll know me dad,' he says, really trying his best to jog my memory. I start on the haircut as he fills me in with his details and family history. It transpires I used to cut his hair more than ten years previously when he was a little lad at school. He hadn't been about for a few years, as he has been 'away' for a bit ('away' is a euphemism for 'in prison'), but he is now in a stable relationship with a nice girlfriend and his life back on track. I am still puzzled over his identity.

'Can you be careful cutting round me neck on the left side? I've just had a tattoo and it's still a bit sore. It's me girlfriend's name,' he tells me. Just below his ear on his neck is a tattoo of the name *DAWN*. It appears quite red, so I keep away from this sensitive area.

As I am finishing the haircut, he says, 'Me girlfriend's here now.' This young girl walks in, wearing a school uniform. The lad pays for his haircut and leaves with his girlfriend.

People live their lives their own way and I never pass judgement on any of my clients, but I was shocked at what I had just witnessed. I was also intrigued as to who his dad was. Weeks later I found out. His dad, who I had never associated with this now grown-up lad, was the quietest family man you would ever wish to meet.

'Did our Robert come for his haircut a couple of weeks ago?' he asked.

'Your Robert?' I asked. 'Who's your Robert?'

'Young lad, just had a daft tattoo of his girlfriend on his neck,' he told me.

'A tattoo of *DAWN*, was it? So that's your lad. He tells me I did his hair when he was little. I do remember him now.'

'Silly lad got himself into trouble a couple of years ago but he seems to be sorting himself out now. He lost his way when my wife died, and he was uncontrollable. No matter what he does or wherever he goes, I will always be his dad, and I love him.'

I tell this tale because I was shocked at the idea of a lad having a tattoo for life of a schoolgirl's name on his neck. We all have freedom of choice and we all make mistakes in life. I used to tell both my children when they were going through those lost, adolescent years that they put rubbers on the ends of pencils because we all make mistakes - but make sure not to wear the rubber out.

I have seen Rob recently, and to his and Dawn's credit they are still in a relationship. She has now left school and owns a pram.

This career I chose, and what seems ages ago to me, can be traced back many centuries. My predecessors not only cut hair but had to attain the knowledge so that they could perform surgery, extract teeth and carry out the odd enema. Can you imagine the scene?

'And how are you today, sir? Is it just a trim or do you require a leg removed? How's your hand? Is it still giving you pain? I could give it a quick amputation; it's buy one get one free today, sir'.

'Both seem to be fine. Just a trim please.'

'Short on the back and sides, is it sir? How's the teeth, sir? I've 15 minutes until my next appointment. I could have a quick fish about and whip a couple of those dodgy peggies out. The deal for this morning is 100 Green Shield Stamps for every tooth up to 6 teeth; any more and you qualify for an Apple iTunes voucher.'

'No, no, I think I'll settle for a nice tidy trim, thanks.'

'How's your seat?'

'My sight? My sight's very good, thank you?'

'No sir... your seat. You know... your seat. Today our special one-off deal is a free rectal bulb syringe with every enema we perform, and we've got quite a big box of those damn syringes to get rid of. Want one?'

'If it's all the same to you I think I'll grow my hair into a ponytail.'

(And we all know what's under a ponytail.)

Because of the longevity of our trade there are some very familiar and recognisable traditions associated with barbering. Probably the most familiar sight would be the barber's pole. A pole with red and white coloured stripes circling the length of the pole; the two colours represent the red of the blood and the white of the bandages. It is thought in later years the United States added blue to their poles, although in some parts of Asia a red, white and blue barber's pole is a symbol of a brothel.

Some traditions will never die, like the barber's pole; the barber's chair is another one of those traditions. A big cumbersome piece of furniture that would be out of place anywhere else apart from a barber's salon. Some traditions lose their appeal as years pass by; the likes of hair pomade, brilliantine, hair tonic, and hair lacquer are all products of yester-year, dated and not contemporary, so disregarded only to reappear under another guise many years later. Today we have such wonderful products on the market like putty, paste, gel, jelly, wax and glue. How our profession has changed with time.

Sadly a tradition that was massive until the 70s but has died out today was the one in which the barber was the main supplier of the never-to-be-mentioned condoms. Probably anybody born after 1975 wouldn't know of the secrecy or the stigma of buying those 'things'. A man wouldn't go and buy condoms in a chemist, particularly if a female assistant was at the counter. This was a taboo subject not to be talked about except by youngsters, who found it all so amusing until they themselves grew up.

The only discreet way to purchase those miniature, square-shaped foil packets (or to give them their posh name, family planning aids) was to either buy them in the pub toilets in one of those wonky condom machines that on many occasions didn't cough up anything and nobody would dare go and ask the landlord for their money back; or buy them at the barber's. This practice was so common-place that the world-famous phrase 'Something for the weekend?' was universally recognised. It was a coy way of asking if a customer wanted to purchase 'those things' without actually having to use that word 'condom'.

It was just gone 5 o'clock and the blinds were closed; the lads were in 'home time' mode and it showed, as they were moving a damn sight quicker than they had all day when there was a knock on the door. As expected the usual 'Sorry we're closed' was shouted towards the door. Then there was another knock. I went to the door to explain that we were closed. Stood outside was a young lad no more than 14 years old in his school uniform.

'I'm sorry, mate. We're closed now.'

'I know you're closed. That's why I've called now. Could you sell me a packet of 'johnnies'?'

I was quite taken aback but didn't see anything wrong, so I sold him a packet of condoms and away he went with a big smile from ear to ear. The week after, the same youngster was knocking on my door, same time after we had closed, and it was obvious what he wanted. As the weeks went by it became a regular habit, only he was buying on a bigger scale, so much so that I bought a large box from the wholesalers, as this was definitely good business. The mark-up on condoms was far bigger than on your ordinary hairspray and shampoo because of the 'secrecy element' about where to buy them. The saga had gone on for probably a few months when all of a sudden it stopped. He didn't appear at our door again.

Weeks later a youngster was having his hair cut, and I recognised the school uniform as being that of the condom buyer. I asked the youngster if he knew of a lad at his school, probably his age, glasses, with a big mop of curly hair. He told me he knew of a lad with that description; it wasn't one of his mates but he knew he had been suspended for selling condoms around school. My large box of condoms sat on my shelf for so long I had to throw the whole box away, as the sell-by date had passed. Another one of my get-rich ventures that backfired, whereas the lad with his flair for business is probably on the board of a multi-million-pound company somewhere on a Caribbean island!

If you can remember the milkman delivering milk in those glass bottles at silly o'clock in the morning, you'll really appreciate some of the notes that Mr Milkman got to read:

Please don't leave any more milk. All they do is drink it.

Milkman, please close the gate behind you because the birds keep pecking the tops off the milk.

Sorry not to have paid your bill before, but my wife had a baby and I've been carrying it around in my pocket for weeks.

From now on please leave two pints every other day and one pint on the days in between, except Wednesdays and Saturdays when I don't want any milk.

Please leave no milk today. When I say today, I mean tomorrow, for I wrote this note yesterday.

No milk today thanks. Please do not leave milk at No. 14 either as he is dead until further notice.

"We always appreciate our school years ... years later!"

Chapter 5 - From boy to apprentice adult

"Steve, will you shag me mate Mary?"

I was raised in a small cottage with no central heating and damp on the inside of the walls, no double-glazed windows and a coal fire that puffed out loads of black stuff on windy days. The kitchen consisted of a washer with built-in wringers, a kitchenette and a posh stainless steel sink. My cot was a hand-me-down, so it was painted with lead-based paint. I ate white bread and real butter, I drank water from a garden hose and soft drinks which contained sugar. I ate worms and lived, I ate gobstoppers and didn't choke, and I sat in the front seat of my dad's car without a seat belt. I watched black and white telly with two channels once the set had warmed up; I played with matchbox cars, not X-box technology, and our telephone communication meant going to our next door neighbour's to use this big heavy Bakelite contraption. As a kid, I sat for hours on a beach watching Mr Punch knock nine bells out of his wife with a stick and thought it was the done thing. Heck, wasn't I lucky to have reached fourteen unscathed?

Everybody made their decisions about where life was going to lead them after July 18th the following year. Some had decided to stay on at school into the fifth year. The rest of the fourth year, which included the truants, the lazy, the part-time misfits and the no-hopers, were thrown to the wolves, or should I say the careers teacher. You didn't make an appointment or ask to see this person - you were summoned. I didn't hold much hope for a positive outcome but that day set the seed for the rest of my life.

'And have you any idea in which direction you wish your career to go, Stephen?' The careers teacher asked the same questions to all the no-hopers and no doubt expected the same answer.

'No, not really, would you have any ideas?' I asked, expecting him to tell me he had a mate that needed a football professional to help out at the local bingo hall.

'According to your teachers and school report, you have a talent for being a good listener. Probably a job working with people, that would be an option,' he told me.

'I can't talk to people,' I tried to explain.

'Then it's about time you started and, while you're at it, have a bit more confidence in your own ability. Be honest with yourself, ask the question 'can I do it?'... Then do it; don't choose the highest mountain too early, scale the lower ones and gain the experience. Some expeditions may not appeal, move on to the next, get to the level you are content with and stop, enjoy the moment and take stock of your life.'

Now half of that was way above my head, but I came out of the room ready to buy a map and my first pair of walking boots and head for the hills. To be fair to this straight-laced teacher with his check tweed jacket and leather elbow patches, he probably told all his victims that they were good listeners, but he threw me numerous ideas that I had never even dreamed of. If it was true and I was a good listener, then what could I do that fitted in with dealing with people and also incorporated a trade apprenticeship so as to keep my mother happy?

A decision had to be made and, looking back, the seeds had already been sown. Though I was unaware of it at the time, I had another twelve months of school life coming my way. Have confidence in yourself; can I do it ... ? Then do it. So I did it.

Anyway, I had another year to find my appropriate trade and to practise the art of talking to people!

I returned to school in September 1968 as a senior fifth-year pupil with the aim of eventually finding the right career and doing my level best in my chosen subjects. To be honest, the last year at school is still quite hazy in my mind, but to my credit I managed to keep up with the rest of the pupils. One thing that became obvious was that the teachers made more time for you; they talked to you on a more adult level and treated you with more respect. This gave us opportunities to talk candidly, to ask the unthinkable (why do we fart and why do they smell?), without getting shouted down. Unbeknown to me, I was gaining confidence by just opening up and talking with these teachers.

It was during one of these chats that a teacher suggested I consider a career as a hairdresser. I shuddered at the thought. What, me be a hairdresser? Only soft lads do them sort of jobs. If I went home and told my dad I wanted to be a hairdresser, there would be hell to pay. I can hear him now: 'No lad of mine is going to be a hairdresser. Get a proper job.'

As the year went by, I gave the idea some thought but was not totally convinced that hairdressing was the road to fame and fortune, although it was an option that was higher up my job list than a steeplejack, labourer or chimney sweep.

I remember one lesson when the teacher was probably having a lazy day and the relaxed chat in class revolved around leaving school and our chosen careers. This casual free-for-all of opinions suddenly took a turn for the worse, as we were asked individually to stand up and say what we wanted to do and give a brief explanation of why. This was a bad idea in my book, as I would have to inform all and sundry of my possible desire to be a hairdresser. The pain and the anxiety was awful as it came nearer to my turn; the ordeal was having a disturbing effect on my rectum. I was close to an accident but I survived.

'Stephen Molloy, what do you want to do?'

'There is a possibility I could go into hairdressing,' I said sheepishly.

I expected the room to erupt, the lads to shout and mock while the girls screamed with laughter. There was not a sound. Nobody spoke.

'Go on and explain why,' the teacher asked. With no negative response and no abuse, I suddenly found an inner strength, a confidence that had previously been alien to me.

'I feel I have the ability to deal with and serve the public.'

'But you could do that working in a shoe shop,' the teacher pointed out.

'Yes sir, but this is no ordinary manual work. You need technical skills for hairdressing and I think I can learn and achieve my goal.'

Where the hell did that come from? I suppose it sounded good but now I wanted to prove it to myself and put that answer into practice.

My first step towards the tonsorial profession was to attend an interview in Chorley at a highly reputable ladies' hairdressing establishment, on a Friday at 6pm after the salon had closed. My very first interview at the age of fifteen, wet behind the ears, very nervous - and he takes his mum along for company. The position was a Saturday job to help in the running of the salon. The usual 'why hairdressing and long days on your feet' were covered, as is the normal procedure in most hairdressing interviews.

'Do you have any questions about the job, Stephen?' asked the nice lady proprietor.

'Remember: have confidence in yourself and show them you were born for the job,' raced through my head.

'Do we have tea breaks?' was my all-important question. Now that took some thinking, Molloy, didn't it?

'Yes, when you've got time. We don't have set times in hairdressing, as the client is your utmost priority.'

My mum rushed into the conversation to help the situation sound more adult. 'What will his duties be?'

'We start at 8.30am and work through until 5.30pm. Stephen will be watching the stylists work. You'll be helping them when asked and generally cleaning and tidying up. It's always an advantage to be excellent with a sweeping brush!' the lady informed us.

I don't think there were many applicants, as I was offered the job and could start the following week.

Thanks, but no thanks. If you think that I am working nine hours cleaning, sweeping and looking after people, you have another think coming, and all for ten shillings a day (yes, that is a whole 50 pence).

How can you learn to be a hairdresser by sweeping and cleaning up? This lad needed some action. Let him loose with some scissors and combs, hairbrushes, hairdryers, that's what the job is all about.

College, that was the place to start. No cleaning up and sweeping at college. It's theory and working in the salon, where volunteers let you loose on their hair. Now we were talking, that was the place for me.

The nearest college that taught hairdressing was Southport Technical College, so I made an appointment. This time I went on my own with my answers ready to all their questions, or so I thought.

The interview went well and, provided I acquired the necessary grades in my exams, they would be happy to enrol me. This was definitely for me. The grades were not too high so the signs were good.

'Would you like to have a look around the classrooms and at our newly-refurbished salon?' asked this quite substantial lady with a big chest.

'Yes please,' said I, now brimming with confidence.

The lady showed me into a large room that looked nothing like a hairdressing salon, but it appeared well stocked with hairdressing equipment. 'This is the salon were you will be taught the practical skills. There will be you and sixteen girls working together in here.'

The journey home from Southport was very quiet. One minute you have found your goal, the next you are on your backside. The thought of being with sixteen girls in the classroom on my own for two years scared me to death. My confidence had evaporated like the steam from a kettle.

The game looked over. I had no Chance Cards or Community Chest Cards left to play, and I felt I had even lost the dice. I completed my final year at school and did as well as anybody expected. With seven CSEs to my name, I left school to join the world of the unemployed, or so I thought.

The very day I finished school, my mum saw an advertisement in the paper for an apprentice gentlemen's hairdresser in Wigan.

I had never considered a barber's job, but two days later I started work in the industrial mining town of Wigan. My weekly wage was £2.50; my weekly bus pass was £2, with ten pence a day for my dinners. In total it cost Mr Thompson the owner £10 for my wages, as I left after a month. It wasn't all bad, as for the first time I came face to face with the public.

As one door closes another one opens. I finished work in Wigan on Saturday night and I started work in a cotton mill on Monday. From £2.50, my wage at the mill for labouring was £7.90. I was rich; I could afford fish and chips for my dinner, and I found out what paying board was all about.

The one major lesson I took away from my brief encounter working in industry was that I found the opposite sex. I had little experience talking to women, let alone working alongside them. I was a very naive young lad working in a large mill shed with numerous females of all ages; it was a bizarre experience. It was very noisy, so all the workers either shouted, used hand signals or handed notes to each other.

Only a few days into the job and one young brazen lass shouted something to me. I hadn't a clue who she was or what she was saying, so after a few whats and ehs and sorry I can't hear you, she casually walked up to me and shouted down my ear, 'Will you shag my mate?' I was off like a shot, red-faced, embarrassed - I was mortified. It wasn't the sort of talk I had encountered in my sleepy village.

I did take a girl out on a date, a quiet, sweet young girl who informed me that the suggestive remark the brazen lass had shouted was one of the usual tricks they played on new young virgin lads. I had been stitched up and my ego was deflated - another lesson in living.

I had been working at the mill for a full two weeks when another advert in the local paper read 'Gentlemen's hairdresser in top Preston salon requires a trainee to join our young styling team'. I rang, had the interview and got the job.

Three jobs in seven weeks - now how long would this one last?

Teacher: 'Jonathan, your composition on 'My Dog' is exactly the same as your brother's. Did you copy his?'
Jonathan: 'No, sir. It's the same dog.'

"The worst bit about Christmas is growing up!"

Chapter 6 - Christmas with all the trimmings

It is the time of year for fun, frolics and flipping hard work. Similar to the pub and restaurant trade, we in the hairdressing trade have to 'wind up' and wait for the onslaught while the rest of the world eases down and waits for Christmas. In both ladies' and gentlemen's hairdressing Christmas is a time of pressure, although ladies in general are more organised and will book perms and technical work earlier than the last minute. Men usually get their haircut on instinct. The clever customers have their hair cut in early December and are then tidy for the festive season, but such characters are the minority; the nearer the big day cometh the busier the salon becometh.

Amazingly enough, nothing changes year after year; it is the male of the species that wander around at the last minute, panic-buying in the shops, so it is no surprise that they leave their haircut until the staff party or the works booze-up, or until their other half simply instructs them to 'get your haircut for Christmas'.

Let's be totally honest about this, lads: in general it is women that make Christmas happen. They are the hub of the wheel; they shop, cook, wrap up presents - organisation skills personified. On the other hand, if you had to wait for a man to organise the festive season, the Christmas dinner would be ready to eat by New Year's Eve and the decorations would still be up when we change the clocks in late March. I have come to the conclusion that if we all stick to our own jobs, all will be well with the world. WOMEN SHOP AND MEN DRINK BEER. This country would be a happier place with fewer problems and very few arguments; the only time the problems arise is when women drink beer and men shop - a cocktail of emotions erupts.

They built a big Trafford Centre shopping complex for the ladies to enjoy their favourite pastime, so why not build a big Men's Crèche next to it for the men? We could watch football and golf on big screens; we could play snooker, pool and cards and all those other sporting pastimes that keep big and little lads happy. We could even wear one of those bibs with a number on, and when it is time to carry the shopping bags back to the car the man in charge shouts out your number and off you go to meet your other half. It couldn't fail; that could well be my new idea for my retirement pension fund: Steve's Men's Crèche, found in all top shopping complexes around the country!

Where was I up to... ah yes, men getting their hair cut at Christmas. It is well documented in this book: haircuts and alcohol go hand in hand like kippers and jelly. So at Christmas, as you work through the pantomime season, you can be certain the proverbial donkey will appear through the door.

Just days before Christmas, two young lads in their late teens bounced into the shop in high spirits. It is strange that at Christmas you always attend to many new customers, whether it is because they don't want to go to their usual hairdresser in a 'popped up' state or they don't have to tip a new hairdresser, who knows, but you do see many new faces. I digress; these lads had had quite a few sherbet lemons and wine gums in the last couple of hours and as they talked to each other the noise rose to shouting level, and then the 'language' started.

'Excuse me lads, can you quieten it down a bit - and no bad language, please,' I said in my quiet but authoritative voice.

'Sorry mate, we were jusht talking,' said the older of the two.

Normality resumed for about two minutes, and then their tones started to rise again.

'You can wait in here, lads, or wait outside, but it's a little warmer in here, so turn the volume down again, please.' Again I sounded stern but not aggressive.

It worked. They calmed down. In fact the younger one fell asleep and the older one tried to read a magazine but found it too difficult as it was upside down.

'Next please,' I shouted. The older lad staggered to his feet, gingerly walked across to my chair, and slumped down.

'Jusht a twim please, mate,' were his instructions.

I had been working on the haircut for about five minutes when I noticed this young lad's complexion was changing to whiter than white, and he started to twitch and sweat.

'Are you OK?' I asked.

'No, not weely, ah'm feelin a bit wuf.'

A warm salon after a skinful of beer and a tight gown around one's neck could be a recipe for a mop-and-bucket activity, so I suggested 'time-out', a breather outside in the cold air. When he agreed to my suggestion, the gown was off like a flash and he was ushered to the door in no time. He had a couple of minutes to recover whilst I made a brew, then he came back inside, sat down, and we were well on the way to completing the haircut. After many years of dealing with boozed-up customers (and I had successfully completed my vomiting awareness course) I had escaped the dreaded mop and bucket saga - or so I thought.

Just as I was finishing the haircut, his mate woke up from Planet Carlsberg.

'All right, Johnny lad, that looks betterrrrrrrrrr.'

The young lad (Carlsberg Cuckoo) throws up all down his shirt, his pants and my floor. He stands up to see what a mess he is in; he stands in the vomit, slips and lays full length in the stuff. I am not amused, to say the least, but I stand and admire the young lad's newly-decorated shirt. His mate gets up off the styling chair, calls him a name that I regularly hear on a football pitch, and then drags him through all the vomit. I open the door and he drags him out along with the contents of his stomach, with added carrots. The lad was covered from his shoes to his hair. He sat outside for over an hour trying to sober up.

To be fair to the older lad, once he got his mate outside showing his fancy shirt off, he did come back into the salon to apologise and to pay for his haircut. That was about the same time as I was searching for the disinfectant and acquainting myself with the mop and bucket once again.

Many years ago another 'popped-up' customer wandered into the salon over Christmas, sat down and waited patiently for his haircut. The usual signs of glazed eyes, red cheeks and a silly smile are always a giveaway when spotting an over-indulgent festive beer monster. Another tell tale sign that a bloke has had more of Rudolph's gravy browning than he can take is that his lips are always moving. Either he is talking to anybody in the vicinity or talking to himself; he is licking his lips, or puckering them to blow a kiss to any takers.

This middle-aged man in his working overalls had most definitely finished work and called at our emporium via the house that serves black Irish lemonade. He was happy with himself - the smile told you so. He was happy with the world and all its occupants as he tried his best to talk to everyone in his vicinity. When other customers entered the salon, he moved up the queue so they could sit down and he could try and make conversation with another new face, as nobody really wanted to engage in his fairy-tale world. After about twenty minutes, the jovial talking had ceased and the noise-box on legs had left the planet; he had fallen asleep.

Nothing new there, then. When it was his turn he would wake up, so what was the problem? The problem being, he fell asleep and he wouldn't wake up. We tried to wake him but to no avail. Wasted Walter was dead to the world. Whatever planet he was on, he wasn't coming home for some time. He sat there with his chin on his chest and slept - no snores, no fuss, just slept. I had this awful thought: what do we do at closing time? Do we contact the police to wake him up, or do I stay in the salon till he wakes? It could be bloody morning.

The customers were using him as a roundabout and still he slept on. Eventually he woke up; he had been asleep for close on two hours. He slowly came to with this puzzled expression on his face, wondering where the hell he was. He got up, walked over to me, and said, 'Alright Steve, I'm sorry for bothering you but I don't know what I'm doing in here. Are you open tomorrow?'

'Yes, Mick,' I answered.

'Then I'll see yer then. I think I'll go and get me 'ead down. I've had a drink, yer know.'

'Yes, Mick, I had a bit of an idea.'

Amazingly Mick came back the following week for his haircut and, when I suggested he'd been asleep here the week before, he didn't even know he'd been in the salon and was most apologetic.

Many years ago, when the pubs closed at 3pm in the afternoon, the last couple of hours before we closed could make or break your Christmas. One year, a new customer walked into the salon straight from enjoying himself in the local pub, had his haircut, gave me a £10 note and walked out. Now he either really liked the haircut or perhaps he didn't know what difference there was between a green £1 note and a brown £10 note, but seeing that haircuts in those days were 50 pence to £1, there really was a Father Christmas that year.

On the other hand, on a different occasion a customer walked into the salon, again straight from the pub on Christmas Eve, and asked if he could have a shampoo and blow dry. He didn't need it cutting.

'Certainly sir, I'll shampoo it right away,' I said, showing the client over to the shampoo basin.

'I only want it washing so that it will sober me up before I go home to the wife.'

I endeavoured to shampoo this wobbly-headed person, who first decided to head butt the sink; there was blood all over it. We sat him up, stopped the bleeding, and then continued with the job in hand. Whilst I was shampooing this boozy bonce, a regular customer called into the salon to wish us a merry Christmas. I returned the compliments of the season, then looked down to the sink to find it rapidly filling with water. I could have drowned the poor sod. I instantly stopped the tap to find carrots and all sorts floating about. He had been sick in the sink. Now mop buckets are one thing, but carrots and sinks are another.

After that we always closed before the pubs closed on Christmas Eve, mainly due to that incident. That was then; today it is customary to close at 1pm every Christmas Eve, waltz off to the pub, and have a few drinks ourselves, whilst meeting customers and friends in many of the town centre bars. Those two hours or so on Christmas Eve are priceless, as it is the time to relax and reflect on all the hard work over such a short period and appreciate the massive two or three days' holiday to come before you crank up them scissors once again.

One Christmas Eve, my work colleague Gary and I had been out in the afternoon as usual, enjoying a well-earned tipple; it is what's called tradition. Gary, a seasoned drinker of two halves of lager, soon found his number was up and retired from the drinking circus to return home by 3pm. Meanwhile I continued on my own little crusade, or should that read 'boozy merry-go-round', to trough until my own sense of standing and keeping both eyes open was slowly evaporating. So I retired back to the salon to ring my 'bestest' wife Jean to pick me up, as this mildly inebriated hairdresser couldn't select the correct bus to transport himself home. There are a lot of buses in that big bus station and they all look the same after three 'lemonades'.

The salon was in total darkness apart from the Christmas lights on the tree. I unlocked the door, entered the salon, turned to lock the door behind me and... He was there, standing in the doorway. This tall figure with a hood moved slowly into the salon. I switched the lights on to try and recognise this stranger.

'Yes mate, can I help you?' I asked. I wasn't intimidated or frightened, the alcohol had seen to that, just shocked.

'Are you closed?' this young man asked.

'Closed? We closed four hours ago, mate,' I informed him, realising he was not a threat to the £1.50 Christmas bonus in my pocket but a lad wanting his hair cut.

'Is there a chance you can just do me?'

'Sorry mate, it would help if I could see you. I've been on the pop for three hours and at present you have three eyes and four ears.'

'I only need a slight trim. It won't take you long, honest.'

'Sorry mate, I couldn't trust myself with a hairbrush, let alone a pair of scissors.'

'Well, where else can I get my hair cut now?' the lad asked.

'It's 5pm on Christmas Eve. There's nowhere open now. Sorry, mate,' I told him sympathetically.

'I'll pay you double if you can do it now, pleeeease.'

The lad was desperate for his haircut, for what reason I didn't find out, but not as desperate as I was for the toilet.

'Sorry, mate. I can't do it, as I have a certain reputation in this trade and that could be severely tarnished if you finished in the hospital and I finished on the front pages of the *Lancashire Evening Post*. Sorry.'

The lad left the salon and I reached the toilet just in time. It was only after the alcohol had drained from my brain cell(s) that I thought, 'Did that really happen?'

When people go back to work after Christmas, it is common courtesy that the usual talking points are related to Christmas. How did Christmas and New Year go? What did you get for Christmas? Did you get drunk? The usual tales of merriment and joy, the happiness with family and friends and also the sadness of missing loved ones. After the decorations are down, the Christmas tales are put to bed for another year. Not so in the hairdresser's salon - these anecdotes are churned out for months, probably until the weather begins to brighten up; a change in the weather brings a change in the conversation. Not everybody goes on holiday but everybody has a Christmas, so everybody has their own account of the festive season.

'I'll never understand women. The more you do for them the more you land yourself in the poo.'

This guy is about twenty-seven, been married a few years, and still has to master the true meaning of life.

'I take it Christmas wasn't too good for you?' I say, knowing the answer.

'I tried my best and it wasn't good enough.'

'So how was Christmas dinner?' I ask, trying to ease the upset.

'Christmas dinner? She didn't even do the dinner - she went off to her mother's for dinner. Just left me on my own.'

'Did you forget the presents?' I ask, not out of sympathy, but mainly because I'm nosey.

'It was because of the presents that she buggered off to her mother's.'

Me being nosey was one thing, but by now I'm really intrigued.

'So was it the wrong colour. Was she not happy with whatever you got?'

'Was she hell. She behaved like a spoilt cow. I wrapped them up and hid them as usual as she likes me to do, and still no good. I've tried my level best for her.' By now he is getting perturbed. He seems quite anxious and upset.

'I'd given her a clue last month when I asked her about colours for board covers. She thought I had bought her a body board like the one we used down in Newquay on holiday last year. I hid it behind the sofa, and Christmas morning I told her to look for her present.

I'd even wrapped it up with this big bow as well.'

'So when she found it, what did she say? What was it you bought her?' I'm excited to find out what he bought her.

'A top-of-the-range ironing board. Best you can buy in Argos.'

I am probably not as disappointed as his wife must have been opening an ironing board on Christmas morning, but even I feel let down. I can't remember whether I laughed or not.

'She started crying and then started to make the Christmas dinner on her own in the kitchen. I tried to help the situation by giving her the other present; that was when she went to her mother's.'

'What was the other present?' I ask.

'It was the ironing-board cover. I thought it was the right colour but she just put her coat on and went to her mother's for dinner, no thought about me. I stayed in on my own all bloody day. Some Christmas I had.'

Ladies, you don't know how lucky you really are. Just appreciate what you received last Christmas from your wonderful man and think: wrong time, wrong place, and you could have married this candidate for husband of the year.

If the lady who received the ironing board reads this book, may I apologise on behalf of your husband. He probably didn't think it through. He should have at least bought you the iron to go with it.

As I write this paragraph, it is early January 2012. My mission this year is to finish this book. I have just completed another onslaught of Christmas working and, as I said earlier in this chapter, most things are very predictable: the inebriated clients, the late rush as lads try to get their leg through the letter box at 1.05pm on Christmas Eve after I have locked the door and closed; the new clients that appear at Christmas so they don't have to tip their usual hairdresser; the regulars that give you fifty pence for Christmas and tell you to 'get yourself a drink'. Most traditions stay the same.

Unfortunately I do see changes in people's lives. It seems parents don't say no to children's wishes these days. If they want it, they have to get it for them, no matter what the price. Here are some of the presents youngsters that sat in my chair this Christmas were getting: a mobile phone for a four-year-old; a laptop computer for a seven-year-old; a metal detector for a four-year-old; piles of money for a nine-year-old; an air rifle for a seven-year-old, and numerous computer war games were top of the list. Over this last Christmas there have been three high-profile shootings of innocent people and, without me sounding like an old fart, air rifles and war games bought for kids in the season of happiness and goodwill to all men do sound like a contradiction of what Christmas is about.

What is Santa's favourite pizza?
One that is deep pan crisp and even!

"I am not a complete idiot - it's just some parts are missing!"

Chapter 7- Committed to the job

'Have confidence in yourself and just explain the situation. He'll understand,' said my mother, who always seemed to have the right phrase for the right moment. I had to inform my boss that, after only two weeks, I had got another job and I was leaving; what an ordeal. The whole morning was spent sitting on the toilet, plucking up the nerve to speak to my boss Mr Wilson, a kind but loud and outspoken man, who had given me the job what seemed only a few days ago. I felt upset, not only for him but the whole factory. I felt I was letting everybody down.

He was walking my way but, with the noise of the factory machinery, it was impossible to speak about such a serious issue, so I followed him to his office and then knocked on his door.

'Come in. Yes, Jim, what's the problem?'

'Er, Steve, Steve Molloy. Well I have got another job and I have to finish working here.'

'That's a bit of a shock, lad. Just as we were getting used to you, and you'd made a bit of an impression with a few of the ladies. What are you going to do?'

'I've got myself an apprenticeship in hairdressing.'

'That's a bloody poof's job. What do you want with that sort of a job?'

'A career where I can prove to myself I have got the balls to serve the public.'

'OK, lad. I'll have your cards and wages made up to 4pm tonight. Collect them from the front office. Come and see me for your job back when you've had enough of serving the public. Thanks again, Jim, and shut the door behind you when you leave.'

That was it. Why all the heartache, the nerves and sickness, all that wasted toilet paper and squeaky bum cheeks? Nobody was upset I was leaving. I hadn't been there long enough. I had made an impression on the ladies because I was the youngest lad in the weaving shed, and as for 'they were just getting used to me,' they didn't even know my bloody name. I hadn't gone to work that day expecting to be temporarily out of work. I'd expected to work my notice, but I was that important to the working day down at t'mill I was gone in a flash.

I don't take any satisfaction from it and I don't take any blame for it either, but sadly the cotton mill closed down about two years later.

'They've rung up from the hairdresser's today and they said you can start next Tuesday at 9am, and you have to report to the Fulwood Barracks.'

'Mother, I'm starting work as an apprentice in hairdressing, not joining the army.'

My mother had this wonderful trick of listening to a conversation and relaying it with important bits missing.

Topline Hairdressing was situated about two miles to the north-east of Preston town centre, opposite Fulwood Barracks. I knew the salon, as I had gone for the interview there a week earlier.

After a cycle ride of two miles, a train journey of thirty minutes, a walk (or run as the train was late) across town to the bus station and then a ten-minute bus ride to Fulwood, I started work on Tuesday 9th September 1969 at 9.10am - yes, I was late. My very first day at a new job and I arrive ten minutes late.

'We start work at nine o'clock, not five past or ten past, Stephen. And what time do you want to go home?' said my new boss, Mr Vin Miller.

'Sorry, but my train arrived late. If I can go early and catch the 5.15, that would be great. Thanks,' said I, not realising that I was answering a sarcastic question.

'This is Jeff. He'll be looking after you today while Michael's away. He'll show you where everything is and all you need to know. The kettle is in the back room. I'll see you in my office at ten.'

What a bloody good start to a new job that was.

Jeff was a tall young lad, about five years older than me, with long fashionable hair, a bubbly character and good sense of humour. Between customers wandering in for a haircut, Jeff gave me the guided tour of the salon and behind the scenes. The ground-floor business comprised a front shop with a large mirror, two working chairs and eight waiting chairs; behind was the back office, for Mr Miller's toupée clients, another shampoo area which led to the toilet, and a kitchen area, which contained the all-important kettle. Jeff told me that he was only working there for the day, as he normally worked at the other salon in town. Another salon in town? Nobody told me about another salon. 'And if it's in town, what the hell am I doing coming all this way out here?' I thought.

It was ten o'clock. Timidly I went into the back office to face the first of many dressing-downs from Mr Miller. For exactly one hour I was given an intense and vivid introduction to the profession - the expectations, its ups and downs, the challenges ahead, the discipline and desire needed to be successful. I listened intently; absorbed by words of wisdom from a man who had won competitions all over the country and now was judging the same events he had won. It wasn't a telling-off or a blasting, which I had expected. He just told me what was expected of me, and asked if I could handle the job, as he had painted it all in black and white. In fact, there were definitely more black bits than white, but my instinct told me that this was for me, and I told my boss I was committed to the job.

During this one-way conversation the phone rang.

'Answer that, Stephen,' said Mr Miller.

I didn't answer the phone at home, so this was a terrifying experience. 'Hello.'

'Hello, who's that?'

'It's me, Stephen.'

'Stephen who? What number is that?'

'Sorry, I don't know.'

'Where am I ringing?'

'It's a hairdresser's, sir.'

This man is now beginning to get irate. 'Where are you?'

'I am in the office, sir.'

'What bloody town?'

'Sorry sir. We are in Fulwood, near Preston.'

'Where's that?'

'Lancashire.'

'Do you cut hair?'

'We do, but I don't yet.'

'Well, when you do, I hope you cut hair better than you answer the phone. Is Vin there?'

'Yes sir, I'll just get him.'

I lowered the phone and told my boss it was for him.

'Who is it?' asked Mr Miller.

'Hello, who are you?'

The phone went dead. Nobody was there. He'd rung off. What a pig's ear I'd made of that.

'Did you find out who was ringing?'

'No.'

'That was Mr Lancaster, a very good customer of ours. You'll have to work on your telephone technique immediately.'

After that experience, I kept away from the dreaded phone but, hours later, I realised I had been set up. The caller didn't know where he was ringing or who he was ringing, but then asked for Vin. Mr Miller asked me who was on the phone, then told me after the caller had rung off that it was Mr Lancaster. I'd been set up, and fallen for it hook, line and what a stinker, on my very first day. This was one of many times that, as a junior apprentice, I succumbed to the inevitable practical jokes.

That first day still is a clear memory in my mind. I was issued with a new working overall, royal blue with navy blue pinstripes, with a small lapel pocket for combs and a large pouch pocket for the neck brush and all the many tips you were supposed to receive.

After lunch on that first day I was shocked and thrilled to be introduced to a part-time member of staff - none other than Mr Alan Kelly. Alan had been in hairdressing for many years as a second career. He was a professional footballer; in fact at that time he was the Preston North End goalkeeper. He came into the shop on a casual basis mainly to 'keep his hand in'. I was in awe of this big, soft-spoken Irishman whom I had watched for many years from the terraces of Deepdale, and now I was working alongside a local soccer legend. What a start to my first day at Topline Hairdressing!

As I had been told on numerous occasions, the main method of learning this job was standing for hours watching. There is no other practical way to do it. You stand and watch from one side of the chair, then from the other side of the chair, then you stand on one leg, and then the other leg. Your back aches, your neck aches, then your mind starts wandering. You begin to feel hungry, thinking, 'Will I be able to last until lunch, or will I faint?' when from out of the blue the customer asks you a question. You don't even know what day it is, let alone 'Am I enjoying the job?' You splutter an answer that doesn't sound English, isn't convincing, and you leave a lasting impression that you are as bright as a ten-watt bulb in a dance hall.

My tea-making skills were fairly inconsistent: one time I served up masculine treacle (too strong) and the next time it was christened 'siren tea' (all clear). Eventually I did master the art of brewing up, but I had this bad habit of leaving the tea bags in the shampoo sink. Not good practice when one of Mr Miller's posh clients arrives for his regular appointment. From the back of the shampoo area I hear, 'Stephen.' I dash into the back to find the tea bags in the sink where I had left them.

'What are they doing there again? Remove them and don't do it again.'

'Sorry. I'll sort it.'

Little more than a week later I had cocked up again, leaving the little blighters in the sink. This time there was no fuss, no shouts of disapproval. Mr Miller walked into the front shop where I was observing as usual, put something into my pouch pocket and walked back into the back of the shop. Moments later, as wet cold tea dribbled out of my overall pocket and down the front of my pale grey pants, I suddenly remembered the bloody tea bags. Never again did I leave those ****** tea bags in the sink.

Within days of starting work I was given my own toolkit consisting of two combs, one pair of ordinary scissors, a pair of tapering scissors, a neck brush and a pure bristle blow-waving brush. All had been used but were my very own, and they had to be looked after with extreme care, as they were my tools of the trade.

So what's so important about a pair of scissors and a comb? Everybody knows what they are and how they function, but a hairdresser's knowledge is a little more specialised and precise.

Our combs are six to seven inches long, made of a hardened rubber compound; one half has thick teeth, the other thin teeth. Usually we have to use the thick teeth. With the thumb holding the spine, the next finger holds the top of the comb in the centre, while the other fingers are used to roll the comb forward and back, over and over.

If you think it's easy, then try it and, after you have dropped the comb for the umpteenth time, give up and take up knitting.

It sounds and looks so easy, but this first task in hairdressing did prove difficult. Just when I conquered the rolling of the comb trick, I was told, now do the same with the left hand. I might as well have had the comb on a piece of string; I got backache from picking the damned comb off the floor.

The next party trick was with the scissors. The thumb-hold works the top blade furthest away from the body, two fingers hold the bottom blade, the third finger is in the finger-hold, and the little finger holds the back of the finger-hold firmly to steady the scissors (that's the easy bit). Now, at arm's length, hold the bottom blade still and just work the thumb up and down, thus giving the impression that the bottom blade is still.

Are you keeping up with play? I will be asking questions later!

The hard bit of the exercise is to hold the scissors against a straight edge, keeping it still, and then speed up the operation. Once you've mastered that little exercise, you put the two tricks together: roll the comb, scissors held against the bottom edge of the comb and work upwards; once at the top, roll comb down to the bottom and start the exercise again.

Pain, frustration and anger are all related to the dreaded scissor over comb technique; it took me an eternity to master, but it was one of the most important elements in my foundation course of hairdressing. Now bring on some bloody hair!

Guinea pigs, mugs or stooges are few and far between when it comes to parting with their hair (or an ear for that matter), so Eddie was my soul mate when learning the art of cutting hair. Eddie was a dummy head with long hair; notice the emphasis on 'long', as Eddie soon lost a weight off his plastic head. He used to sit in the spare working chair, propped up on an adjustable stand with a gown round his neck, whilst I practised working on him.

The customers knew that Eddie was a dummy; well, nearly all could see that, except old Fred. At first glance it could look like a customer sitting in the chair having his hair cut; to old Fred, with his bad eyesight and jam-jar-bottom glasses, it was a customer he knew as Bill off the allotments.

'How you doing, Bill?'

Nobody spoke, as we didn't know who Fred was talking to.

'Are you not talking, lad? It's me, Fred,' looking towards Eddie.

Then it dawned that Fred thought that Eddie, my dummy model, was Bill off the allotments. Michael, my work colleague, replied quick as a flash, 'Am doin' ol' reet, Fred. Ow's thee-sel?'

'Gradely, if it stays fine for me tomatoes.'

By this time I was in tears. I couldn't laugh, as Fred hadn't a clue he was talking to a dummy. I had to bite my hand to stop the noise of my giggles.

'Are you down there today, Bill?' asked Fred.

There was no answer, so Fred looked at me and came out with the classic statement, 'He's not saying much 'cause he's bloody deaf, you know. Probably not got his hearing aid in.'

That was it; I nearly choked. I ran out of the shop and collapsed into a heap, crying with laughter. You know when the chuckle button is pressed and you can't stop laughing; the belly wobbles, you gasp for air, the tears stream down your face - well, that was yours truly on that day. I composed myself, then went back into the shop to see Fred leaving. As he was walking past the chair, he shouted towards Eddie the dummy, 'See thee later, Bill.'

He looked straight at me and said, 'Bloody deaf as a post, yon bugger, and his seet isn't much better, tha knows.'

That just started me off again. I often wonder what Fred said to him when he met him at the allotment later that day.

Husband and wife are celebrating their Golden Wedding Anniversary. The next morning whilst eating breakfast, the wife says to her husband, 'Darling, my nipples still get hot after fifty years of marriage'.
The husband looks up from his newspaper and replies, 'Yes, my little fruit loop, no wonder. You've got one in your coffee and the other one in your porridge.'

"*RICH* is relative ... The richer you are, the more relatives you have."

Chapter 8 - The complaints department is now closed!

The customer is always right. Now whoever thought that one up, I can assure you he was definitely not a hairdresser. In fact, I don't think he had ever dealt with the paying public. The person who came up with the saying: 'You can please some of the people all of the time, and you can please all of the people some of the time, but you can never please all of the people all of the time,' definitely dealt with the public. In fact, the author of that saying must have been a hairdresser.

Many people go to the hairdresser's to give themselves a lift, to make themselves feel and look better, to relax and unwind, to enjoy a little 'me' time, and to enjoy pleasant conversation. The hairdresser's can also be an outlet to let off steam. We are the last line of defence, the sympathetic ear, the only people in the world that listen without passing judgement. Hairdressers are good at this sort of therapy. It comes with the job; only sometimes hairdressers can also have a bad day. We're human beings too, so we are bound to have the odd hiccup.

If a joiner makes a mess of a piece of wood, he gets another piece and starts again. If the builder has a problem with his wall, he knocks it down and rebuilds it. If a hairdresser is told to cut one inch off the hair and then the client says it is too much, we have just boarded the cock-up carousel. We work with hairnets; we do not have any safety nets. We use hair gel; we do not do use hair glue. When hair is on the floor, it's too late. We aim to please and we strive hard to achieve our goal, but on some occasions it may not be appreciated or good enough.

In my business, the majority of clients are regular visitors, but with no appointment system I know them mainly through friendship and experience. I know where they live, where they work, where they drink, what football team they support - but I know the names of very few.

This guy had been having his hair cut by me for many years. When he got married, I did his hair for the big day; since then he had been divorced and had been playing the mating game for many a year. Even though I knew him very well and I knew how I cut his hair, I followed the accepted practice and ask him how he wanted his hair cut.

'Just tidy it up like usual?' I asked, knowing the answer.

'I'll leave it to you, you're the boss,' was his reply, and we continued with the usual everyday chat. The guy contributed to filling my till and he left my establishment a happy chappie, as was usually the case.

The peace was shattered about 10am the following day. In fact it must have been earlier, as we hadn't made a coffee and I hadn't reached the television page in the morning paper.

'Are you the boss?' I was asked by this large lady, who reminded me of a rugby prop forward.

'Yes, that is correct. How can I help you?' I asked, somewhat puzzled.

'You cut me feller's hair yesterday and it's far too short,' she said abruptly.

'Are you sure it was here he had it done? I can't remember anybody complaining about their haircut yesterday,' I explained, trying to soften her tone.

'No, it was you who did it. He said it was the boss and he was bald,' she smirked.

Well, that narrowed it down to one; it must have been me that had done this haircut, as there is only one boss and I may have lost a few strands of hair over the years.

'So what was wrong with the haircut?' I asked, trying not to look frightened even though she was a damn sight bigger than me.

'It was far too short. I want him to grow it long but he won't.'

'So let's get this right: he was happy with his haircut, I was happy with his haircut, but you weren't happy because he got his hair cut when you told him not to,' I countered, not wanting to sound too sarcastic as I valued my ears.

By now I was starting to smile, as I thought she had made an appearance for a bit of a laugh, but this was definitely no laughing matter and 'Mrs Prop Forward' was definitely not laughing. To ease the tension I came up with a compromise.

'Next time he comes for his haircut, either send him with a note or you come along with him so you can give me all the instructions,' I said, not wanting to sound too cocky as my wind-pipe was working fine and I wanted to keep it that way.

'Next time! There will be no next time,' she bellowed. 'I will cut his hair from now on.' She turned and stormed out of the salon.

I never did see that guy again in my salon. I lost a customer and he probably lost the will to live.

Whilst travelling in America, I observed that if things are not as they should be, people complain. In this country the majority of people will avoid complaining because they do not want to make a scene. In a restaurant a table of diners will moan to one other that the soup isn't hot enough, the steak is too tough, the peas are cold, but when the waiter arrives to ask if everything is good we tell him, 'All is just fine, thank you.' Improvements can't be made if nothing is said.

My own children have heard certain phrases many times that I have used that will stay with them all their lives and I am quite sure they will use them when bringing up their own children. One important phrase that I learned as a young apprentice is: 'It's not *what* is said - it is *how* it is said that matters.'

If I said to the wife during a war of words, 'You're stupid,' then the odds are I would be subjected to the silent treatment, make my own meals and sleep in the shed. Alternatively, if in conversation I joke, 'You're stupid,' because she bought three bags of carrots that we didn't need, I would be subjected to a full-on, two-minute talking-to on how good carrots are for my eyesight (same two words, different outcome).

When many people complain, they expect an argument. In some cases they *want* an argument. Their voice gets louder until they start to shout. I find it a good policy to listen intently, then speak when there is a question to be answered, as I did when this lady started bellowing at me on the other end of the phone.

'Hello, Toptrend Hairdressing,' I answered.

'Hello. Is that the hairdresser's on the bus station?' this upset lady shouted.

'Yes it is,' I said. 'Is there something wrong?'

'My son had his hair cut at your place this morning and he is not happy,' she yelled. 'What are you going to do about it?' She started to cry.

'Now please stop shouting and stop crying, and tell me what the problem is,' I said, feeling a little bemused.

She went quiet for a few seconds, blew her nose and continued: 'My son had his hair cut today at your salon and it's wrong. He's shouting at me.' She started to cry again.

'Will you ask him to speak to me and we can sort this out?'

'He won't speak to you. I've told him to talk to you but he won't,' she sobbed, while I heard shouting in the background.

'Ask him to come back to the salon today so we can sort it out. Then you won't get into any more trouble,' I said.

'I'll send him on the bus right away.' The phone went down with a thud.

I asked the lads if they could remember any youngster in that morning who was not happy with his haircut. We had no idea who this mum-threatening, mini-thug could be - but we didn't have long to wait.

Unfortunately for this lad, the salon was busy when he returned to confront us. I had done his haircut no more than an hour and a half earlier. This mini-thug, who had gone home and reduced his mother to tears, was about twenty-five years old and had the softest spoken voice you ever heard. He walked in and stood at the door.

'Hello. Was it your mother that has just been on the phone in tears?' I asked, speaking so that everybody in the shop could hear.

'Yes, that's right,' he squeaked.

'So what's wrong with the haircut?' I asked, making sure everyone heard the question, as I knew that there was nothing wrong with it. I had done as he had asked.

'I think I could do to have it a little bit shorter at the back,' he whispered, hoping nobody was listening.

'So instead of coming back to see me about your haircut, you went home and reduced your mother to tears.' I was beginning to get a little uptight. My exhaust mechanism was getting a little heated - I was in free flow. He stood there and took it. I was more upset for his mother than on my own account, but all of a sudden I stopped the ridicule. Like a bolt of lightening the thought struck me that, if I gave him any more stick, his mother could well be the loser again. I didn't say another word to this mild-mannered wimp - I just cut his hair shorter. I didn't charge him any money but I scribbled a letter and sealed it up in an envelope and asked him to give it to his mother. The letter read: 'Mother, sorry for the upset today.'

I don't think I have ever been more angry with a customer than I was that day. He never came back for another haircut and the letter probably never arrived home, but for me it drew a line under the episode and made me feel better.

In life, the older you get the more knowledge you gain. Whether you use that knowledge is debatable, but at certain times of your life you come face to face with a problem or situation and realise you have been there before. In reality, you should draw on your experience and know what to do the second time around, but life isn't like that, as I'm sure you'll agree when you read the next two tales.

It is Saturday morning and the salon is full of the patient, pleasant people of Preston waiting for their haircuts. All is well in Toptrend Hairdressing, and Gary and I are fully operational in trying to make a crust. In walks a tall young Afro-Caribbean guy carrying a small parcel. He stands waiting at the door, as there are no seats. As we finish with our clients, the queue moves along and this guy sits down on the first available seat. After several minutes, I realise that the young guy has left the salon and left his parcel on his seat.

My first concern is for the safety of the people in the salon, as this could be a bomb (it was about the time of the Manchester town centre bombings). I ask the man sitting alongside the parcel where this guy is, expecting a toilet break must have been necessary; he informs me he has gone shopping and he has asked the man if he would move the parcel along the queue to save his position in the queue for him. What a bloody cheek! Then yours truly moves the parcel from the seat and starts to examine it. Now if it had been a bomb and this cuckoo was meddling with it, we could all have been given a harp that day. It turns out to be a box containing an electric shaver. I place the parcel on the coat stand and wait for the elusive customer to return.

More than an hour and a half later, the guy arrives back, first looking for his parcel and second expecting to be next in the queue for his haircut.

I shout for the next customer to climb aboard my working chair, knowing we are in for a confrontation. The big guy walks forward to be seated. 'Sorry sir. It isn't you next. There are all these people waiting,' I inform him.

'Yes it is. I came in earlier and left my parcel to queue for me,' he pointed out.

'Sorry sir, but you have to sit and wait your turn. We do not cut parcels' hair,' I explain, trying to make light of the situation.

'I had to go shopping. You are being totally unreasonable,' he says and his voice begins to rise. 'You do not want to cut my hair. You do not like black people, you are a racist,' he shouts.

I give him his parcel from the coat-stand and ask him to leave the salon.

It was mid-afternoon on a busy Saturday and I had just finished this lad in his mid-twenties. We had been having the usual banter whilst I was cutting his hair, and I could not have envisaged what was about to happen. The lad paid, turned to leave and … wallop. He collapsed full length on the floor. He was out cold.

With my limited knowledge of first aid I felt a pulse and eased him into the recovery position. Gary rang for the ambulance as I went fishing with a pencil to make sure he hadn't swallowed his tongue. Nobody moved from their seats. They all just sat and watched, not that there was anything to see. We waited for the ambulance to turn up. Movement was slowly starting to return in his arms and I spoke quietly to the lad to find out some details.

'Hello, you've fainted. Can you hear me?' I asked, trying to get some sense out of the lad. Nothing appeared to get through, so I asked again, 'Hello, you are in the hairdresser's, can you hear me?'

He slowly started to come back to Planet Earth and ramble. The rambling got louder; he opened his eyes and started to shout at me.

'You're against me, you. Get away. Leave me alone,' he shouted, then started hurling insults and foul language at me. I tried to calm him down but to no avail. He was having none of it. A customer came over and tried to ease the lad's anxiety, but he continued to shout at me.

The blue-light brigade arrived none too soon. One of the ambulance men walked in, saw the lad on the floor and shouted, 'Get up, Jimmy. Come on, Jimmy, get up.' It was like a story from out of the Bible: I witnessed a miracle in my salon that day. The lad picked himself up and walked out of the salon unaided.

I walked out with the ambulance man, who told me it was a regular occurrence; Jimmy often had these epileptic fits. They came on when he had forgotten to take his tablets. Rumour had it that Jimmy sometimes deliberately forgot to take the tablets so he always had a very quick taxi service home, because he lived near the hospital!

Two different circumstances, but both times I was involved in an odious situation. I have had foul language hurled at me on many occasions, having been a football referee for more than thirty years, but I have never been accused of being a racist except in this case. In any situation where I have been subjected to a volatile confrontation, I usually listen, act and later analyse what I could have done to prevent that situation happening again. These two tales I considered for ages and didn't find any answers. It was another day in the salon dealing with everyday life.

The up-side to dealing with everyday life is that you never know what is coming your way, what you will have to face and what idiotic questions you may be asked. We are not talking silly questions like: What does a Blackpool donkey get for his dinner? Answer: Half an hour like his owner; or a common enquiry like, 'I'm in a hurry. Could you do me in five minutes?' How bloody stupid.

We are now talking dumb answers to some dumb questions.

Harry had longish hair compared with today's styles; it reached to the bottom of his ears and over the collar at the back. He had very wavy hair that grew into a tight curl if left to its own devices. Like the majority of people in the world, Harry was not happy with his hair. People with curly hair want straight hair, people with straight hair want wavy hair, people with thick hair want thinner hair, people with thin hair want thick hair, and I would just like some hair of any sort. Very few people are happy with what they have.

Harry's middle name must have been Vanity. Each visit, he would have his hair shampooed, cut and ironed flat. It was many years before men would own up to using straighteners, so I would spend ages blow-drying and ironing his hair as flat as it would allow. Just before he left my salon, he would look at himself in the mirror, smile and blow a kiss to himself, then vacate the premises.

This particular day it was damp, miserable and blowing a gale. The usual masterpiece had been achieved and a can of hairspray was exhausted to make the hairstyle stay put. Harry left the salon with the customary smile and kiss - to arrive back within forty-five seconds. The hair had been ravaged by the seventy-five-mile-an-hour hurricane and he looked like Marge from The Simpsons. Harry was not a happy cartoon character.

'Look at this, Steve,' he announced, rushing back into the salon like a rabbit glad to find his warren. 'It's bloody windy out there. Look at your masterpiece. It's ruined,' he moaned, not happy at his mirror image now. There were no smiles and certainly no kisses.

'Can you sort this out, Steve? Will it go flat like before?'

'Harry, with that wind out there, the only chance of keeping your hair flat is covering it with cling film and tying it under your ears,' I said.

Without a moment's hesitation he asked, 'Will that keep it flat? We could give it a go if you think it will work,' not taking on board the fact that I was being a little ironic. After another half-hour's action replay, Harry left by a different route.

As I've been in the same town-centre location for more than thirty-five years, it is fairly obvious that on a few occasions I must be getting some haircuts right!

Hairstyle trends change and people occasionally want to change their own image, as well as their hairdresser. Children grow up wanting a new makeover and a different person to do it. People move to new locations for work and have to find another hairdresser.

The one thing I find amazing is that a handful of people want to try a new hairdresser every time they get a haircut. Whatever the situation, it is common practice to see new faces walk through the door every day you are open for business.

The majority of customers are loyal to one hairdresser, whether it is for the hairdresser's personality, his skill and professional ability, or his reliability and friendship with the customer. Whatever it takes, the business is built on regular customers, and regular can mean every week, every month or every year. That is the nature of the business but all hairdressers know that things will never stay the same.

Analysing why you lose customers could send you barmy. It would be easier to push a piece of string up Scafell Pike. The ones that really upset the thinking mechanism in the brain are the customers who you try to help, but then they leave you with a big pile of do-do and no brush and shovel to sweep it up!

These five short stories start with the letters N M M N G. You'll see why at the end!

<u>Naughty</u>: I was revamping the salon and throwing the old waiting chairs away. I had cut Johnny's hair since he was a kid when he had come with his mum after school. He was in his early twenties now and had recently taken over running the local scout group in his area. He wanted my old chairs for his scout hut and I kept them in the back of the salon till he collected them. Eventually I had no room to store them so I put them on the roof of the salon until he collected them. Outcome to my benevolent story: he never came back for the chairs so didn't come back for his haircut. Resulting in one lost customer.

<u>Misleading</u>: I had cut Herman's hair for well over ten years and

he and June, his wife, became close family friends; we had been out for meals together and spent many an evening looking for the bottom of a wine bottle. Whilst out in the car one day, Jean got a text to say Herman had packed his bags and left the matrimonial home. He had been having an affair for more than two years and he had given his wife notice only to cook for one in the future. June was devastated, Jean was shocked and I was bloody miffed. I didn't know; what do they say? 'Never mix business with pleasure.' Resulting in one lost ...

<u>Mistrusting</u>: From a very early age, Graham used to come with his dad for his haircut. He was a well-respected lad from a good family background. As expected, he started to come on his own as he got bigger. We had a very good rapport as he grew up. He started working as a chef at a local restaurant and was getting on his feet. One day he called in for his haircut about 4.30pm and when he was paying he suddenly realised he had no money with him. No problem. He got out his cheque book out and started to write me a cheque, only instead of making the cheque for £7.50 he made it out for £30 and asked if I could give him the change in cash so he didn't have to go to the bank on his way home. Need I say more (rubber cheque; bounce, bounce)… When we eventually went round to his house, his dad paid back the £30 with no hesitation with the words, 'Has he done it again? He's always doing that.' Resulting in: lost…

<u>Negative</u>: Eric was a three-weekly regular. You could set your watch by him. Friday at 3.45pm, Eric entered the building. He knocked off work early on Fridays and a haircut was top of his list every twenty-one days - a creature of habit. A joiner by trade, and always looking for work. I was under pressure at home to decorate the hallway, and spindles were mentioned for the stairway. I asked Eric to come and look at the job and price it up. Didn't turn up. I phoned him and he was coming round the next night … didn't turn

up. He called on Friday for his haircut and told me he had lost my address and phone number but he would be round tonight. Eric doesn't open my door on a Friday at 3.45 every twenty-one days any more. Resulting in: you guessed it!

<u>Gullible:</u> Christmas Eve fell on a Sunday. Jim was in the armed services and was due back home for Christmas after serving abroad. On his last visit he had asked me if it was possible for me to cut his hair on the Sunday as he was only getting home late on the 23rd. He confirmed he would be there on Sunday at 11am as we had agreed by phone a week earlier. Outcome to my helpful story: he didn't turn up, didn't phone and I had to eat all six mince pies. Net result: … read as above!

So, what do the letters **N M M N G** equate to?
No More Mister Nice Guy.

I am still trading and after many experiences like those last five tales, I bought a brush and shovel (*I learnt sense*), and I have less doo-doo to clean up these days!

Extracts from complaint forms to a council office somewhere near you.

The toilet is blocked and we cannot bath the children until it is fixed.

Our kitchen floor is very damp. We have two children and we would like a third.

My water is a funny colour and not fit to drink.

I am writing on behalf of my sink, which is running away from the wall.

This is to let you know there is a smell from the man next door.

"One minute is a long time on the wrong side of a toilet door when you're bursting!"

Chapter 9 - The passing of time

Months of determined effort saw me master the art of brewing up and answering the phone, not to mention scissor work. The main change to this young, wet-behind-the-ears youth was that I was gaining in confidence, a necessity for success in this career. Not to say I was brimming with the stuff, but I could hold a sensible conversation with customers and cut hair, albeit on a dummy or on very old pensioners who would insist I practise on their grey hair to learn the 'tricks of the trade'. To be honest, I never did find many tricks of the trade cutting a three-inch band of grey fine hair... But the lift it gave when I attended to a customer from entering the salon, cutting, chatting and charging him, made me feel not quite master class but I was on my way. When that same customer came in again and asked specifically for me to do it - then I was nearing master class.

While progress in the use of the scissors continued, running concurrently was the learning process of what was then called blow-waving: an art form for making waves in hair, bending hair to a desired form and creating lift and movement for a specific style with the use of a hand-held hairdryer. Sounds complicated - it bloody well is.

Hairdryers years ago were heavy and cumbersome with a very

wide nozzle, and the aim of the game was to hold the hair in the desired shape with a bristle brush and direct the air flow to dry the hair, thus creating the shape. The boss, who had many catch phrases, would issue the instruction 'Hold and Mould', although my efforts were more like 'Steam and Dry'. I can tell you that Eddie, my trusted dummy, came out in many hot sweats as I practised this wonderful art.

The two technical and most difficult exercises were applying the hot air flow to the roots of the hair, and the rolling forward and reverse use of the brush. One soon became skilled in the application of hot air on human guinea pigs, as they either screamed with pain or they slowly slid down the chair to escape the excessive heat from the dryer.

The second of these skills became a huge problem for me. I spent hour after hour rolling the damn brush forwards and back, over and over, using one hand then the other. Every spare moment, I had a bristle brush in my hand, practising. One particular night I was travelling home on the train, minding my own business, hand in my large coat pocket, rolling the brush back and forth. You can't read with one hand in your pocket holding a bristle brush so I was in another world, concentrating on making this action second nature. As the train slowed down approaching a station, I returned to Planet Earth and noticed this middle-aged lady across from me, looking my way with a really nice warm smile on her face. I smiled back and thought nothing of it. Minutes later, as the train was pulling away from the station, I swapped pockets with the brush and continued with my practice. This time I slyly looked across at the lady sitting opposite; she still had this broad smile but looked away when we made eye contact. 'Nice lady,' I thought. The train started to slow down for the next station and she made a move to get up and leave. I looked up to smile and say 'bye', when she leaned over and said quietly to me, 'It's a shame these stations are too near. You just can't get there can you, love?'

I honestly hadn't a clue what she was talking about but like a näive clot I answered, 'No.'

She alighted from the train. I thought, 'What a pleasant lady. What the hell was she talking about?' Further down the line, the penny dropped. A young lad playing about in his pocket with hand motions and then changing pockets… I went all hot and sticky, my mind was racing and I felt physically sick. It was more than two weeks before I ventured on the train - and luckily I didn't see the lady again.

With the passing of time the confidence and skill factors increased, giving me the satisfaction that I had found my vocation in life. The boss was happy with my progress, so I was given the opportunity to sign indenture forms as an apprentice hairdresser. My sentence to deal with the public consisted of a three-year apprenticeship and two years as an improver. To this very day I am still technically an improver, as I never did receive my passing-out papers.

Early in my apprenticeship I was introduced to another important and exciting piece of apparatus: the open razor, also known as the 'cutthroat razor' - a splendid and useful tool, to be treated with the utmost respect. The open razor is still often used today but in a different form, as most of today's razors have replaceable blades for which no sharpening is necessary; you just throw away the used blade and snap in another. To be honest, I guess the blades are better now and will keep their edge much longer. But in the dark ages you had to learn to look after your prize possession, your very own open razor.

The large blade, usually made from Solingen German steel, was kept well-oiled for obvious reasons, but the hard work was to achieve the edge. A carborundum stone about eight inches by two was oiled and the blade was laid flat on the stone. Now comes the clever bit that took some time and effort. I learnt to move the blade slowly, edge towards me, then in a figure-of-eight movement turn over the blade to stroke away from me, keeping it perfectly flat to the stone. This exercise sounds complicated, but it was one of the tricks that I picked up quickly for a very special reason. As I explained, you had to keep the blade perfectly flat to the stone. Well, my boss showed me the only way you can tell the blade is flat to the stone is by placing a finger from your other hand onto the stone, letting the edge slide under your finger. I learned very quickly, as the sight of blood made my legs wobble.

The work on the stone would take any nicks and bumps off the steel; the finishing touch was to polish the edge on a leather strop. This was done by pushing the blade away from you with the edge trailing nearest to you and, again in a figure-of-eight movement, turning over the blade so as to strop both sides of the blade. It is quite obvious to me now why the blade is trailing; if it was pushed edge first there would be no leather strop, as it would cut into the leather. It wasn't that obvious then because I demolished many a leather strop, cutting them to ribbons.

Using the razor as a tool is an art form; it gives some wonderful results on wet hair, but it could be also used as a very serious weapon. In the early 70s a cutthroat razor was a prized possession: our salon was burgled one evening and the police thought the main target of the thieves (apart from the money, of course) was the cutthroat razors. It was a strange world even then!

Whilst on the subject of the razor - it was a fairly common event for our hairdressing business to go out to church halls and youth clubs, to put on hairdressing shows. This gave the staff experience in showing off their work and performing in front of an audience if they were going to do competition work; plus, from the boss's point of view, it was a good way of drumming up trade in the surrounding areas.

This particular evening, we had finished our demonstration and the boss, who was never short on fun and games, decided to hold a quick competition for the audience, as we had finished a little early. He got three willing volunteers out of the audience to come up on stage to shave a balloon. This sounds harder than it is, but there are certain tricks to doing it. Firstly, he showed the audience how it was done centre stage, whilst backstage the three stooges were kitted up with overalls and given strict instructions on dos and don'ts. The balloons were covered in shaving foam and each volunteer was given a razor and a box of tissues to wipe the foam off the razor. They were shown how to do this. It wasn't a race, but two of the balloons soon popped. The muppet at the far end was doing ever so well, in fact he was doing too well as he got a little excited and proceeded to wipe the surplus foam off the razor with (you guessed it) his fingers. There was blood everywhere, and that really put a dampener on the whole evening. I suppose nowadays there would be lawsuits all over the place. Luckily, no long-term damage was done but that trick was never performed again in any of our hair shows.

When learning the art of hair craft, working on blocks with implanted artificial fabricated fibre to replicate hair was a start, but once you gained the skill and the confidence, real human hair was the ultimate goal.

It didn't come as any surprise that to find guinea pigs to practise my skills on was as hard as finding glider engine mechanics. Fast-forward two years and my nights could have been spent doing the same job that I was doing all day, but for little reward.

'Steve's a good barber. He'll do you a favour, he'll cut your hair,' and in most cases I did, at all times of the day. One bloke who lived up the road, who never spoke to me or even recognised me, rang one Sunday evening at 10.30pm pleading for his haircut as he had an interview the following morning. The mug was the guy holding the pair of scissors at 11pm.

I can't remember many volunteers offering their precious locks when I needed practice on human hair early in my apprenticeship.

I had cut Maurice's hair for many years at home. It fitted in with my schedule and it was convenient for him - but suddenly he stopped calling. Months later I bumped into him in the local pub.

'Hi Maurice,' I said as naturally as I could, as I didn't want him to feel embarrassed.

'How are you doing, Steve? Not seen you for a bit,' he said, with an uneasy smile. 'You see, I get me hair cut by this woman that comes round to cut the wife's hair. She doesn't do it as good as you - in fact she cocks it up a bit. I'm not really happy with the way she does it but she's got a belting pair of tits!'

'Sorry Maurice, I can't compete with them,' I conceded.

There is a golden rule when it comes to haircuts: when you find what you require in a haircut, whether it is price, convenience, personality, jokes, professionalism or a belting pair of tits, then stay with that hairdresser.

Happy with your hair? Then you'll feel happy in your life.

Just been to the gym today and - wow! They have a new machine. I only used it for half an hour then started to feel sick. It's a good machine and it does everything - Kit Kats, Snickers, Crisps, Mars Bars a really good variety.

"Don't take life too seriously- it isn't permanent!"

Chapter 10 - The ups and downs and ins and outs of life

Tuesday morning 9.15 and it's raining. I have already been soaked just getting to work, and the odds are it will be raining when I go home. I find to my delight that there are no tea bags for a brew and the milkman has not yet arrived. All my colleagues have assembled in the staffroom to discuss their weekend activities whilst I am left in the salon keeping watch, awaiting any early clientele. I am the junior in the salon and nobody is interested in my weekend adventures, as they don't live up to their own nocturnal habits.

Hairdressing is unique, as it is probably the only profession that has a belated weekend. In my early years most hairdressers would close on Monday, thereby giving you two days off work together, but it also meant it was customary that hairdressers had that dreaded Monday morning feeling on a Tuesday morning. I was having that feeling now and, knowing my luck, it would be a long Tuesday morning.

'Hello, Steve. How are you doing?'

This soft voice brought me back to reality; I was miles away, contemplating another working week at the asylum.

'How are you doing?' I answered, but for an instant I couldn't recognise this grey-haired, oldish man of about sixty.

'I'm not too bad and getting better as every day goes by,' he answered, as he sat down on my big chair.

I tried to instil some energy into the haircut but also tried to recognise him. He obviously knew me, as he knew my name.

'You don't know who I am, do you, Steve?'

'Go on, give us a clue,' I said with my cheeky, boyish humour.

'Don, train driver. The last time you cut my hair was May last year, remember?'

Now, unless you run an appointment system, you do not know many people's names but you do remember most people by where they work, where they drink or some other distinguishing feature. Unfortunately this face was not ringing any bells.

'No, it still hasn't clicked, has it?'

'Sorry but… No,' I said. I was intrigued, but not without a certain amount of embarrassment.

'I came for my haircut just before I went on holiday to Devon and Cornwall.'

'Were you going with your wife, driving down and doing a spot of fishing?'

'Correct, that's it. Well I've been poorly since then. That's why you haven't seen me for some time.'

To look at this man now from what I remembered of him only a few months ago, dumbfounded me. He looked sixty; he was in fact thirty-eight. Once a strong and physically active young man, he was now a shadow of his former self. His hair was very thick with a slight wave; though he still had a thick mane of hair, it was now grey. I was probably only eighteen myself and I had never seen a decline in a person to the extent that I couldn't recognise him. I was shocked, I was upset, but I was also curious as to how this rapid decline had come about.

'So what's been happening? Did you go on holiday?'

Don started to explain his fight for life: his anguish, his pain and sadness. I listened with awe to his compelling story.

'We were having a wonderful holiday and the weather was very kind to us. On the third day I thought I'd had too much sun, as I started with this blinding headache. The upshot was that I collapsed and ended up in hospital with a brain haemorrhage. You'll see the cuts on my scalp.'

I combed the hair and found a massive circular scar on each side of his head, starting at the temple hairline and looping round to behind both ears.

'Are they sore? Is it all right to touch them with my comb?' I was apprehensive about hurting this guy.

'No problem. That's why I had to wait to let it heal before I could come and see you. I was down there in hospital for five months before they let me return up north, and the wife had to find accommodation for all that time. The wife drove us back and it took us eleven hours to amble home with frequent stops.'

'So how are you feeling now?' To be honest I couldn't say he looked well because he didn't; he was a different person from the one I remembered.

'I'm feeling much better every day and you don't know how that feels until you have been so close to the boss upstairs. I look older and I feel tired but I am still here to tell the tale. When I saw the doctor for the last time before I left the hospital I thanked him for giving me my life back. I hope you can do as good a job with my hair as he did with my head.'

I remember thinking, *It's raining, there are no tea bags, no milk and nobody wants to listen to my weekend. WHAT THE HELL HAVE I GOT TO BE MISERABLE ABOUT?*

I don't know how long it took me to cut his hair that day. It seemed an eternity but, thirty-five years on, I can still remember that day. I had started with the world on my shoulders and learned another valuable lesson in life. To this day I will never use 'knowing my luck' as a figure of speech because I know I am a very lucky individual.

It is three days before Christmas Day and, as is customary, we are packed to the doors with the Christmas rush.

'Next please,' I yelled, over the repetitive Christmas music on the radio. I waited for my next contestant to jump into the hot seat.

A gentleman in his mid-fifties whom I had never met in my life climbed aboard and we started the usual chatter, how he wanted his haircut, and no he wasn't working on this particular day.

'Are you on holiday for Christmas now, sir?'

'I'm on holiday permanently. I've retired.'

'What a lucky man. What do you do with all that time on your hands?' I enquired.

'I take it easy. I was a dentist working down in Surrey for many years but I had to retire through ill health.'

'So you live up here now, then?'

'No, I'm just visiting my daughter for Christmas and spending some quality time with my family.'

I don't know what it was, but the voice seemed to falter as he spoke.

'It's been some time since you've seen them?' I asked trying not to sound too nosey.

'No, quite the opposite. I see them fairly regularly, but last week when I visited my doctor he advised me to stop driving.'

'That must have been quite a shock to the system.'

'Not as much as when he told me this would probably be my last Christmas!'

There are not many times this hairdresser is ever stuck for words, whether it be sympathetic words, one-line humorous insults or just pleasantries, but this time I had no wind in my sails. I stood there for a few seconds, then tried to pretend he hadn't said what he had said. Words would not come. There was just nothing to say; I tried, and my mouth was about to open but nothing happened. He saw that I was in no man's land, probably by my facial expression. To his credit, he helped me out of this void in time.

'I knew it wasn't good, but when you get news like that you either sink or swim, and I aim to swim until I sink.' He spoke with confidence. He was going to enjoy this Christmas come what may. He had this purposeful smile all the time we were speaking and the hairdresser had nearly lost it! 'This Christmas I'll be with my family for the last time, but I aim to enjoy it and then I can say goodbye to them all.'

I was struggling to hold it together but managed to keep my composure.

The customer was pleased with the haircut. He paid; I shook his hand and wished him all the luck in the world. He left the salon and I went and sat down in the back for a few moments to understand what had just happened.

A person I had never met before had made such a big impact on my way of thinking. He hadn't told me because he wanted sympathy; he'd told me because I asked. That Christmas Day I had that person in my thoughts many times and hoped he really did enjoy his last Christmas.

Jonathan was a quiet, shy lad who lacked confidence. In his mid-thirties, he'd never had any meaningful relationships with any ladies but longed for one. I had done his hair for more than ten years on a weekly basis, so I was well up his Christmas card list and qualified as one of his best mates, probably because he didn't have any others. Each week he would tell me about how near he was to finding a girlfriend, only for this fictitious dream girl to let him down at the last moment. Even with one of my expertly styled masterpieces on his head, the ladies found Jonathan a no-go area. His mother had died when he was in his early twenties, so he lived with his dad in a large house on the outskirts of Preston.

This particular day Jonathan waltzes into the salon with a smile from ear'ole to ear'ole.

'Someone's looking in a good mood. Have we won on the pools?' I enquire, hoping the lad has found some female company.

'There is a new lady in my life again, Steve.'

I don't come with the cynical comment about the word 'again', as I have heard this so many times before. 'So this one must be special to put a smile on the dial that big,' I say.

'She's a wonderful lady and we have so much in common.'

That was the start of a romance. Over the next couple of months the relationship grew and grew, and each week Jonathan came with more pieces of news about this bizarre courtship. On one occasion he announced that she had been married before but that was in the past; her future was with him. Then the following week she owned up to having two children. The week after he told me he'd met the children and he would be glad to look after them, as he and his lady were thinking of looking for a place to live together. I was glad for the lad because he was a changed man, but I was very sceptical. He was older than me but not as street-wise, and he seemed to be running in quicksand. There were too many flaws in his very odd story.

I tried to tell him without him becoming aware of my concern. 'What's all the big hurry, Jonathan? There's plenty of time. Slow the job down, don't rush into such a big decision.'

'We want to have children of our own so we need a place to live - and soon.'

While they were looking for a house to buy, Jonathan's father sadly died and so the perfect answer was to move into his dad's house. This seemed to be the makings of a happy family.

After they had moved into his dad's house I rarely saw Jonathan, as he said his new lady was doing his hair for him.

I met him walking through the town centre about fifteen months later and he was a shadow of his former self. I invited him to the salon to sort out his once proud hairstyle that was now a thin and untidy mess.

Jonathan was embarrassed to let me know about his new lifestyle in the local shelter for the homeless. The missing months since I had seen him had been a total catastrophe; the lady he was in love with took him to the cleaners and then hung him out with cheap clothes pegs so he would fall back into the mud again and again. It transpired this that lady had four children and moved them all into Jonathan's house. He paid for everything and even put her name on the deeds of the house. After a few months she shipped in her existing husband and poor Jonathan was beaten up and kicked out of his own dad's house.

Tales like this happen in every town in every country all the time, but when I am so close to them, it leaves me upset and concerned for such vulnerable people.

Not too many weeks after I spoke to Jonathan, I read in the local newspaper that his body had been found behind some waste bins. Supposedly he had died of hypothermia.

∾

Jim arrives in my salon with a large, two-piece collar on his neck; the obvious question would be 'What happened to you?' but with Jim it is 'What happened this time?' If you cut Jim down the middle of his body with an axe, the words 'Beware, Catastrophic Disaster Area' would be written through him like a stick of Blackpool rock. This is the lad that was pushed down the stairs at a night club; thrown out of the club for causing trouble; lost his money in the chaos; whilst walking home was mugged by a group of lads; jumped over a fence as he ran away to escape their further attentions; caught his finger jumping down from the fence and lost the finger. It definitely did happen, as I've seen his hand. The lad is a walking catastrophe. I think his rocking horse died when he was ten, and thereafter 'Miss Fortune' was his regular girlfriend. This debacle happened to Jim in 2004, and it just shows us all how fine a line we walk each day.

Jim finishes work early and heads for the pub (as he is starting his holidays), has two pints, goes home, picks his girlfriend and the cases up and drives over to Manchester Airport to stay the night before flying off early the next morning. They are staying at one of the posh hotels on the airport complex. His girlfriend wants a shower and Jim is itching to find the bar, so he arranges to meet her downstairs when she is ready. Jim walks down the stairs, as the lift is full. Just as he leaves the landing to get to the bar, he misses his footing and tumbles all the way down to the bottom of the stairs. He tries to get up, with a sore shoulder and neck, but the hotel porter asks him to stay still as an ambulance has been called for. He is rushed to hospital.

Meanwhile his girlfriend has sorted herself out and ambles down to the bar to meet Jim for a drink. With no sign of him, she assumes that he has gone into the airport to look at the planes, goes back to their bedroom and goes to sleep. She wakes up in the early hours with no sign of Jim and with the flight only three hours away. She rushes down to the bar to look for him and then asks at the reception if they have any information about him, as they have to check in for their flight. She is informed he was taken to hospital the previous night. She gets a taxi and rushes to find him.

In hospital Jim has it confirmed that he has broken his neck. He's transferred to Hope Hospital and fitted with a large metal cage - two metal rods through his temples exiting at the back of his head. I saw the marks on his skin after the rods were removed.

'So that collar is to keep your head still?' I ask. 'And you are feeling much better now?'

'I was, but I got an infection on one side so I went into Preston Hospital. The rod was tightened, the infection burst and I was in hospital another week. That was more painful than the break,' he tells me.

'So how long is it since the fall?' I ask.

'It's fifteen weeks since. I'm now on the road to recovery, just having to wear this large collar.'

On that particular day Jim seemed upbeat and confident about his future, but I could sense there was an element of despondency. His girlfriend had ended the relationship, as she blamed him for losing the holiday and, to add to Jim's misfortune, the insurance company was refusing to pay out for the holiday, as he had smelt of alcohol when he had had the accident.

I have cut Jim's hair many times since and he has made a remarkable recovery. When you look at the big picture of what could have happened, he was a lucky boy that day.

Every day has a different story; every time I open my door for business there is another tale to tell. What other job can make you cry with laughter one moment and put you on the seat of your pants the next? All my working life I have dealt with the public, and I am privileged to be part of so many people's lives. It just makes me realise how fortunate I really am.

Last week I went to the cemetery to lay some flowers on Nan's grave. As I was standing there I noticed four gravediggers walking about with a coffin. After I had cleaned up Nan's grave I noticed the four gravediggers with the same coffin going the other way. About twenty minutes later as I was leaving Nan's grave, the four gravediggers were still wandering about carrying the coffin. I remember thinking to myself; they've lost the plot!

"Shouldn't common sense become more obvious the older you get?"

Chapter II - Naïvety

After eighteen months I had taken to this job like wine to a bottle and the job seemed to like me. I was a settled young man. I had moved to the busy town-centre salon under a new boss, I had my own position and my own mirror, I had passed my driving test, was the proud owner of a mini-van with seats in the back and, oh yes, I nearly forgot - I found out about girls. I was now making my way through life knowing full well that I had no more learning to do, as I knew all I had to know.

Most Saturdays, four of the Croston mob would meet up and leave the sticks to go up town to booze and boogie. It was probably more like 'Watch with Mother', as there was more action in a bag of marbles. Before the pubs shut we would make our way to our usual haunt, the Top Rank nightclub (they used to be called discothèques), and get a good position to spot all the 'fit birds' as they walked down the stairs. We would pair off and see if we could score with the chicks, meet up, change the pairs, and go wandering in hope once again, meet up, change the pairs and stand at the edge of the dance floor and ogle; then we would meet up and go home. All the way home in the car we all crowed about how each one of us could have scored but 'didn't want to leave a mate on his own'. What a load of codswallop!

On this particular night my luck was in - or this nice young lady felt sorry for me - as I scored in the pub before we got to the nightclub. She had to be home early so I volunteered to take her. The lads went on clubbing. We both had another drink, went outside and then I realised I wasn't driving. I took her home on the service bus; my wages didn't stretch to taxis. We got off the bus somewhere up Blackpool Road and I walked her home. We stood and talked as my nerves started to jangle and my legs started to shake. How do I kiss her? When do I kiss her? Do I move to kiss her or does she move to kiss me? Just then we both had the same idea and we banged noses. I was so embarrassed I couldn't get away fast enough. I said in a hurried tone, 'See you later', and went.

What a bloody start to my wild days of passion.

Tuesday morning and I was full of myself. All the usual questions from the lads at work: 'How did your weekend go, Steve? Did you manage to score?'

Very casually I informed them I took this bird home on Saturday night. Now that stopped all the stick. I was one of the lads and I had scored with a girl, when in reality I had banged noses.

Dave was interested. In fact he was a nosey sod. 'Come on then, Steve. How did it go?'

'I met her in a pub in town, then I took her home.'

'Well, go on then, did you go all the way?'

'All the way where?' I asked, not wanting to divulge the fact that I took her home on the bus.

'You know. All the way?' Dave said, inquisitively, getting quite excited.

'No, no, I didn't have to go all the way as the bus went on to Blackpool but she only lived in Lea.'

I didn't know what I had said but all my workmates were told about my exploits and many customers were given the story, too. I was left wondering 'why the humour?' as, living in the sticks, if you went all the way you took the bus to the terminus. I was as smart as fishing bait, the green patches behind the ears were showing for quite some time, and I found there was a lot to learn about life at the age of seventeen.

~

My adolescent years left a lot to be desired. As far as learning fast, I was able and willing but the brain was taking a little longer. If brains were taxed, I would have had a rebate.

I was working quite happily on this particular day when a customer I knew as Mick, one of the boss's clients, came in and sat on my chair. I immediately thought that he was checking out my artistic talents so he could report back to my boss on how I was progressing. As I placed the gown over Mick, I noticed a hearing aid had been placed on my shelf in front of my mirror. I hadn't realised that he had a hearing problem, so I cautiously moved into customer-friendly mode and with a raised voice I enquired, 'How are we today, sir?'

Nothing of a reply was forthcoming, so I thought I should speak louder. 'Is it just a trim, sir?'

'I'm all right, thank you,' said Mick.

I had made an impression, so now I knew the level at which to talk to this customer. 'Have you got the day off today?'

'Yes please. Just tidy it up if you will.'

Bloody hell, I thought to myself, delayed action or what? How long does it take to sink in between the ears? I raised my voice a little and tried again. 'Not such a bad day for October, is it?'

'Just having a couple of days off with the kids, while they're on holiday.'

I was concentrating on the haircut because I thought there was a spy in the camp checking up on me, and by now I was almost shouting in a slow but very meticulous voice.

'Been anywhere nice?'

'We do get some nice weather in October usually.'

That was it. Somebody had pressed my chuckle button and I started to giggle. I was on the way to losing it. I composed myself and told myself I was a professional and I couldn't let this customer see I was laughing, or he might think I was laughing at his affliction. I took the easy way out and got on with the job in hand and kept quiet.

To my surprise Mick said in a quiet voice, 'How long have you been working at this job now, Steve?'

I wanted to make myself understood so I used sign language and shouted very slowly so he could at least lip-read if he didn't catch the answer: 'NEARLY THREE YEARS'.

I finished the haircut with no complaints, just a nod of the head to show his satisfaction. As I was shouting the charge for the haircut to Mick, my boss arrived in from lunch.

'Hello Mick, how are you doing?' my boss asked.

'Fine thanks. You're looking good yourself,' Mick replied.

'Stephen's been looking after you then?'

'Yes he's done a good job, and we've just had a quiet chat.'

Quiet chat? I was nearly hoarse with shouting - in walks my boss, and Mick has perfect hearing. Like a complete dumb idiot I then said to Mick, 'Don't forget your hearing aid, sir'.

'It's not mine, Steve. I found it in the street outside.'

Realisation dawned. I had been had, not for the first time. Mick wasn't deaf but he had picked up on my inability to work, listen, shout and understand until it was too late. That's when I nearly lost it with the fit of giggles. It was another one of those idiotic moments in my life that I look back on and smile about. You live and learn, and I learned to live through another cock-up. They were a regular occurrence in the early years.

~

Just after my nineteenth birthday in 1972, I came out of my time as an apprentice and was then classed as an improver for another two years. I left the Fulwood salon to be second-in-command at the town-centre salon under Eric, my new boss. Eric was a quiet-spoken, well-educated, very unassuming gentleman - a genuinely decent man who helped me through those tricky years.

I was given a smoker's pipe - why I haven't a clue, but I was given one. A regular customer always left the salon with this really nutty fragrance that used to billow out of his smoking gun. I'll have some of that, I thought. I bought some, but hadn't a clue what to do with it. Enter Eric.

'I've bought some of this tobacco but what do I do with it?' I asked.

'Get your money back,' said Eric, and persuaded me to take it back to the shop. He was a very heavy smoker and working alongside him for many years I probably inhaled my fair share of the dreaded weed, but it was my only attempt at the habit and at a very early age I was lucky to stop before I started.

It was while I was working at the town-centre salon that I was introduced to Jean, a young girl two years my junior, who was to make a major impression on my life (and my wallet), then and still to this very day (definitely the wallet).

Meanwhile, back at the ranch, the town-centre salon was a major change to my lifestyle. The clientele were completely different: more cosmopolitan, all ages, all styles ranging from skinheads through feather cuts and punks, to Elvis quiffs complete with DAs. This was a whole new challenge, with new customers to show off your skills to and impress with your talents and techniques. It was like giving a child a box of crayons and a pad of paper.

Call it misunderstood, confused or just plain deluded, but in those yesteryears of the 70s I did struggle with my inability to understand the jargon and trends of the 'new age'. I couldn't understand the very flowery pungent smell many of the young lads breezed in with. It wasn't the obligatory Brut for Men Aftershave or anything that strong, but it lingered in the shop for ages after they had disappeared. One customer of mine tried to explain to me in simple English that many of these rare odours were probably derived from amphetamines. 'Sorry, you lost me. Can we speak in one or two syllables?'

It's completely different now, but drugs and the like were seldom mentioned. You heard people talk about Purple Hearts but you never saw them. What actually were they? Were they purple pills? I still don't know to this day, not that it has hindered me in any way, but I suppose if you wanted to know you would make the effort to find out. Then, the main drug on offer (as it is today) was tobacco. That dirty, smelly, smoking habit that is intolerable today was fashionable in those days. The likes of 'grass' were for mowing in the garden, 'Coke' was kept in a bunker outside and was burned (though we also drank many gallons of the stuff), a 'Joint' was cooked on a Sunday lunchtime and 'Pot' was what the joint was cooked in. How little did I know and how streetwise I wasn't.

It's Saturday afternoon and Johnny, a trendy young lad I had attended to for many months, arrives for 'the works': shampoo, cut and blow-dry in readiness for his big night out. His passion is dance music: Northern Soul, Motown, all very loud and fast, and he travels all over the country to enjoy his 'all-nighters' with his mates.

'So where is it tonight?' I ask.

'There's a club we go to in Stoke, The Twisted Wheel Club.'

'Late night, early morning occasion is it?' I enquire.

'Late night and late morning really, as we stay till it comes daylight.'

'That's some dancing. How the hell do you manage to stay awake all that time, let alone dance?'

'When we get there, we all start off with a few beers to get in the swing of things and then start dancing. You tend to dance with your mates, so we all finish together and get another beer. You sweat all the time so you need to take plenty of liquids and the 'Speed' keeps you going.'

'What's 'Speed'?' I innocently ask.

'It's a substance that gets you there quicker and keeps you up there longer.'

I was not aware of 'Speed' or any other substances that could 'keep you up there longer'. I didn't know what it was or what it did, and I remember thinking, 'But how does it get you there quicker?' So the 'Dumbo' with the scissors then asks, 'Do you add it to the petrol before you leave Preston?'

The lad just smiles and takes it that I'm being sarcastic. I'm not, I just don't know. The sad epilogue to this tale was that many years later I found out that the lad died of a drug-related illness. What is it they say - innocence is bliss?

Another big lesson in those early years was to assess the clientele: who you could trust, who was the genuine article, who was a total waste of space, the people that wallowed in bull-excrement, and the ones that you knew always told lies because their lips were moving. As a youngster, you tended to believe everything people told you; call it green behind the ears but you trusted people more then, you had respect and, on some occasions, you were the one to look the donkey.

Jim, a regular customer, would always come for his haircut on a

Thursday afternoon and wait for me to cut his hair. Why? Because there was only me working and I was gullible enough to believe his stories. He had told me he worked for Cunard, the shipping company, and travelled all over the world on board cruise liners. Any time I fancied a holiday he could fix me up with a nice winter break, as the ships were quieter then, although it was only for me that he could fix a free trip, keep it quiet, don't tell anybody else, nudge, nudge, or he could get into trouble. Me going on a cruise liner at the age of eighteen? Now this lad is going places, or so I thought.

Whilst I was cutting his hair we talked about me joining him on his liner in late February, and that he would ring me with the final details when he arrived home from his next trip. I booked my time off work and was set for life on the ocean waves. No phone call, no details and no contact so, as I knew where he was a regular drinker when in port, I went to find him at the Cockpit Bar at the Bull and Royal in the town centre. I knew where the bar was, but I had never been in or heard anything of its reputation.

I went after work at about 5.30 pm and the bar seemed moderately busy for a Thursday evening. As I walked to the bar I was not aware of anything strange or unfamiliar, only the usual noise of voices talking.

'Half a bitter, please,' I said, as I had no intention of staying long, only enough time to find out if Jim was due home sooner or later. It wasn't long before I was approached by a gent in his mid-thirties making pleasant chitchat. I looked around but, with no sign of Jim, I casually asked if he knew Jim and briefly described what he looked like.

'You're not with the police, are you?' he asked very warily. I ask you, a lad of eighteen in a blazer with brass buttons doesn't actually resemble the Flying Squad, does he?

'No I'm looking for this man who works on the liners for Cunard, blond hair?'

'Oh, are you looking for Bent Jim?'

There are times in life when you know you shouldn't be there, there are times in life when you want that big hole to be in close proximity, and there are the times when you are in desperate need of an adult nappy. I asked with a splutter, 'Who's Bent Jim?'

'He hasn't conned you about a cruise liner or a flight on his airline, has he?'

I was too stunned to speak.

'Sorry, me old son, but Jim is a fraudster, a con artist through and through. The last I heard he had been sent down for a stretch - Wakefield, I think. Can I buy you a drink?'

I had had the wind taken out of my sails good and proper. I was sitting in a gay bar in the town centre, talking to a complete stranger who had just asked to buy me a drink. I made my apologies and scuttled out of the place, hoping nobody had seen me or - worse still - recognised me.

An enormous lesson in life is not to trust everybody. You read about stories in the paper where youngsters are conned, with fearsome consequences. I was green, I was taken in, but I was one of the lucky ones. I wasn't scared (at the time), but it gave my confidence a dent for quite a while.

One of my all time boo-boos that I am happy to relate in these pages is one of those situations that are so 'cringeworthy'. I only asked a simple question. Could anybody be so thick? Answer ... yes. It was me, the man holding the scissors with little substance between the ears.

This tale involves a regular customer in his late twenties, a customer I held in high regard, a well-educated person who not only told a good tale but was also a good listener. After many months of attending to this client I found out the reason for this gentleman's good character traits ... he was a priest.

We chatted about all and sundry; I had not only found a good customer but had gained a genuine friend. This particular morning the salon was fairly quiet. I was working one chair and my boss was working on the adjacent chair. I was in my customary mode of 'if you're nosey, you find out things', and the conversation went something like this:

'So how long have you been a priest?' hoping not to sound too pushy.

'I started at college here in England when I was eighteen. I was born and raised in Ireland.'

'So have you any brothers in the clergy?'

'No. It was my own idea. No pressure from the family, it must have been a calling from above.'

Before this particular conversation, we had talked for many hours on a multitude of topics. I was not intimidated or ashamed to question this young man about anything.

'But what about the sex thing, or should I say the lack of it?'

'I made a commitment and I am strong enough to see it through,' he explained without any embarrassment, and I tried to understand his meaning.

'So if you have no brothers or cousins in the priesthood, what made you decide on being a priest? Was your dad a priest?' I asked, not knowing what a ludicrous question it really was. I suppose it's true what my dad said: 'Eh, lad, if yer brains were made of gunpowder, you wouldn't have enough to blow yer bloody cap off.'

The priest didn't speak. He hadn't got an answer to that, he just sat there and smiled. I knew there was something wrong. Had I overstepped the mark? Was I being rude to ask such a question? I looked across at my boss. He just looked at me, smiled, then raised his eyes up into his forehead and said, 'Sorry, father, but Stephen isn't a member of your flock.'

I sometimes think back to those early years with a wry smile. Did I say that? Did I really ask such a stupid question? Was I that naive? The answer is 'yes,' but you have to do absurd and senseless things so that you can learn from them and continue to find more answers to more stupid questions.

Näivety of children.
These are answers from a Sunday school test.

In the first book of the bible, Guinness's, God got tired of creating the world so he took the Sabbath off.

The first commandment was when Eve told Adam to eat the apple.

The seventh commandment is thou shalt not admit adultery.

The Jews were a proud people and throughout history they had trouble with unsympathetic genitals.

"Marriage is a wonderful
invention - and so is a
bicycle puncture repair kit"

Chapter Twelve -
Actions speak louder
than words

Look pal, you're supposed
to be the expert.....
cut it 'flattering' like!

There you go mate...
that one's on the house.

I wake up; so it must be another good day. I arrive at work at 8.50, unlock the door and the lights go on, coat off and blinds up, check temperature, fire on or not, cash register switched on, then collect the newspapers, a quick glance in the mirror to make sure I am dressed presentably and finally check all my own 39 hairs to make sure all is well, then ... We are open for business.

Isn't life good when a plan comes together? But in our line of work it seldom does. It is the organised chaos or the amazing unfamiliarity a day can display that makes this job what it really is ... unique.

When I open the blinds I find there are three people stood waiting at the door for me to open the salon. I smile and greet them all as they enter the salon. My first observations tell me that not one of these old lads will see three score years and ten again. They all have bus passes but can't use them because it is before 9.30 and they all want to be first on the chair to get their hair cut. They all sit down together and then start to enter into conversation about who arrived first and at what time. The volume of the chatter then starts to rise and I am thinking we could have a showing of teeth or throwing of caps if I don't intervene.

'Right, what's the problem? Who's first?' I ask, knowing this is not going to be easy.

'I am,' they all chirp together.

'I haven't a clue, so you'll have to tell me why you all want to go first,' I say, so that we could make a start as soon as possible. One has an appointment at the hospital, another has a funeral to attend, and the other is in a hurry to get to the Post Office to collect his pension. All worthy explanations as to why they have arrived at the salon early. I picked the old lad that has an appointment at the hospital, then the old lad that is going to the funeral, then the Post Office pension man. They all left in good spirits with no animosity towards me or their fellow chair stealers.

Weeks later when they returned separately for their haircut they all coughed up an amazing coincidence of stories. The man who had a hospital appointment HAD a hospital appointment but it was at 2.30 that afternoon. The man who had a funeral to attend HAD a funeral to attend but it was the day after, on the Thursday. The man who had to go to the Post Office had an idea the other two were not telling the truth so he said that because he couldn't think of anything better, although he admitted he had collected his pension the day before on the Tuesday. Behaviour you would expect from children but, as I have found, the older you get the more inclined you are to revert back to your childhood. Age is a very high price to pay for immaturity.

It is 9.20 on a Saturday morning. The salon is busy and in walks, or more accurately bounces through the door, Arfa Brain. He is well dressed, as he hasn't reached home after a night of booze and kebabs. These are a give-away, as the shirt still has the remains of chilli relish and the salon is filling up rapidly with alcohol fumes, although I have to say he was not drunk.

'Excuse me, mate. Could you cut me hair today?' Mr Brain asks.

'Yes. If you want to sit and wait, we'll be able to look after you soon,' I answer with an uneasy reluctance.

'See, me hair's really fick and it needs finning out.'

'Yes, that's OK. We'll be able to sort that out for you,' I reassure the young lad.

'How much will it be, mate?

It will be about eight pounds, I answer.

The lad then starts rummaging through all his pockets searching for all his worldly goods. I continue to attend to the client on my chair when I am interrupted once again.

Excuse me mate ... do it any cheaper?

'No, sorry. That's what it'll cost,' I say.

He has another root about in all his pockets, then comes out with:

'What can you do for pound twenty-three?

'You can't even hang your coat up for that.' I say, wanting him to leave ASAP.

'Can you just fin it a bit then for one pound twenty-three?'

'No sorry, not even a bit, sorry.'

He sits down and needs time for the floating brain cell to settle.

He now is thinking over his next move, or is going to attempt to go to sleep. After five minutes he has regrouped his brain cell, stands up, and walks over to me.

'Excuse me, mate. You're a decent sort of a bloke. How about if you let me borrow yer finning scissors for 5 minutes and yer can have me last one pound twenty-three? I'll do it me self.'

'Shut the door behind you as you leave,' I say in my most official voice.

The lad left still with his fick hair and one pound twenty-three still burning a hole in his pocket. My customer that I was attending to as the circus performance developed told me that if he hadn't have seen that for himself he would never have believed it.

There are stories within this book that beggar belief and, as I have said many times, some people are just unbelievable. We are all guilty of stupid actions in our daily life. Some people do amazingly daft or stupid actions and are quite happy, unlike your author, to own up to them. There is an old saying that goes something like: Never trust a man who, when left alone with a tea cosy, doesn't try it on.

It is common knowledge that nobody is perfect, although I have met many that thought they were the closest thing to it. One particular client really thought that he should have had as his middle two names Almost Perfect.

Can you imagine Billy Almost Perfect Plonker as a name?

On first impressions he came across as a well-educated person that had boundless knowledge of a wide range of topics. After only a few months of cutting his hair I realised that his aerial didn't really pick up all the channels in our area. His mate, who also frequented my salon, once told me that Billy was known as a well-educated accident. He was a good team member in a sports quiz but when it came to DIY he was as smart as fishing bait. He had fallen through the ceiling whilst lagging the loft, drilled through the cooker cable whilst putting up shelves in the kitchen, and he managed to knock over a full tin of paint on the lounge carpet whilst painting the ceiling whilst (simultaneously) watching the football on the telly. Geography wasn't his greatest asset either. He decided for a special surprise treat he would take his wife to 'Shakespeare Country', as she always wanted to visit Ann Hathaway's Cottage. I would have loved to have known what his explanation was as he arrived in… Stafford. He was convinced Willy Shakespeare lived in Stafford, which is nowhere near Stratford on Avon. *Billy has deprived a small village of its very own idiot.*

This lad had been waiting for his haircut for about 20 minutes, and as I observed him sitting waiting he constantly played with the hair on one side of his head. He was stroking it and pulling it, trying his best to flatten what looked like a frizzy patch of hair just behind his ear. The lad had a good head of hair, quite long and very thick, and this odd patch spoilt the effect. He climbed on board the chair and as he looked in the mirror he appeared quite embarrassed about the unusual frizzy patch.

'Could I have a trim please, and could you please try and sort that frizzy bit out on my right?' he asked.

'Just a trim? What's happened to that frizzy patch of hair?' I asked knowing it was self-inflicted. I had never seen a patch so damaged.

'Don't know what happened. I just dried it like usual and it went frizzy there,' the lad explained, although not too convincingly.

'Did you stick your head in front of a flame or the fire?' I asked, knowing it had been scorched with severe heat.

'No, it wasn't the fire. I was in a hurry to go out last Saturday night and my sister's hairdryer is useless, so I used the hot air gun my dad uses for stripping paint. It dried most of it; there was just a problem on that side.'

There probably wasn't any brain to damage, but it's a wonder the lad had any hair left to cut.

When I started working in this job, hair-styles were on the change. Most people had short back and sides but the Teddy Boy hairstyles were the high fashion alternative - waves and crests, hair combed into the centre at the back of the head to produce a DA (a duck's rectum by another name). It turned heads, it made you look; it was an era of radical change. Men were getting used to growing their hair longer, and following closely by came the long-haired Beatle haircuts. It was then the turn of the very long hair, and competition as to who could grow it the longest. Running concurrent with the long hair was the Mod hairstyle, a short-cropped tidy hairstyle with the recipient wearing a furry-hooded Parka jacket and riding a scooter.

The wow factor entered with the punk era. Now that was a real fashion statement. To do these styles went against everything I had been taught; you totally destroyed the everyday haircut to hack and bludgeon the hair into a shape that would need mountains of hairspray, and after all the time and effort only a handful of the nation liked it, and it had to be hairsprayed back into a shape again the very next day. In all honesty it changed the world of hairdressing. The hairdressing industry was transformed to another planet. Hair creams took a back seat. There were hairsprays, there were multi-coloured gels, there were gel sprays, mousse foam, wax - the list was endless. When I had done one of these styles and painstakingly spent ages cutting and sticking hair up in spikes, or a Mohican Style stuck up 6 inches or more vertically from the head, it did make me feel good. Probably because I had conquered the void; I had gone where not many people had trod; I had used my ability to turn heads.

From the extreme of big hair and punk came the complete opposite, and we were now taking the bloody lot off. Enter the skinhead movement. I call it a movement because in that era if you had a skinhead haircut you were part of a gang; hatred, anarchy, abuse, riots ensued, and rebellious disorder was commonplace. By cutting all the hair off it made a statement; having it stuck up made a statement. The style showed which sect you belonged to and which beliefs you subscribed to.

Strangely, today, in 2014 the majority of males from 16 to 60 have short-cropped and skin-head type haircuts, but thankfully today short hair doesn't bring the upheaval it did in the 80s and 90s.

You wouldn't dream of going to the pictures and just asking for a ticket to watch any film; the nice lady behind the desk wants to know what film you want to watch. You would never go for a meal in a restaurant and order something on the menu if you didn't know what it was. But in the hair clairvoyant's tent at the barber circus:

'I'll have a 0 on the back and sides and a 4 on the top, please,' I am told.

'Do you want it bald on the sides and a ¼ inch left on the top?' I ask.

'No, I don't want it that short. That will be far too short.'

'Well, why did you ask for it?'

If a hairdresser did what was asked for, the hairdresser would be out of business within six months. A hairdresser's reputation depends on the public's inadequacy to know what they want!

Two young lads walk into the salon both wanting short haircuts. One lad jumps on Gary's chair and the other jumps onto my chair. Both lads are about 16, and although still at school they are very confident, verging on the cocky side.

'I want it very short please, a number 3 all over,' says the lad on Gary's chair.

'I want a number 2 all over, please,' says my youngster, obviously trying to outdo his mate.

'I'll have a number 1 then, please,' Gary's bright spark chirps up, trumping his mate's bravado.

'I'll have a zero, please,' my little ray of sunshine chirps up, with this huge smile straining his face muscles. I then spend the next five minutes telling him of the downside of a zero - from ear ache from parents to school discipline to bald heads taking time to grow, and still he insists that I cut it with a zero blade.

'You are absolutely sure you want it bald?' I ask, just to confirm what he wants.

'Yes please', he instructs me. I start on the left side, just cutting a 2-inch band so that he can see the severity of the cut. I have cut from his temple to above his ear when he shouts,

'Stop.' He looks at it close in the mirror and then he has a feel at his instant alopecia spot. He gulps hard and I can see traces of dampness appearing in his eyes. He just sits and stares at the mirror. He is speechless, numb with shock.

'I didn't want it that short. That's too short. Can you cut the rest a bit longer than that and make that look longer? he asks in a hesitant and shy tone.

Now I am good... but not that bloody good that I can make hair grow, and if I could I wouldn't have stood behind this chair all those years with a bald head. I sorted it out to almost unnoticeable, but the young lad had learnt a lesson in daring whilst his mate left with a huge smile on his face.

Over the last 10 to 15 years or so it has become popular to raise vast

amounts of money through programmes encouraging a certain element of the general public to make complete idiots of themselves doing strange and hideous tasks. Meanwhile the rest of the world stand on the sidelines, watch and laugh at them, and find it much safer shelling out cash for the cause than to take the embarrassment and endless ridicule. So when the lunatic asylum has had a day release for the cause, what better place to go to make one look a complete TW-T ... correct, the hairdresser's.

The lad is about 20, medium to long dark brown hair, and sporting a small moustache. He is well-dressed and when he asks if I can cut his hair now he speaks softly, politely and with quite a posh accent.

'Yes, sir, I can do your hair right away. Please take the big chair,' I say, but am shocked at his reply.

'I am having it cut for the charity event on the television tonight. How much would you pay me to have all my hair cut off?' he asks.

'Sorry, I may be missing something here; did you ask me how much I would pay you to have your hair cut?' I enquire.

'Yes, that's correct. How much is it worth for you to pay me to cut my hair off?'

'Nowt. Why would I want to pay you? I've seen many people with bald heads and it's usual procedure that when you walk through my door to get your hair cut you pay me for the privilege. That's how it works.' I'm not rude, just indignant.

'Come on, it's for charity, and if I'm on local TV tonight I'll mention you,' he says.

'Sorry. Doesn't work like that,' I say, expecting him to leave.

'OK, how much will it cost to cut it all off and draw some snazzy design on the head?'

'If you want a design drawing on the head, we're talking quite a bit of time and money,' I say, but actually I'm was quite excited to be given the chance to produce my own design work on this posh bloke's bonce. There's no way he's leaving now; I'm salivating at the thought of producing my own little masterpiece.

'If it's for charity, I'll try and keep the price down,' and before he had chance to answer, the clippers spring into life. Hair is flying at the same pace as turkey feathers at Christmas. With the head supporting short stubble, I'm ready to design.

'Any preference? Do you want the charity's name writing on your head?' I ask.

'No, no writing. Just random design. I'll leave it with you,' he instructs. I am like a pig in sh-t: there are lines, stars, squiggles - I scribe all sorts until I run out of head.

'How good does that look?' I ask, chuffed to bits with my creation.

'Yes, that's certainly different. Watch out for me on the TV tonight,' he says.

He's happy with his new look and I pay the amount I charge him into the charity box.

Result: Customer Happy, Charity £10, Hairdresser Ecstatic.

Another regular money-spinning event results in half the country walking around for the day in red; outrageous and flamboyant outfits are the norm for the day. That said, there are clowns that wear wigs and then there is Ben.

Ben wanted to have a laugh, he wanted to be the office jester and he thought it would be a good idea to dye his hair red ... but didn't really know how to do it. With fence paint it does what it says on the tin; with red hair dye it doesn't. Ben didn't think it did either, so he left it on his head an hour longer than it said on the tin. The dye ran everywhere, down his back, in his ears, over his face. He looked like he had been invited to join a Red Indian tribe and the cowboys had won.

Instinct tells you there is something untoward when Ben arrives in my salon in his hat and scarf on a hot summer's day.

'Hiya, Steve. Could you help me? I'm in a bit of a mess,' he asks, as I ask him to remove his make-shift mask.

'I tried to make me hair red for the charity day but it went wrong.'

'Yes, I do believe that wasn't what you had in mind,' I say.

'Can you cut it all off so that it'll look better than this?'

'I can cut it all off, Ben but I don't think it will make it any better. Your head's stained with the hairdye, I tell him.

'Anything's better than this. Please just take it all off,' he pleads.

I cut the hair to a very short length and realise the dye has made a patchwork pattern all over his head. I stifle any giddy laughing and show my true professional training. With the hair cut very short he resembles a red Friesian cow. It looks idiotic. But then again, people on this particular day are dressing up and looking an idiot to make money. That said, I have an idea. I don't know if it will work but I ask Ben for his approval and he agrees. I go for it.

With a red felt tip pen I join up all the patches and draw a big red bunny rabbit on his head. What I had to do is join up the red bits that are already there so that it looks as if the resulting bunny is all done on purpose. It works. I don't charge him and he assures me he is giving the money to charity.

Result: Customer, No1 Office Jester; Charity, £8; Hairdresser, Now Exhibiting Red Rabbits.

It is 10.05am and Barry is late for work.

'Hi Steve, I haven't got time for my haircut now, I'm on my way to work. I'll be in after lunch. Can you sponsor me please?'

'What's it for and what are you doing?' I ask.

'I'm doing a Mars Bar eating sponsorship at lunch-time. I've been to the supermarket for 12 bars and I have to eat as many as possible in five minutes.'

'Put me down for a quid a bar. Do you want the 12 quid now?' I ask.

'No, it'll do later today after I've done it,' Barry tells me.

Barry arrives at 4.36pm. He does not look well; in fact, a snowman has more colour in his face.

'Hi Barry. How did you get on with the Mars Bars? How much do I owe you?' I ask.

'Can't talk at moment. Me mouth is too sore; me gums feel like I have eaten rocks for dinner.'

'Why, what happened? How many did you eat in five minutes?' I ask, feeling a little sympathetic for the lad.

'Four. When I left here, I went to the office and put me Mars Bars in the fridge to stop them melting and forgot to take them out. They were rock hard. I bit, chewed, nibbled and just managed four. Went to the lavvy and threw up.'

The lad was off work for two days, had to pay for an expensive visit to the dentist, and made less than he told the supermarket manager he would make.

Result: Customer, Sensitive Mouth; Charity, Less than Expected; Hairdresser, Saved £8.

Bloke at a horse race whispers to Fred, 'Do you want the winner of the next race?'
Fred whispers back, 'No thanks. I've only got a small garden.'

"Appreciate what you
don't have today; it may be
toothache tomorrow."

Chapter 13 - Big Events that Shaped my Life

It was now the mid seventies when long hair was commonplace, young men and women challenged one another as to who could grow their hair the longest, and when walking behind a person you were clueless as to their gender. It was definitely not a good idea to strike up a conversation with the words 'excuse me luv,' as I found to my amazement and embarrassment when asking this 'blonde' for a dance. He had a beard… it was quite dark!

Way back in those dark ages, when you went out looking for a girlfriend most lads fell into two groups: the cocky, confident, loud-mouthed Jack the Lad who scored by just being cheeky, or the quiet, shy, timid, self-conscious type of lad that went home regretting not asking that girl for a dance. I definitely flopped into the second group. After encountering many knock-backs and eventually after drinking all night and gaining the confidence to get to talk to a nice girl, I was too pissed to say something sensible. I remember asking a girl if she wanted a 'dwink', and then when we sat down to talk the brain cell slipped into giddy mode and I asked her if she was wearing her own teeth. No wonder there were numerous embarrassing rejections.

On our first date I asked one young lady what she wanted to drink.

'I'll have a rum and blackcurrant, please,' she answered.

'Bloody hell,' I thought, 'I can't afford one of them on my wages,' so I bought her half a lager.

'That's not a rum and black,' she said.

'No, sorry. If you're going out with me you're drinking half a lager.'

I'm still married to that same lady after more than 36 years, and she still doesn't drink lager.

My dancing days had now been curtailed, as I was courting the lady of my life, Jean Margaret - a cracker, as I was once reputed to have called her. Over the months we had been together we had formed a good relationship and her family had made me very welcome.

After only twenty months of us being together, her dad died at the age of 53; Jean was seventeen. This was a major disaster for my beloved little girl but it was a really significant time in my life.

I had never been confronted with death before. I had seen dead bodies, I had been to funerals of distant family, but I had not been emotionally involved as I was then. Jean's dad's death just blew me away, so to speak; the heartache, the numbness, the apprehension, a young head full of confused emotions; it was a very poignant time and I learnt another hard lesson in life.

If the path to true love was all about sailing off into the sunset, well, we most certainly must have boarded the wrong ship. Our vessel did take in water on many occasions but the ship was never in danger of sinking, so eighteen months after the death of her dad I asked Jean to marry me - well, not in so many words. After we had skirted most of the jewellery shops (as was common practice during our lunchtime strolls), I walked her back to the bank where she worked. As I was leaving her to go back to work, I said, 'Do you want to go and get that ring that you like?'

Silence, then she said, 'What did you just say?'

'Do you want to go and get that ring you like in that jeweller's window?'

'Is that a proposal of marriage?' Jean asked in a very giddy tone of voice.

'Suppose it could be. Do you want me to go down on one knee?'

We were standing outside the bank in the middle of the town centre. I was just about to bend down when she said, 'You do and you will be on your own when you stand up.'

She set off to walk into work, turned and said, 'Yes,' with this silly, smile on her face, and disappeared into the bank.

Days later we went to visit Jean's grandad to tell him the exciting news.

'We've come to tell you that we're going to get engaged, grandad,' Jean said with a beaming smile.

'That's good news,' he said, then he turned to me. 'It's like buying your first motor-bike and you can't ride it.'

I laughed; then to keep the conversation light and amusing 'Blunder Pants' replied with, 'Yes, but you can still tamper with the spark plugs.' Now that wasn't one of my better remarks, seeing as Jean's mum was with us at the time.

Twelve months later we bought our first house, a semi-detached costing £6,900, in Walton-le-Dale. We spent a year doing it up and I got married to Jean on 25th June 1977.

Earlier that year the business was given notice to leave our premises, as the owners were going to sell the property for redevelopment. Eric, my boss, was a worried man, but more to the point so was I, as I had now got a mortgage and was soon to be married. After months of searching, the business acquired a small rented property on the recently built Preston Bus Station.

This was purely a speculative venture. There were hairdressers in airports and hairdressers in some big city stations but a gentleman's hairdressers in a bus station, now that was a gamble. The property, small in area, had two floor-to-ceiling walls constructed of glass. There were no hiding places; I was told in no uncertain terms that the work must be right, as you were in full view of the world and his wife. It was like performing in a goldfish bowl.

The business took off better than we had expected, although it took some time to get used to seeing people walking past the salon, as the previous salon was three floors up and Peter the Pigeon was all you had for conversation.

People soon took note of Toptrend Hairdressing, and many recognised us from working within the 'goldfish bowl'. On several occasions I was referred to as 'that barber on the bus station'. More to the point, we were working at eye level with, and introduced to, an all-new Joe & Josephine Public: the nosey people, the smelly people, the arrogant people, the friendly people, the rude people, the abusive children, the well-mannered people - the list goes on. I mention the multifarious masses because it is these people that have given me a good living for many a year and, to be honest, this book would have very little content without them.

After only a few months, the business at our new premises was on its feet and running with the wind. It was busy enough to employ three hairdressers, and everything on the allotment was weed-free.

Two and a half years after we got married, my wife Jean presented me with a little daughter, Nicola Marie, and wow - what a change in lifestyle that brought. Everybody warns you of the hard work and sleepless nights ahead, and the joy and pleasure of being a parent cannot be envisaged until you have witnessed it first-hand. Significantly, I remember thinking that all the effort, toil, love and affection that you give your own child, your own parents did for you many years previously and you never give it a thought ... until you have your own.

Thursday afternoon 3.45pm. The phone rang and I answered it. 'Good afternoon, Toptrend Hairdressing.'

There was silence and then I heard what seemed like someone sobbing and crying:

'Is that you, Stephen?'

'Yes, is that you, Dad?'

'We've lost our mum.'

'Dad, Dad, what are you talking about?'

'You had better come home, lad.'

'I'm on my way.'

I can't really remember much about the journey to Leyland but, on arrival at mum and dad's house, I found my dad being comforted by a neighbour. Mum had suffered a massive heart attack whilst out shopping and died walking back home.

My mum was my best friend; we were best mates.

That day in January when mum died, Jean and I decided that we should try for baby No.2. December of the same year Emma Louise arrived (this lad is very high on the ladder when it comes to sperm count!).

Over the years, the business continued to grow, although Eric, my boss, was spending less time in the salon. He was approaching retirement so only worked Fridays and Saturdays. Meanwhile I was made senior partner of the business.

1984 is the title of a book written by George Orwell, but little did I know 1984 would hold twists and turns of its own for me. In May of that year Steve, the young lad I had trained up from school, decided that he wanted a change of scenery and went to work at a plumber's merchant. Not only did it seem a waste of a career but it left the business short-handed. Eric came back to work full-time but, due to his age and the timeless days he had become used to, he lacked the interest he once had for the job. I interviewed many a young person who claimed they had the inclination to study and learn the profession; a few were given the opportunity to sample daily life in the salon. Several tried, but to no avail.

July 14th was just like any other Saturday: a steady flow of customers, finished on time, cleaned up and away for the weekend. On the Sunday I was in the garden when the phone rang. It was Eric's daughter informing me that Eric had died during the night of a brain haemorrhage. Nothing can prepare you for shocks like this, although I had dealt with a few in the past. The principal figure in my hairdressing career had gone, having cut his last haircut and without even a 'ta-ra mate'.

I remember thinking that this vessel needed two oars to sail a straight course and now it seemed like I was the last man standing. It wasn't long before the cavalry arrived in the shape of Gary, a time-served hairdresser who had trained at the same establishment as myself. We worked in the same way and we both knew what a good haircut looked like. This was an alliance that was to last for more than twenty-one years.

The business was now being run by two young lads: me as the captain of the ship at the tender age of thirty-one, and Gary (Gaz) as the galley lad, aged twenty-five. Over those twenty-one years together, the boat's crew changed seniority on many occasions.

It didn't take long for Gaz and me to develop a strong bond which meant Toptrend Hairdressing was sailing a good and steady course once more. Gaz had his own sense of humour: dry, cynical, and on occasions mildly sarcastic, although I never heard him tell a joke. On an ordinary day he allowed himself three smiles, and one of those was reserved for closing time. Customers would ask me if he ever smiled on a regular basis but were soon told only when he had wind.

Coming up to Christmas, we used to hold a competition to see who could get the most boring customer, someone with few interests who talked in a monotone and wittered on about nothing - the person you would hate to be sitting next to on a plane to Australia. We called it our Christmas Party List. It was our own competition, so nobody else knew, but to inform each other we used to use a coded phrase: 'another one for the Christmas Party'. This told your opposite number to listen to his conversation.

'Yeah, and I fix me own bike when it breaks and I fix punctures as well,' says Weary Willy.

'Bet that takes some doing?' Gaz smirks.

'I'm good at fixing cassettes as well; I splice the two ends together when they break.'

Willy is on a roll and Gaz is working quickly to eject him from his chair. Then I hear, 'Steve, is the Christmas Party List full?'

'I don't know Gaz, there aren't too many places left for this year,' I say.

'Party, do you have a Christmas Party? When is it?' Willy asks.

'We shut early on Christmas Eve and go out with all them on the Party List.'

'Can I put me name on yer list? I'm doing nowt over Christmas.' Willy says.

'Course you can. We're always looking for puncture-fixers and cassette-tape-splicers on our Chrissy do,' Gaz jokes.

He thought it was funny. I knew he was joking, but Willy was serious. Two days before Christmas Eve Willy turned up to ask what time the party started and did we supply food? Thinking quickly on his feet, Gaz told him we had had to cancel the party due to lack of support. Where's Willy? - we never did see him again!

The business premises comprised a small shop unit inside Preston Bus Station measuring approximately forty feet by thirty feet, with a back store room, a private area for fitting toupées that served as the lunch area, and the main working area, which contained three working chairs and a small area with a sink for the shampooing. We had enough space to seat eight waiting customers at any one time. Two of the four walls were plate-glass floor to ceiling so, as I mentioned before, we were goldfish swimming about in this small goldfish bowl. A very small arena when tempers flared and arguments erupted, as all workmates do let off steam on the odd occasion, but in our salon many people on the outside world saw the rants but had to strain to hear them.

Working on a bus station, we had no appointment system so clients would wait their turn for a haircut. On many occasions we were asked to adopt an appointment system but we felt the business didn't warrant one. When Preston Bus Station was built, it was reputed to be the second-largest bus station in Europe. A large building with a tiny hairdressers; it could work, it would work, and it damn well *did* work, because Gary and I put in the effort needed to make it work.

Above the salon, there were enough car parking spaces for 1100 cars on five floors, so parking was no problem. Within a hundred yards of the front door of the business were numerous ten- and twelve-storey office blocks with many working people, so we were very rarely bored.

I write about the layout of the business to give you an insight into Toptrend Hairdressing - a small business in a humungous building - so that you can visualise the setting of many of the events that have occurred. However, the future of the building is somewhat precarious. The local council has announced that the bus station complex is to have new owners. At present news of the eventual outcome of our bus station is still a mystery

The future? Eventually, the powers that be will make some major decisions that will affect Preston Bus Station, as well as Toptrend Hairdressing. God willing, I hope still to be of service to the public somewhere.

I was driving to work this morning when I spotted an
RAC man parked up in a lay-by.
The driver was sobbing and looked really miserable.
I thought to myself, 'that bloke's heading for a
breakdown.'

"Women need love to have sex; men need sex to feel loved."

Chapter 14 - Sex in the city

"Evening ladies, might I interest you in my show?"

"Filthy bugger!"

Confidentiality is of utmost importance when dealing with the public. People in high-profile jobs are duty-bound to safeguard the identity of their clients. The law of the land provides us with a Data Protection Act. Doctors, solicitors, police personnel, financial staff dealing with money, clergy and ministers, the list is endless; they all have a code of conduct when it comes to the security and protection of an individual's data and identity.

I have never heard of a hairdresser signing a confidentiality agreement but customers still tell their hairdresser their most personal secrets on a regular basis. Why? Because they trust their hairdresser. Hairdressers usually have their own code of conduct and keep these personal tales private, thereby safeguarding their business.

The hairdresser has an individual persona. The more you get to know this person, the more you can trust him. He doesn't just make you look good, he also makes you feel good. The client offloads all his cares and problems and the hairdresser listens. The hairdresser is off the radar from family, work colleagues and close friends. He isn't too close but close enough for customers to tell their life-changing decisions, their attitude to matrimony and their sexual encounters - including with whom. From my point of view I feel privileged that my clients look on me not only as a hairdresser, but as a friend and an ally with whom they can share their private and intimate secrets.

I had known the family for more than twenty years: mum Helen, dad Tony and their lads, Barry and Greg, who was the younger by seven years. The lads had been coming for their hair cutting way before they first started school so, as with my own family, I could see the physical changes over the years. Barry was more street-wise while Greg was the quiet one with the brains; he watched his brother, noted his good and bad points, then filed away the information for later in life. On leaving school, Barry had followed the wrong crowd, drinking, smoking and taking drugs, and inevitably had visited the police station to sleep off the effects on many occasions. By the age of nineteen, the lad was lost; he was in another world and at times sleeping rough, as his parents could not tolerate all the upheaval.

The lad confided in me on many occasions; I was somebody to talk to. His parents loved him but had no idea what to do, and they had to protect Greg.

One night Barry's mate died through drugs. I remember Barry coming into the salon days after that event and just wanting to talk. He was totally spent with anxiety - he reacted like the little lad I once knew. He asked me if I would mind having a chat. I could tell he needed to talk to someone so I obliged. He called back later that day with a tale to which I was happy to listen. His main problem was that he couldn't understand why his mate had died; the drugs - it was only a bit of fun. To look at him in such misery reminded me of when my own mum had died many years previously and the unacceptable knowledge that you wouldn't see somebody you loved ever again. We talked for ages - he was filled with mixed emotions that came flooding out. He wanted to say sorry to so many people but he couldn't.

Barry got his life back to some semblance of normality. He got a job, went back home to live with his family, found himself a girlfriend and contributed to life in the ordinary lane. I had regular contact with his dad for his haircut and, although life was not always harmonious, Barry had left the dark days behind him.

'So how are things going, Barry?' I asked.

'Yeah, it's good, fings are OK,' he answered, with little emotion in his voice.

'Doesn't sound too good. Still going with the same lady?' I asked, suspecting a break-up was on the cards. Knowing him all that time, I sensed there was something not right.

'No, did I not tell you? I finished with her after three years. Too much earache, got meself another one.'

Barry was not coming across as his usual self.

'So what's the problem?' I asked, sounding like I was his dad.

'Nowt,' he snapped.

I backed off, not wishing to intrude nor tangle with his aggressive attitude. He sat there in a sort of daze, not looking in the mirror, but into space. I left him to his thoughts.

'She's pregnant,' he said in a quiet and remorseful tone. He told me as if he was telling his own dad. I wasn't surprised by his announcement but didn't want to sound too laid back about the situation.

'So what have your mum and dad said about it? What have her mum and dad said about it?' I asked.

'Nobody knows yet. I don't know what to do.' The lad looked bewildered. He tried to smile but it was a nervous attempt - he was petrified.

Later that day, by a strange coincidence, his dad came in for his haircut. We chatted, and nothing was said about Barry's predicament. It was obvious his dad wasn't aware of this thunderbolt coming his way.

Weeks later, Barry called in to the salon for his haircut and catch up. He was a different person. The lad had cast off a cloud. He was upbeat and a happy individual, but not for the reasons I thought.

'You seem to be in good spirits. Everything sorted and well with the girlfriend and both mums and dads?'

'Yeah, everyfink good now,' he said and completed the story. 'Me bird had a miscarriage, so fings went well in the end.'

'Did you tell your mum and dad about the baby?' I asked.

'No, didn't bovver. There was no point 'cause I split with her when she lost the baby. Got meself another woman know, quite a tasty lady this one.'

And the world keeps spinning!

I suppose you learn to accept that some of the tales you are told may be exaggerated to make the tale sound better, bolstered up to give the person more credibility - or they are just plain lies. Like the middle-aged bloke who told me he was going to hospital soon for a major operation. He and his wife had decided they were not having any more children so *he* was having a hysterectomy. I tried to explain that it was a fairly common operation for his wife but it would be a bloody major operation for him.

'The wife has had the kids so we think it is only fair that I do my bit,' he told me.

'Is it a vasectomy you're having?' I asked.

'No, it's not a vasectomy. Me mate had one of those and it wasn't much good. It didn't work; she got pregnant again. No, we are going to get the job done properly,' he said in no uncertain terms.

I didn't pursue the matter, though I haven't seen that bloke in my salon since to ask him how it went!

I presume people confide in their hairdresser because they feel comfortable with them knowing their intimate secrets, and they can also boast to the hairdresser knowing the hairdresser will not get involved. But in one case, as a result of many coincidences, I ended up slap-bang in the middle of a very precarious situation.

Ronny was a young lad in his mid twenties - smart, good-looking and he looked even better after sitting in my barber's chair for twenty-five minutes every three weeks. He was the typical 'lad about town,' loud and cocky with a good disposition. Enjoyed the usual lifestyle of a working lad, earned money during the week to blow on beer and women at the weekend. He enjoyed life and he enjoyed the ladies even more. Every visit he had a tale to tell, usually more than one, and he confided all the sordid details to me.

His recent acquisition was a lady in her mid-forties, who enjoyed life to the full but only 'played out' on a Thursday night due to her commitments. She was married. I was told the full script: where she lived, where she worked, where she shopped, their weekend nocturnal activities - and even her hairdresser's name. Ronny's affair with Mrs Married Lady went on for months and, with his regular three-weekly updates, it felt like I knew this lady better than her husband did. Discretion was not one of Ronny's traits, so not only did he enjoy boasting to me about his randy rendezvous, he also amused the entire salon, as he hadn't been blessed with the quietest voice.

Mr Ordinary had been a client of mine for many years, a quiet nondescript sort of bloke that spoke when spoken to, had little conversation and seemed to amble through life at a snail's pace. It was round Christmas time when I saw a different side to my client, as he had been out at the works party and he had been drinking loony juice. He was a different person, jovial, bubbly and witty, and he made little sense with his conversation. Months later I found out more about Mr Ordinary. A family man with grown-up children, played golf, and worked locally. His wife worked at an accountant's office in town and he had to work away most Thursdays and Fridays down south but always made sure he was home for his weekend golf matches.

Now, what you the readers are thinking took me months to piece together!

The plot wasn't thickening. It was already pea soup. To add a few croutons into the broth, I slipped in the odd enquiry to confirm my suspicions and, as expected, I knew the pan was boiling and I had to be so careful so as to not dish out any confidential tit-bits.

At the time I thought it was just a silly episode in somebody else's life - it didn't involve me - but I was *already* involved. I knew both parties; they were clients of mine. I was actually worried about somebody else's dilemma and Mr Ordinary didn't even know he had a dilemma. I pushed it to the back of my mind and expected it to either sort itself out or just go away. It wasn't my problem - but it became my problem, a bloody big problem.

It is a busy Friday afternoon about four-ish and all is well with the world; Gary is watching the clock looking forward to home time and I am rambling on to a customer about football. There are probably four people waiting and the radio is producing the usual background music. The door opens and in walks Ronny in his work clothes, armed with his usual tales.

'All right, Steve?' Ronny enquires as he sits down.

'Yes thanks, Ron. Just finished?' I ask noticing his work clothes.

'Yeah, bit tired today. Had a late night last night, round at hers, yer know.' As he informs me, he has this grin a cat has after he's finished the last drop of milk from his bowl. I am talking football to my client and Ronny wants to engage me (and the rest of the salon) with tales of his late-night frenzy.

'Ronny, just have a kip and you can tell me all about it later,' I say, trying to shut him up. He takes the hint and reads one of my out-of-date magazines (probably *The Morris Oxford Car for the Modern Man* manual).

The door opens and Mr Ordinary walks in and sits next to Ronny. If I didn't think it was my problem before, it is now. Talk about squeaky bum moments in life - well, that was most definitely one of mine. My mind is working overtime. I am sweating buckets, my stomach turns upside down and I need the toilet. I can't go now. I have to deal with my somebody else's dilemma. I look at them both in the mirror. They haven't a care in the world, they don't know who the other one is, and they read their magazines and wait for their haircut.

Ronny is quiet for now but that won't last for long; I have to make sure I get Ronny on my chair before Gary does, or he will tell Gary about his exploits in cinema surround-sound whilst I'm cutting Mr Ordinary's hair. The thought of that! I am wetting myself already but I have to keep calm. I keep saying to myself, 'It isn't my fault, it isn't my problem, relax, I've done nothing wrong' but I still need the toilet.

My next customer is a little lad and, providing I can sort him out quickly, I will be able to attend to Ronny. The boy fidgets for England and (I have to be totally honest) I don't check to see if he ends up with both ears, but from what I remember I sort his haircut very quickly and to my relief I have Ronny jump aboard my chair.

'Bloody hell, Steve what a good night I had last night. I stayed over at you know where,' he says. He can't wait to tell me all the details.

'Ronny, is that all there is to your life. Why don't you train to be a referee like me?' I ask, trying to drag him away from the subject.

'I'll be round there again at t'weekend, yer know,' he tells me.

I keep him talking about everything and anything, and all he wants to tell me is about last night's nocturnal activities. Meanwhile Mr Ordinary is enjoying having his hair cut, sitting on Gary's chair, listening to the outrageous 'man-talk' that is spilling over from my chair.

Ronny has one of the quickest haircuts of his life. I have him paying for the privilege before he realises he is leaving. With Ronny out of the equation, I have a quick chat to Mr Ordinary, who tells me he was away last night down south but called in for his haircut on his way back today. He will be playing golf in a tournament as usual over the weekend.

Ronny went to work down south and I lost touch with him years ago. Mr Ordinary still pops into the salon to tell me about his grandchildren and the happy family life he leads now he is retired.

I never met his wife.

Years later, I smile about this particular incident but at the time it wasn't what I call fun. People confide in their hairdresser whether he likes it or not. Sometimes it is a relief to tell somebody their problems and sometimes it is just good to boast about one's encounters. Confidentiality wasn't in my vocabulary when I started this job; I didn't know what it was. In fact I probably couldn't spell the word and it certainly wasn't in my hairdressing syllabus, but it is something you have to observe... or you could soon gain a reputation that nobody wants.

I had known Harry for many years. A retired gentleman, always dressed very smartly. He was married and had a middle-aged lad who lived at home with him and his wife. Harry's wife was quite a bit older than Harry and wasn't that good on her feet, so didn't venture out often. Harry did all the shopping and looked after the household chores. His enjoyment was bus rides. He would finish up at Manchester Airport one day, Blackpool the next, but always made sure he was back to look after the family each night. Everybody has their own way of life and this suited Harry. He had his responsibilities to the family and he had his days out.

I nearly forgot to tell you that he liked the ladies as well.

'I'm going to Blackpool tomorrow,' Harry told me, with this childish smile on his face.

'Will this be a solo trip or are we having company?' I asked.

'Little Mary said she'll be coming along for the ride,' Harry informed me. 'She likes Blackpool.'

'I bet she does,' I quipped. 'And which one is it that likes Southport?'

'That's Elsie. She loves Southport.'

Harry had been going on romantic rambles for years and he told me each of the ladies didn't know about any of the other ones and - more importantly - his wife didn't know about any of them. Harry had a really clever trick he would use when he was out with one of his ladies. He would buy two tickets to go to Southport, give one ticket to his chosen lady and then meet her on the bus. Before he sat down, he would introduce himself to her loudly enough for the other passengers to hear. Anybody who knew Harry would assume he didn't know the lady he was about to sit next to.

'If anybody sees me holding Elsie's hand in Southport, they'll just think I'm a fast worker,' Harry told me.

Harry had liaisons with many ladies for many years. This particular day he arrived with his son. I had never seen them together; they both wanted their hair cut, as it was Harry's wife's funeral the following day. I offered my condolences to them both and hoped all went well the next day.

A month later Harry arrived for his haircut with a lady in tow. 'Steve, I'd like you to meet Doris. She's helping me through my bereavement. She's a big help to me,' he said, with that childish smile painted across his face.

'Take it easy, Harry, don't be overdoing it,' I said.

'He's doing all right now I'm attending to his needs,' Doris chipped in, at which we both smiled.

Weeks later his son called in for his haircut and told us his dad was doing fine. 'Yeah, I don't know for sure but I think he's got himself another lady-friend, nothing too serious. He needs a bit of company now mum has gone,' he said.

I just agreed.

I started this chapter with the word 'confidentiality' and, as you have just read, hairdressers must have total discretion with their clients.

You may question how I can write stories about other people without breaking that confidence. In most of my stories there is usually only one main player. All names and identities are fictitious. The tale is told as I saw it, although if the main players were to read this book I am quite sure they would be able to recognise themselves, even though they wouldn't own up to it.

Also in that first paragraph, I mentioned the clergy having a strict code of conduct regarding confidentiality. I make no apologies for this tale being included in my book because it happened to me many years ago.

Jean and I had been together for three years when we got engaged, and we got married more than five years after that fateful day, 7th March 1972, when I first took her out. I wasn't from a religious family, so it was never a big issue in my life. I went to church whenever it suited. I was christened and confirmed but religion never dictated my life. The 25th June 1977 was our wedding date, and it was Jean's wedding day. I always say I attended my wedding on Jean's day; it was the bride's special day. Whatever she wanted she got, so we were married in her church. I had no problem with that, although I had to attend a few lessons before the wedding to be able to marry in church.

I listened to these lessons intently. I was made aware of what was expected of me and the importance of the church in our lives together. The lessons were delivered to me as if the priest was trying to impregnate me with his beliefs. I asked questions which were pushed to one side like a batter playing cricket. I was taking him seriously and he wasn't taking me seriously at all. Now, I've always been accepted in the family as the proverbial clown, the joker, but on this occasion it wasn't the time or the place. He told us the significance of telling the truth and the values of confidentiality, and how it is so important in the church and our daily lives.

'A good friend of mine in Liverpool was taking confession when a young man entered the confessional. He had come to tell the truth about owning a gun and was asking for forgiveness from the father,' the priest told us. He was telling a tale to highlight the importance of truth and honesty.

I wasn't trying to be clever but with all the negative vibes I had endured I asked, 'How do you know what went on in that confessional?'

The priest thought for a while about my question, got up from his chair and said, 'I think it is about time we finished for today.'

Confidentiality, discretion, call it what you will, the priest had fabricated a story or his good friend wasn't all that good at keeping a secret.

You would not believe the earache I received when Jean got me out of that meeting. The wedding was nearly called off.

Three sons and their wives were invited to hear the reading of their late father's will.

'To David I bequeath all my outdoor equipment, my garden implements the plants and all the shrubs. You enjoy all the aspects of gardening and you even married a girl called Poppy.

'To Michael I bequeath all my cash in the bank, as money was always a big part of your life. You even married a girl called Penny.'

Jonathan stood up and said to his wife 'Come on, Fanny. We are not staying here to be insulted!'

"Experience is something you don't get until after you need it"

Chapter 15 - Finding the answers

I had now given three years to this career and completed my apprenticeship - or so I thought; you had to complete another two years as an improver before you were a fully qualified hairdresser. After three years I was earning nearly £20 each week, was working my own chair, had acquired my own customers (even though some were smelly people that nobody else wanted to work on), and was making a few pence in tips for my lemonade shandies - it used to be half of Boddington's beer but the landlord from the next-door pub knew my age and put a stop to that.

I mention smelly people, as this job is about dealing with the public at large, the well-to-do and the low-lives. College gives you a good understanding of the job, the different techniques and skills required; you are encouraged to bring friends and family along to practise to gain the skills, then you use that ability on the paying public. Nobody takes along a smelly person to practise on, or an argumentative loud foul-mouthed half-wit that can't put three sentences together without swearing. The public is made up of people from differing backgrounds - and you have to deal with them and learn fast.

I remember one Christmas Eve many years ago, a regular customer of ours arrived to get a quick trim for the festive season but unfortunately he arrived at a very busy time. He disappeared, to arrive again after 3pm when the pub next door had shut. This normally soft-spoken regular had changed his character, his appearance and his manner whilst downing 'eleventeen' pints of 'Loony Juice'. Some people drink from the fountain of knowledge; this guy only gargled.

By this time on Christmas Eve, we had had enough of serving the public and were looking forward to sampling our complimentary can of beer from the boss and going home. I don't know what it is about this job but no hairdresser I know likes to work on boozed-up customers; you humour them and you have to tolerate them but there is no satisfaction in dealing with them. We try to avoid such customers by slowing down or speeding up with our present customers so somebody else can have the pleasure. I 'won' the raffle and attempted to not just cut his hair, but to make any sense of the verbiage that sprayed from his mouth.

'Give ush a nish trim will you, luv?'

'Yes sir. How short?'

'How dooo I know? You're the barbra.'

I started to trim his hair whilst he grumbled to himself and then took leave of this earth and went to sleep. Now that might sound an easy way out for me, not having to listen to his drivel, but when somebody goes to sleep their head has a tendency to nod in all directions. Now I had a fight on my hands with 'Mr Wobbly Head'. I managed to trim his hair and achieve a reasonable result, then had to wake him up with a few hefty shoves.

'Is that what you wanted, sir?'

'No luv, cut it shorter,' he instructed, and went back to sleep.

I struggled again as I took the hair fairly short, and woke 'Noddy' up once again. 'Is that better for you now, sir?'

He opened one eye and said, 'No, not yet luv. Jusht keep going until I tell you when to shhtop.'

He went back to sleep and left me to it. I was not too happy with the proceedings and was looking for answers to my problem. I didn't take any more hair off, but woke him again and said, 'There we are, sir. Is that better?'

He looked through two slits of alcohol-fuelled eyes and said, 'No luv, cut it all off.'

'Are you sure that's what you want, sir?' I was waiting for the ultimate answer to make my Christmas; 'Go on, Noddy,' I thought, 'say yes if you dare.

'Go on, luvvy. Take the whole bloody lot off.'

I didn't need telling again. The clippers sprang to life and three minutes later the shop floor was warmer and my task was complete. I woke him up uneasily, wondering what his reaction would be.

'There we are. It's all done now, sir.'

He looked in the mirror and said, 'That's enough. Don't tek any more off, luv,' which was a good job because there was nowt left to tek off.

He got up, paid and walked out into the dark cold December evening air. I always wonder what his wife said when he got home, and imagine what he must have thought when he woke up on Christmas day with a bald head. Whether he couldn't face us or took exception to me cutting all his hair off I don't know, but we never saw him again.

Since time began and hair needed cutting, there have been manufacturers that have made money by selling tools and gimmicks - newspaper advertisement that claim: 'Cut your own hair and you can save £££££'s on your hairdressing bills'. These miracle implements can produce a wealth of revenue not only for the manufacturer but also for the miracle worker that has to use all his professional skills to create some resemblance of a style from a catastrophe.

Many years ago, a firm brought out a tool to trim and thin dogs' hair. The invention was a plastic double-ended comb about four inches long with a razor blade incorporated within the comb's teeth. The idea was that you combed through the dog's hair and at the same time it trimmed its coat. Now how simple can that be? Well, it must have worked, because they sold many thousands, and then some bright spark had the idea to adapt the tool so that you could cut your own hair. The principle could work, but the logistics certainly didn't save people money; it cost people ££s in repair work and weeks of humiliation and embarrassment.

This young lad walks into the salon one very warm sunny day with a 'Bob Hat' on his head. Experience tells me that we are in for a laugh as there is usually some sort of disaster lurking beneath a woolly tea cosy.

'Can you sort me hair out? It's a bit of a mess,' asks the lad sheepishly.

'I can have a good try if you take your hat off.'

'I'm a bit embarrassed. Promise you won't laugh?'

'No problem. No doubt I'll have seen worse,' I say, trying to give the lad a bit of moral support.

The lad slowly removes the hat from his head to reveal what can only be described as a patchwork quilt. I have to admit I hadn't seen many worse than this catastrophe and to this day I still haven't.

'What on earth happened here?' I ask with amazement.

'Me mates cut me hair with one of those wonder combs. You know, the one with the razor-blade? We'd all been out drinking and went back to me mate's house where we hit the whisky bottle. I fell asleep and woke up with this mess.'

'So I suppose you were the unlucky one?'

'No, not really. I was one of the lucky ones. One mate had his hair cut with the hedge shears and that was a right cock-up, but Johnny had the worst job. When he fell asleep we shaved round his willy and his balls with a razor blade.'

'What? And he didn't wake up while you were doing it?' I ask.

'No, but he soon woke up when me mate poured after-shave over his balls. He jumped two foot off the settee.'

My eyes still water at the thought of that ordeal but it's the suicidal cocktail of mixing alcohol and hair cutting that always spells disaster for the drinker and amusement for the miracle-worker.

I have been in this profession more than forty years and still things puzzle me. You tend to know many of the answers but definitely not all of them. One of the most important rules in this job is to send the client out of the salon HAPPY. Do that small task and you are on the road to success.

Nothing prepares you for the public. After all these years there are still many questions I would like to find the answers to. I don't think there are answers to some dilemmas; you just face them head on, deal with the situation and analyse it after the event, wondering if you found the correct solution.

A few sticky situations that I have confronted with over the years I share with you now. I handled the situation at the time but to this day I don't know if I arrived at the right answer.

I am not averse to people with body odour. People work hard and sweat. I have no problem when people do not shower or wash their hair every day. Even when they're old, people that struggle with bathroom skills through no fault of their own find it difficult; I can handle that. It's not good, but that's life. I struggle with the people who don't keep their bodies clean because of plain laziness. The odour is left in the salon long after the smelly client has gone, a legacy that can leave the newly arrived customers thinking it is the salon itself that smells. These waiting customers are not aware that the source of the smell left the salon ages ago. From a selfish point of view, it is not a pleasant situation and should not happen in this day and age. Unfortunately it still does.

Regrettably I had to terminate my services for a customer that I had dealt with for many years - under sufferance, might I add - just because of the smell. When I say 'dealt with for many years,' he got his hair shampooed and cut *twice a year* and then didn't touch his hair until the next visit. Never combed it and never shampooed it in six months. The hair was a mass of filthy, tangled pads, and just to help the aroma he didn't appear to shower, ever. When you were shampooing his hair you had to hold your breath or try your best not to throw up. To be honest, I felt sorry for this mild-mannered, soft-spoken, middle-aged man, which is the only reason I continued to do the job for so many years.

One evening, something caught my attention on the TV about airline companies that were refusing passengers with excessive body odour. The programme went on to say that such passengers would have to shower, and then the airline would loan them clean clothes for the duration of the flight. The programme started me thinking why we, as professionals working in close proximity to our clients, should have to deal with exceptionally smelly people.

After watching this programme, I changed my way of thinking. Although concerned with how I should handle the situation, I had to deal with it in a dignified manner. The day arrived when this customer appeared at my door. I honestly felt upset for the man but before he had chance to take his coat off I said sympathetically: 'I'm sorry, sir. We can't cut your hair today.'

'Why not?' he asked.

'You'll need to have a shower and shampoo your hair before we can cut it, sir.'

'Well, can't *you* wash it for me? You usually do.'

'But it's all tangled and matted,' I said, trying to defuse the situation.

'It usually is, so what's the problem today?'

It was now becoming a difficult situation and I was being pushed to explain my reasons for not cutting his hair. It would have been easy to say we were closing early or make some other excuse, but that would only have delayed the problem. The only way was to hit him with the truth, little though I liked the idea,

'Before I can cut your hair again, you'll have to shower before you enter the salon because of your body odour. Sorry about that, but you are upsetting some of our regular customers,' I said.

'But I'm a regular customer; I've been coming here for years.'

I suppose getting your hair cut twice a year for many years makes you a regular customer. As my ordeal came to an end, my sympathy went out to this lonely man as he slowly, without fuss or embarrassment, walked to the door to leave. As he opened the door, he turned and said, 'It isn't just getting my haircut; I have a problem finding a dentist as well.'

I realised I had made the correct decision, but it didn't make me feel any better.

A blind customer I have known for many years arrives at the salon one busy Friday morning. As he enters, I welcome him and tell him how many are waiting in the queue, and then guide him to the nearest waiting chair.

'Are you all right there, lad?' asks Joe.

'I'm doing fine thanks, Joe,' I answer, as I thought he was talking to me.

'Now sit down and be good, that's a good lad,' Joe says but, unbeknown to me, he is holding a conversation with the dog.

The whole salon thinks it is so funny. There is laughter and titters from around the salon, all except from Joe. He presumes people are laughing at him instead of laughing about the situation. Joe is not amused and gets a little upset.

'I think we will leave my haircut, Bobby, until Steve has learned more manners,' Joe snaps.

Now Joe is not a happy bunny and thinks I am belittling him in front of all my customers. He gets up to leave the salon. I try my best to reassure him that nobody was laughing at him and we sit him down again. Bobby the dog then lies down full length in front of the entrance door; nobody can get in or out.

'Joe, can I ask you to move Bobby to one side of the door, as nobody can get in the salon,' I ask.

'It's me bloody dog's fault now, is it?' Joe retorts.

Now I have to say, it is not one of Joe's better days; more to the point it isn't going too well for me, as Joe once again decides to leave. Again people start to titter, and through sign language I ask them to be quiet, as the situation is now getting a little awkward. We calm Joe down again; now he just talks to Bobby, as he is not friends with the world.

After half an hour, Joe is sitting in my chair and I am attending to his mass of grey hair. I am still not on his Christmas card list but things aren't as tense. Just as I am finishing off his haircut I notice Bobby walk over to the waste bin in the corner of the room and cock his leg up against it. This time there is louder laughter, but I pass that off as somebody telling a joke on the radio.

Joe left the salon on his third attempt with a good haircut, but was still uncertain of my conduct. I never did tell him that Bobby had a weak bladder but, as the world has come to know, I am bloody good with a mop and bucket.

Herbert came to me for his haircut for many years. He didn't have a dog to help him. He always relied on his white stick and plenty of cheek. He would amble down the bus station tapping his stick until he knew he was in the vicinity, then he would say out loud so any passer-by would help him, 'Is the barber's near here?' If nobody was about and I hadn't seen him, he would say it louder until either I would go and bring him in or somebody would show him to my door.

He would always ask if I had a new apprentice and, if there was, he'd tell me, 'Let them loose on me. I can't see, and if they make a mess, it doesn't matter; it'll grow again.' This was always very helpful to the new starter, as it was probably the first time he would have the chance to practise on real hair on a real human being and have the added relief that the client wasn't watching what he was doing.

Believe me, the first time you cut hair on a real person and they are watching every move… now that is frightening.

The amusing punch line to this tale came at the end of the hair cut. Michael, an apprentice, would finish cutting Herbert's hair, check it, ask me to check it, then when we were all happy he would show him the back of his head in the mirror and shout, 'IS THAT ALL RIGHT FOR YOU, SIR?'

Herbert would feel his hair to check it was short enough, and then would say, 'I'm bloody blind. I'm not bloody deaf!'

Once upon a time, a guy asked a beautiful girl 'Will you marry me?'
The girl said, 'NO!'
The guy lived happily ever after and rode motorcycles and went fishing and watched football and played golf a lot and drank loads of beer and had tons of money in the bank and left the toilet seat up and farted whenever he wanted.
The End

"The early bird may get the worm but the second mouse will always get the cheese."

Chapter 16 - Strange but true

As I've noted many times in this book, you can never presume how a day will unfold, never guess how the public will react and never understand how a grown-up mature person can come out with the most absurd, stupid and insane claptrap and honestly believe it. I am the first to admit everybody has their own opinions and makes their own choices in life, but at times you wonder whether some people live their lives on another planet and just visit my salon on their day off. I honestly believe these stories, mainly because I know the people who told me the tales, but I will leave it up to you to make up your own mind.

After many weeks, it came to my attention that on busy days when the salon was full, this lad of about fifteen would call into the salon, read the magazines until it was his turn for his haircut, then make a quick exit. Because this only happened when we were busy, it took us a few weeks to cotton on to his game. On his next appearance I was ready for him and said, 'Do you want your hair cut today?'

'Yeah,' was the answer, at which I was quite shocked.

I worked as he read until it was his turn for his haircut. 'Next please,' I said, expecting him to come forward for his haircut.

'You can go next,' he said to the man on his left, and continued to read his magazine.

When he had finished it, he walked over to me and announced politely, 'I will get me hair cut next week when you've got some new mags in. I've read all those. See yer next week,' and walked out.

The lad wasn't rude or offensive, but he didn't return a week later … he returned about ten years later. I recognised him immediately. It wasn't busy, so I asked, 'Yes sir, can I help you, or are you here to read my magazines again?'

He looked puzzled. 'No, I haven't come for my haircut. I've called in to see if you sell books.'

'Books, what sort of books?' I enquired.

'Do you sell an instruction book on how to cut my own hair, or if not, how to cut other people's hair?'

'No, sorry sir, we don't sell books.'

As he turned to leave, I bade him good day and said, 'If you do find an instruction book, I wouldn't mind having a look at it when you've finished with it. Would you like to take one of my magazines for the time being, sir?'

He declined my offer.

It is early January 2009, the economy has taken a nose dive over the last six months and much, or should that be most, of the country's population is feeling that it's harder to make their wages last out the month. Big name stores are closing every day, none more popular or famous than Woolworths. Credit cards need paying after that expensive Christmas, the days are dark, damp and cold, and the main talking point is not holidays but job losses and short-time working.

I arrive at the usual time and make my emporium ready for business although, as things are at present, I am not expecting my till to be ringing the tune 'It's a hap-hap-happy day' too often.

By 9.30 my second client is leaving the salon and both the first two have had the same tale to tell: both redundant and looking for a job. I try to encourage both lads and give them confidence about their future, as I am sure I would appreciate that sort of support if I were in their situation. My next lad has a ten-minute moan about having to go to work and how five o'clock couldn't come soon enough. I have little tolerance and politely tell him that I knew where there were two lads who would be very happy to work till five o'clock in his place. He leaves happy with his haircut but has difficulty dragging his tail from between his legs as he goes off to work.

As I am sweeping up, in walks my fourth client of the day: a big lad of about twenty-seven, short hair and many visible tattoos. In fact his skin was probably darker than our coalman.

'Hiya Steve. It is Steve, isn't it?' he asks.

'Correct, that is me,' I acknowledge; with that many tattoos I do recall attending to him in the distant past.

'It's quite a while since I've seen you in here,' I observe.

'Yeah, it is. About eighteen months, but I always come here for me haircut every time I come out of nick. After having it cocked-up in prison, I like to come here to get it done right. I got out this morning.'

Now if there is anything to lift your day it is the knowledge that this lad always comes to me after he is released because I can do the job better than the lads in prison; and people doubt my ability!

On the subject of Her Majesty's Porridge Palace for the unwilling visitor, I have attended many customers who have had the privilege of serving time in such establishments. As my business is situated at a bus station less than a mile from the prison doors, the hairdresser is often high on the 'when released list,' although usually there is another stop off that comes top of the list before me (*any ideas?*).

The main objective is to go home looking better than when they went inside. Probably due to the number of years I've been standing behind that chair, I usually find it easy to spot a person that has just been released from prison that day, as most of them have the same traits. No matter what time of the day, they almost certainly smell of alcohol (*did you get it right?*). As you would expect, they are usually in high spirits and very friendly. They always want to call me 'sir' or 'boss', and in most cases they are very open and want to tell me all about life in prison; what job they had, how much they got paid, how often they received visitors. In my experience, most of the people who have experienced the 'naughty step institution' have been extremely polite.

Brian had been a customer of mine for many years and, although he never arrived at my door drunk, he was a heavy drinker and made no secret of the fact. Unfortunately, due to extreme amounts of the 'falling-down fizz', he finished up sitting on the adult naughty step for quite a lengthy stretch. On his return to the land of normality, we had many a chat about his time behind bars and the experiences that had changed his life forever. He admitted enjoying prison and admitted it probably saved his life. On occasions towards the end of his sentence, he was allowed weekends at home, providing he returned early on Sunday evening. Many times he returned to prison hours early because he found it boring at home. The last time I saw Brian he was a reformed character, didn't drink, ('never touch the stuff, it should be banned' were his words), although most nights he was content to while away the hours with a little magic plant extract added to his cigarettes; he is now a happy man. In his words, 'it helps me and the world to stay calm'.

A sad case was when this bloke of about thirty entered my salon with a young girl of about five, who was his daughter. Sad, because this bloke was quite drunk. Waiting for his haircut he fell asleep, whilst his daughter amused herself with a doll she had brought with her. He was aroused from his slumber by his daughter, telling him it was his turn to get his hair cut. I tried to engage him in conversation, but his words were incoherent and he fell asleep again. When I had finished the haircut I woke him up and, thankfully, he seemed a little clearer in his speech and he could stand more steadily. He paid, waved for the little girl to follow him and departed. I watched him get on a bus with the little girl tagging along behind.

Weeks later when he came back, he was sober and very much alert. When I asked him if the little girl that was looking after him was his daughter, he couldn't remember calling in before. Effectively, a five-year-old girl was looking after her drunken dad. Sad but true.

Working in one town for so long, you tend to know a lot of people. Although I don't know many of their names, their faces are familiar. I still find it odd to see pictures of individuals who have passed through my door appear in the local media for misdemeanours far beyond my wildest dreams. I have attended to at least three convicted murderers. They appeared ordinary, friendly, pleasant people and, like everybody else in my little city of Preston, they have their own agendas in life. I cut hair; I do not judge people.

People tell their hairdresser intimate details of their lives. I cut hair and I am a very good listener, although if they want my opinion I will say it as I see it; I have never been one for telling people what they want to hear. On many occasions I have lost customers because I gave honest answers that weren't what they wanted to hear. But I can say I have helped many people through their problems and predicaments, because many of them have returned to report on their progress.

The first time I met Dave I thought, 'Has he got any money to pay for a haircut?' He wore relatively clean, worn-out clothes with a tired old raincoat that had definitely seen better days. He spoke with a soft northern accent and had a well-lived-in face with really red cheeks.

'Yes sir, can I help you?' I ask.

'How much is a haircut, please?' he asks politely.

'For your haircut it will be £7, sir,' I inform him.

'Can you cut it right away, please?'

'Yes sir, if you would like to sit on this chair,' I say - although what I'm really thinking is 'Have you enough money to pay for the haircut?' I don't ask the obvious, as that would be an insult and I don't want to prejudge the man.

During the haircut he is happy to tell me about his lifestyle; he is living in a hostel, although if he was involved in another drunken escapade he would have to leave. We talk at length about his drinking and, although he says he drinks quite often, he won't admit to having a problem.

'I just want to get my life back on track. I'm a proud man. I've let myself go and I need some help. Any ideas?'

I am being asked for help from a person I didn't know fifteen minutes ago. The guy does come across as genuine, and I really believe that he is asking me for help.

As a youngster, I saw my father in many alcoholic-related states. He was never abusive, nor was I ever beaten or hit, but his unreasonable behaviour and mood swings caused sadness in our usually happy family. As a youngster, I learned to keep out of his way when he had been drinking, but as I grew up I tried to understand the reasons behind the once-infrequent binges that had become regular weekend benders. They disrupted the household and upset my very caring mother. I am sad to say this, but the older

I became the more I started to lose my respect for my father. I learned about the sadness that alcohol can bring. My father became selfish, irresponsible about his family. He fabricated the truth to fit his unbelievable stories, and our biggest concern was that he couldn't admit he had a problem. Living with this dilemma from an early age, I felt I knew enough to pass on some useful advice.

Over many months Dave used the hair-cutting visit as therapy for his problem. We exchanged views and opinions and, unbeknown to me, he listened intently to my limited knowledge. On one occasion I told him he had to face the truth; I told him he had a drink problem and the only way forward was to admit it to himself. That statement was as welcome as a parking ticket, and there was definitely a tense atmosphere. Sometimes the conversations reached levels way above the usual hairdressing pleasantries. Sometimes I wondered if he would find another hairdresser, as the lad was not getting much sympathy from me; sympathy is in the same section as syphilis in my dictionary, and I don't have either.

It took him months to confront his drinking habit. Then one day he arrived in my salon not just for a haircut; his main purpose was to tell me he had acknowledged that he had a major problem to his family and friends and had contacted the relevant authorities for help. His words to me that day were: 'I'm on the road to regaining my self-esteem.'

More than ten years have passed since the day that Dave arrived in my salon for the first time to chat about his lifestyle and his state of health, and I still cut his hair. He has beaten the booze and made life worth living for himself and his family. He has regained his self-esteem, and every time he leaves my salon he shakes my hand and thanks me for my help.

Dave's story is only one of many tales in this book, although for him it was probably a stepping-stone to his new and happy life. I don't think for one moment that I was the man to put him on the straight and narrow. All I did was listen, ask him to be truthful to himself, face the dilemma and be honest.

Writing this tale has given me confidence to face one of my own demons, to lift the lid on my own father's drinking habits. Until I wrote this account, I had never really accepted that there was a problem. I purposely forgot about the unhappiness and shut it in the 'do not open' box in my memory bank. My thoughts of my happy childhood could be poisoned by opening that box. In reality, by sharing that very private period in my life with you, I feel a strange sense of release and contentment.

With owning a hairdressing business on a bus station in a city with communications that connect it to much of the country, I have attended to many people passing through on their journeys. I have been privileged to meet people from all corners of the globe and gained knowledge from their visits. A half-hour conversation whilst cutting the hair of a complete stranger from a different country has brought invitations to meet up with them in their native land. I regard that as something very special.

It is bizarre, but I find meeting people for the first time in my private life quite an uncomfortable experience. Every day of my working life I meet new people and that is no problem; it is on my territory, my domain; it is my job as a professional to make people feel welcome and attend to their hair. I suppose it is mainly down to experience, but within as little as two minutes you can sense whether the customer is the genuine article and you can form a bond with him, or if he is just a client wanting his haircut.

This unfamiliar face was quite a welcome sight, as trade had been quiet all morning. A man in his early forties, blond wavy hair and a strong Yorkshire accent. He told me he was travelling down from Scotland and was changing direction to go to his home town of Barnsley. His haircut lasted a considerable time, due to the fascinating adventure he was embarking on. I was captivated by the tale. Initially I was very sceptical but...

He was going to Barnsley to find his girlfriend of yesteryear. He had planned to marry this lady and was engaged to her for quite some time whilst he was studying at university. He finished university and, days before the wedding, he got cold feet and left. No note, no explanation - just upped and left. He went to live down south.

It was now *twenty-three years* later. He realised that he had made a mistake and wanted to see her again. He had hired a private investigator to find out where she was living. That's where he was heading that day on the bus to Barnsley.

At this point in the conversation I was not in the market for fairy tales and was not convinced. Then he showed me the letter from the private investigator with the address of the lady he wanted to find. He had got my attention and I was hooked.

His plan was to stalk her house (his words) so he could see what she looked like after all the years, and see if he still fancied her. If he did, and only if he did, he was going to engage the private investigator to find out if she was married, had any children, and what her present family situation was.

I had to ask the obvious. She had a new life; what if she was unrecognisable? People change their appearance after twenty-three years; what if she didn't want to know him? He had let her down big style many years earlier.

He told me that, providing she wasn't married and not involved in any long-term relationship, it would only be a matter of time before he would woo her back into his life! Was this middle-aged man having a mid-life trauma? Was he in need of a brain transplant? I wondered, if you gave him a penny for his thoughts, would you get change?

He told me of his plan to meet the lady, providing all the jigsaw pieces fitted into the puzzle. His friend travelled abroad on a regular basis so he was going to write a letter for him to post on the Continent, saying that he had found out where she was living and that it would be good to meet up with her again. Would she meet him at the airport when he arrived in the country?

The haircut took so long that he had to leave in a hurry, as he was late for his bus. The whole episode seems weird; even as I write the tale I can't believe that I was witness to such a stupid story, but all those years ago I believed him. He really did convince me he was the genuine article.

If they make a TV drama out of this story, you heard it first in my book!

There are only two four-letter words that are offensive to men: 'Don't' and 'Stop'.
Unless they are used together.

"To steal an idea from one person is plagiarism; to steal from many is research."

Chapter 17 - From pupil to teacher

After the death of my partner Eric and young Gary joining me, the business got back on track. Gary and I were a good team and had a good working relationship. Even early in my career, I was aware of the responsibility of owning a business; if anything went wrong it was down to me; if we had a quiet time with little or no trade, it was me who didn't get paid. The buck stopped with me.

The really long hair styles were now on their way out and the new shorter haircuts were bringing more trendy young lads through the door - styles that were artistic. Flat-top haircuts were the height of fashion, a style that needed a good head of hair and a person with creative talent to master the job. If you got it right, they brought their mates to have their hair done. The younger lads of school age were looking for something different like the wedge haircuts: hair cut short on the back and sides with a thick line cut symmetrically around the head about an inch above the ears. Such a stupid, way-out haircut brought the youngsters flooding through the doors of good men's hairdressers all over the country. We do what is asked; we don't have to like it!

As the business started to pick up, I decided to take on a young apprentice to help with the workload and give a young person the chance to sample this wacky world of hairdressing - a mission that probably started the demise of my soon-to-become-thinning hair!

I interviewed many applicants. One question I always asked was, 'We start at 9am and close at 5pm. Would you find it any problem to stand on your feet all day?'

I remember one school-leaver said he probably couldn't stand all day, as he helped out with a milk round from 5am till 8am and he was really looking for a sit-down office job. Another memorable interview was with a school-leaver who had brought his Record of Achievement - a portfolio of the important and impressive feats he was proud of. I looked at the book and there was nothing of any note written in it. I asked, 'There isn't much in the book, is there?'

The lad thought for a moment, then said 'That's because I've dun nowt.'

On many occasions the youngsters didn't even come back for a second interview even when asked. The search for a good junior was a hard task.

Michael started work on Tuesday morning. He was waiting outside the salon when I arrived at 8.50am, appearance clean and tidy, though he was quite flushed as he was nervous at the thought of what was to come. I showed him round the salon (which took all of two minutes), introduced him to Gary, then a couple of customers arrived, so Gary and I started work.

'Michael, the first job you have to be successful at in hairdressing is making a brew. The cups and all you will need are over by the sink. Can you make a brew to start with, please?'

He was in the back for ages, then he appeared with a cup of tea, walked over to the customer waiting area, sat down and started reading the paper.

'Michael, where are our brews?' I asked.

'Didn't make you one. You said make a brew, so I did.'

He had been with us thirty minutes and had made himself a brew, sat down, and started reading the daily paper. I can remember thinking, 'It must have been me; I didn't explain properly.'

When anyone learns a trade or job of any sort it is only a matter of time before it comes easy, although some people learn faster than others. Learning to drive is a prime example; you struggle with the pedals, the other road users are not helpful, bends arrive too quickly for you to change gear, and cars are always too near even when they are parked. Months later, after you have passed the test, it all becomes straightforward; you don't have to think what you have to do. It is all plain sailing.

Frustration is probably the most frequently used word when learning this simple-to-the-eye occupation. From the learner's point of view it looks easy, but after trying time and time again it soon becomes obvious that it isn't. You are told to keep practising - but on whom? All your family and friends are really pleased you're learning this job, because when you are qualified free haircuts will definitely be an option, but while you are training see how many people volunteer their prized locks for you to practise on. From the teacher's point of view, routine and simple tasks of the day develop into an 'endurance of sanity'. To find a five-letter word that goes after 'good' and 'common' could take many months. It was only when I had my own apprentices to train that I thought how hard others had struggled to help me master this trade.

Michael had been with us a few weeks and he had learned everyday tasks that helped the salon tick: cleaning, keeping the salon tidy and also realising we all drank coffee. He was proficient at seating and gowning up the client, a simple task but one you have to learn. The next instalment was to show him the 'performance epilogue', the finishing off. We had talked it through, I had shown him and he said he understood.

'Is that OK for you, sir?' I ask, as I show my client the back mirror.

'That will do fine, thanks,' my client replies.

'Michael will look after you now, sir,' I inform the client

Michael brushes the client off and, because he is apprehensive, manages to empty the gown's contents of the client's hair all over his trousers and jumper.

'Sorry sir,' says Michael.

'No problem, we all have to learn,' says my client.

'Right Michael, can you give Mr Brown's clothes a brush.'

Now common sense would tell you and me that... No, what's common sense?

'There yar, mate. There's a brush for yer pants,' is Michael's reply as he hands the brush to the client.

Frustration with a capital FRUST.

Now, I know that you do not gain experience in hairdressing by going out doing errands for the business but it is always a job for the junior. At the same time, it gives everybody a good laugh at the junior's expense. I remember as a young apprentice being sent to the local cobbler's for the boss's shoes and instructed to get a 'Long Weight' and bring back a 'Bucket of Steam'. As an enthusiastic youngster, all you want to do is your best to show you are good at whatever you are asked to do.

'I've come for Mr Ormerod's shoes,' I said, as I produced this little green ticket with a number handwritten on it. The old man came out of the back of the shop with the shoes in a brown paper bag and handed them to me. I remember paying him £2 10s 6d.

'Is that all?' the old man enquired.

'No, I've been asked to get the Long Weight and take back the

Bucket of Steam.'

'Aye, alright lad. You just wait there and I will get the kettle on for your steam. Have you brought your own bucket?'

'No, sorry, I wasn't given one. Should I go back and get a bucket?' I asked, trying to be helpful.

'No lad it's all right. You can make do with mine, but it's got a little hole in it. You'll have to rush back to work quick or you could lose some of the steam.'

I sat and waited for ages, thinking about the quickest way back to work without losing any steam. As well as carrying this bucket full of steam, I had to carry the long weight and I hadn't seen how big that was going to be. I could hear the old man in the back of his workshop hammering away. Every so often he would come in to see if I was still there and say, 'Sorry about your long wait. I'm having trouble catching the last bit of steam; it just won't stay in the damn bucket. It's probably the bucket. It's one of my old ones.'

I was completely taken in. Talk about green behind the ears - I was cabbage-looking. I sat there for over two hours.

'I've just had a phone call off your boss and he's told me to send you back to work. You've had a long wait and he says he doesn't need the steam now. He's made some of his own.'

I was puzzled. I still hadn't understood, although I soon found out I was the plank of the day when I returned to work. The shoes were the decoy. I had gone for a 'Long Weight' (long wait), and how does anybody collect steam? I can still raise a smile thinking about waiting in that old cobbler's shop. Could anybody be so thick, so naïve, so stupid... I was!

Michael had gone for the sandwiches at 11.45am as he did every day, only today it was 1.15pm and we still hadn't seen a meat and tattie pie, a cheese and tomato butty or Michael. Gary was mad and I was getting anxious. Gary was mad because he had to have his dinner before 1pm or he turned into a green monster. I was anxious because it wouldn't look good applying for another apprentice and explaining we'd lost the last one on the way to the butty shop.

Michael appeared at 1.20pm with our supplies. 'Before you ask, I didn't get lost. I lost the £10 note,' he said.

Gary did not stick around for any explanations, as the pie had priority.

'So when did you find out you'd lost it?' I asked.

'When I came to pay. I searched in my pockets and it wasn't there.'

'So what happened then?' I asked.

'I left the food there and walked back looking for the £10 note on the floor,' was Michael's reply.

'You were bound to find it on the floor,' chirps Gary, pebble-dashing the mirror with a gobful of tattie pie.

'I didn't find it on the floor, so I went to the police station to see if anybody had handed it in,' said a bemused Michael.

'Did they have a box of tenners and you had to identify your own before they let you take it?' said the sarcastic pie-eater.

'No, nobody had handed it in, so I went back to collect the butties and told him I couldn't find the money. He said I could pay for them tomorrow. That's why it took me so long,' said Michael.

Gary threatened to tie a big balloon to Michael's coat and pin a badge to him with the words IF LOST, PLEASE RETURN TO TOPTREND, PRESTON BUS STATION.

Another one of Michael's classic encounters happened outside the salon. He had a tour of duty to pay money into the bank, collect stamps from the Post Office and deliver a letter to the Tax Office in town. He wasn't away long and the whole tour was accomplished with no problems, or so it seemed.

'Everything go well, Michael?' I asked.

'No problems. I soon found the Tax Office and there's a post box outside on their wall so you don't need to go into the building,' Michael informed me.

On inspection, it transpired that he had bought a book of stamps and one of the stamps was missing.

'Michael, did you check the book of stamps when you bought them? Was it full?' I asked, a little puzzled.

'Yes. There was a full book but I needed a stamp to post the letter at the Tax Office.'

'So let's get this correct. You stood outside the Tax Office, put a stamp on the envelope and then posted it through their own post box?' I asked, knowing the answer.

'Yes. Don't all letters need stamps?' Michael asked.

It wasn't long before we decided that this career was probably not for Michael, and we parted on good terms. Weeks later I received a letter asking if I would give a reference for him, as he had informed his prospective new employer of his previous employment working for me. He had applied to be a postman.

Now where was I? That's it: perfection, an art that most hairdressers strive to achieve. Some days it is so easy to attain the desired effect, it happens like magic; the hair is the right colour, the right texture, the head is the perfect shape, the bone structure of the person's face is faultless, the neckline is textbook. You blink and the perfect haircut appears with ease, the client is over the rainbow and goes out like the Tin Man skipping with Toto. That happens on one of those few and far between days. Then there are those other days...

Guy arrived to work at Toptrend Hairdressing after leaving school - a slender, fresh-faced young lad with confidence way beyond his years. His aptitude for dealing with the public and his ability to master the job were incredible.

When you have got the unenviable title of salon apprentice, it is only a matter of time before the door will open and Mr Unreasonable will be sitting on your chair expecting you to perform miracles.

Mr Unreasonable is in his early twenties, dressed smartly in quite expensive gear, wearing overpowering aftershave, sporting a good tan, with loads of attitude and thinking he is the dog's best bits. Instantly there is a clash of personalities.

Guy is polite but wary. 'Yes, sir. How would you like it?' he enquires.

'I would like my hair restyled. I want something different. Would you be able to do that?' asks Mr U. in a patronising tone.

'Yes, sir. What did you have in mind?' asks Guy.

'I don't really know. Have you any styling books I could browse through to help me decide?'

The styling book is unearthed from the depths of the back room. All the cobwebs are blown off, all spiders are evicted from their homes, and the book is presented to the client.

Many years ago we stopped using styling books because a person would find a style that they liked and expect the hairdressing miracle worker to transform this dull lifeless person into a Hollywood film star. Talking to a client and asking the right questions usually gives the hairdresser the basic guidelines, clarifies what they want and what can be done. It was easier to say we didn't have a styling book than to explain some unwanted home truths.

Guy wants to show this clever sod he can rise above this predicament and show his skills. After ten minutes Mr U. has found a style in the book. The photo shows a young lad of similar age dressed in tennis clothing, long wavy shoulder-length hair and wearing a headband. The photo portrays him as having just walked off the tennis court, as he is sweating. I have an idea what is to follow, but am not expecting the punch-line.

'I would like you to create something like that,' he says to Guy, showing him the picture.

Guy smirks. 'Well, sir, that could be a little difficult. Firstly, your hair isn't as long as the guy's hair in the picture, and secondly your hair is straight whereas this style is very curly.'

'Is it because you haven't enough experience that you can't do it?' asks the impertinent clot.

Guy stays very calm; he doesn't rise to that comment. 'No, sir. If you had the length and the same sort of hair that person has in the photo, then I could recreate that look.'

'Is there anybody here that can do it for me if you can't?' he asks.

'No, sir. The problem is that you haven't got the necessary material for anybody to accomplish your desired style,' says Guy.

'I think I'll leave it then and grow my hair longer, so somebody can get it right for me,' Mr U. says as he gets up to leave the salon.

'Do you play tennis, sir?' asks Guy.

I think to myself 'Now what's coming?'

'No. Why?' Mr U. asks.

'That style you picked in the book was of a young tennis player. Well, with your hair and your facial bone structure, the nearest I could get to that picture is wetting your face.'

Mr U. leaves the building, and we don't laugh until he is out of earshot.

How smart is your right foot?
This is hysterical. Try it and see if you can outsmart
your right foot ... you won't!
It takes five seconds of your time.
Without anyone watching you, and while sitting down,
lift your right foot off the floor and make clockwise
circles.
While doing this, draw the number six in the air with
your right hand.
Unbelievably, your foot will change directions...
Told you so!

"Don't take yourself so seriously. No one else does."

Chapter 18 - Just another day in Paradise

For more than forty-five years, I've been devoted to my chosen career. The highs have certainly outweighed the lows, but there are a few customers who insist that getting a haircut is a means to an end, and the person that does this menial task was probably stacking shelves in the corner shop last week. In their eyes, the hairdresser does one job - he cuts hair. The less time these clients spend on this exercise the better. Three haircuts a year is fine. One-word answers; no dialogue is music to their ears. Enter Mr Important.

A tall middle-aged gentleman with a mass of red curly hair walked into the salon and said in a stern, loud voice, 'I need my haircut today. Is it convenient now, as I'm in a hurry?'

I was always told that customers get their first impressions of you as they walk through the door, but you should always delay forming your opinion of them until you have taken time to weigh up the situation.

'Yes sir. I will be with you shortly, if you would like to take a seat,' I said politely.

'Where do I sit?'

The obvious answer was too easy, so I pointed to the available chairs.

He sat and read his daily newspaper, regularly glancing at his watch and giving loud sighs.

'Yes sir, I will take you on that big red chair right away,' I said courteously, perhaps betraying just a hint of sarcasm.

'Short and tidy' was his only instruction.

'Is it your day off today, sir?' I asked.

'No,' he replied curtly.

Experience tells you that certain customers don't want to talk. The sooner they can leave your premises the better. One-word answers tell you to shut your mouth and get them out of the chair as soon as possible.

This customer started to read his newspaper, with an occasional glance at his watch to keep me on my toes. The haircut was going well and I was in full control of the situation. Mr Important didn't want to talk to me and I didn't feel like singing or humming a tune, so I started to read his paper with him. He occasionally looked up, so I pretended to be deep in concentration. I remember reading something about Kyle Minogue, and there was a picture of the lady, when suddenly from nowhere … HE SNEEZED. His head shot forward. With the technique of a craftsman I miraculously guided the clippers that were erasing some minor neck hairs away from the nodding donkey's head.

'Sorry about that,' said the heartless Mr Important.

'Not as sorry as the mess that sneeze did,' I said with some concern.

I deviously parted the hair from the nape of the neck up the back of his head, thereby making it look as though there was a botched line in his haircut. I showed him the back mirror with this 'pretend scar'. I only did it to bring this full-of-himself Mr Important down a peg or two.

'Oh no, look at that! Can you make it look better? Can you sort it out, please?' This once stuck-up soul had lost the sharpness in his voice. He now required the services of a skilled hairdresser who ten minutes ago was somebody that usually resided on the bottom of his designer leather shoes.

'It is a big problem, as you can see, but we'll try and sort it out,' I said reassuringly.

From that moment, he was my mate. He wanted to talk and told me he was not in that much of a hurry; he just wanted to 'try it on.'

A good haircut accomplished and a pleased customer left the salon, although I told him he had made the wrong first impression when he entered the salon, and it isn't clever to 'try it on'. But I suppose it isn't clever to mislead people either, especially when they are paying for the privilege.

Sport has been part of my life since I was big enough to bounce a ball. I have been lucky enough to participate in various activities, so I have a vague knowledge of the whys and wherefores of many of these pastimes.

I had often been fishing with my brother and my mate Peter at the local pit, but I had to learn to swim before I was allowed to go on my own; it was a parental rule. Another strict rule was being home from fishing on time. There were no mobile phones; I wasn't old enough to own a watch, so I had this large green 'Big Ben' alarm clock that alerted me when to pack up and head off home. The thing was, it alerted half of Lancashire too. Once that clock sounded, nobody caught any fish for ages. In fact, the last time I saw the clock it made many a ripple after one of the bigger boys took a dislike to it and 'splash,' it was now waking up tiny fishes in the bowels of the pit.

I thought I knew about fishing, but there are some details that fishermen keep to themselves.

'Next please,' I called out making myself heard over the radio. This lad of about twenty-five made himself comfortable on my working chair. He wasn't dressed up; in fact, he looked as if he had just left the field after standing in for the farmer's scarecrow.

'Could you take your glasses and bob hat off, please?' I asked, sensing he hadn't arrived on the clever people's bus trip to Preston.

'Aye, alreet mate, I just want a twim,' he informed me, taking off his hat.

From under this hat springs out a mass of curly hair, shiny clean and in good condition.

'How much of a trim? How much are we taking off?' I asked, a little bewildered.

'Just tek a bit off, I'll leave it t'you,' That didn't help much but I decided on a mid-length haircut, leaving the hair just over the top of his ears, taking about four inches off.

'It's been a bit since I had me haircut. If I'm not workin,' I'm fishin,'' he informed me. 'It woz bloody cold yesterday, it snowed and it was below freezing. I've got all't tackle and I get me stove going inside me bivvy. Bloody brilliant.'

'Did you catch anything yesterday?' I asked.

'Nowt much doin,' just a few little uns.'

After about twenty minutes my floor had acquired a brand new covering, a red curly-haired carpet. This young man had lost half a stone in weight and I'd transformed him into a younger, stylish fisherman. The haircut was nearing completion and I was feeling quite good about my efforts when I saw it... Just behind his left ear was a maggot. A real live wiggly maggot. I stood back in shock. It wasn't as if I was scared of a tiny maggot, I had handled many when I was fishing - but a maggot wasn't a creature one would expect to see whilst cutting hair. I think it was the shock on my face that made the bloke realise there was something wrong.

'Wot's up, mate?' he asked, not with any great concern.

'I have just come across a maggot in your hair,' I explained.

'It'll be reet. Towd yer it was bloody cold. I had 'em in a plastic bag under me bob hat yesterday keeping 'em warm. They're no bloody good too cold. They go hard and dee off. One of the little divils must have escaped. If it gets really cold I keep a few at a time in me mouth,' he said, matter of factly.

I was happy with the results of his haircut. I don't think he looked at it when I had finished. He just put his bob hat back on his head and paid.

Two issues come to mind: what would have happened if he had gone to a ladies' hairdressers and a maggot had dropped out of his hair; and secondly, he had them under his hat *yesterday* and he slept with his wife last night; now, do we really know how many of them little divils escaped?

The pinna - a flabby piece of cartilage covered with skin - can be a hairdresser's worst enemy. They come in all shapes and sizes with differing characteristics: some floppy, some rigid. They commonly come in a pair, though this isn't always true. The pair are often similar, though this isn't always true, and they are usually positioned symmetrically on each side of the face. I'm quite sure hairdressers would be more content with life if we didn't have ears - cutting hair would be much easier. Every hairdresser has accidentally drawn blood whilst cutting around the ear and every hairdresser at some stage of his or her career has cocked up by using the ear as a guide, only to find that one ear is considerably lower or larger than the other. It is the hairdresser's occupational hazard!

Some time ago Ian, a regular customer of mine, had the misfortune to have his ear cut off in an accident. The surgeons tried to sew the ear back but to no avail. Although he still had his hearing on both sides of his head, he grew his hair longer to cover the scar. He told me that, in time, the doctors were going to construct a new ear and hopefully graft it into position so it would give him more confidence in his appearance. In the short term, they had made him an artificial ear that was stuck on with spirit gum. To be honest, the ear was slightly too light in colour, which made it look like it was plastic, but since he kept his hair long over the ears it wasn't that noticeable. It helped with his confidence and it wasn't long before he would quite happily talk about his new hearing aid (his terminology) and make fun of the situation.

This particular time when Ian called at my salon, it was a warm summer's day and the salon was quite busy.

'Next please,' I shouted to make myself heard over the football commentary on the radio. Ian sat in my chair with a big stupid grin, beaming from one ear to - the artificial one.

'Somebody looks happy with himself. Have you won the lottery?' I asked.

'No, just in a daft mood,' he told me. With his hair quite long, I started by just spraying a fine mist of water and combing it into position. That's when it happened… *His ear fell on the floor.* That instant I nearly collapsed. My legs wobbled and my whole body froze with shock. I didn't know what to do or where to look.

Three seconds felt like three minutes. Then Ian said in a loud voice, 'Bloody hell - he's took me ear off.'

I was down on the floor in a flash, picking up this bloody plastic ear, hoping nobody was aware of my predicament. The embarrassment was worse than anything I could ever imagine.

'Give it here. I'll stick it back on so I can go out tonight,' Ian said. He told me that he was low on spirit gum, so he had purposely not put any glue on; he knew it would fall off as soon as I touched his hair.

Another one of his fiendish tricks was that whilst he was out with his mates clubbing, the gum would slowly lose its grip as he sweated. He would take his ear off and quietly slip it into one of his mate's drinks. He said he had tried it as a chat-up line with the ladies but it definitely wasn't a winner!

Now, this next tale doesn't fit into this chapter. It should be included in an earlier chapter related to those precious tiny tots, but this happened just after I had finished writing the book. I couldn't leave it out, as it was far too good a tale.

A young mum opens the door and asks, 'Excuse me; can you cut my little lad's hair for me now? I am in a rush to catch my next bus.'

'Yes, I can do it right away,' I say. The little lad takes his coat off and climbed up onto my big kiddie's seat. Mum sits and waits, reading a magazine, and it isn't long before he wants to tell me all about his mum and his sister and his weekend dad (his words). We discuss football and Father Christmas and presents - and his name is Simon. He never stops talking and it's fun to listen to him rabbiting on.

'So how old are you, Simon?' I ask.

'Next week it's my birthday. I'll be seven, but my mum says I am four and a half when I am on the bus!'

I smile and glance in the mirror to see his mum slowly raise the magazine to cover the guilty look on her face. Simon doesn't tell lies!

Jimmy's racing snail is not winning races anymore. He decided to take its shell off to reduce its weight and make him more aerodynamic. It didn't work; if anything it made him more sluggish.

"If a relationship has to be
a secret, you shouldn't be
in it."

Chapter 19 - Toupée or not Toupée

A nother aspect of my career is acquiring the artistry to reupholster the head, to thatch the male roof, to take years off the ageing father figure. This is done by the tried and tested use of the syrup of fig: a wig, or what is more formally called a hairpiece or toupée.

As a young lad I just couldn't understand why older men were so vain as to cover up what nature had dealt them. That was my opinion then - and as a middle-aged man of fifty-plus years my opinion today hasn't changed. To offer a vote of confidence to all toupée wearers, a good-quality human-hair, well-cut and colour-blended hairpiece can look very effective, taking years off the man and giving him immense confidence.

Over the years I have been told numerous times: 'You can't fool me. I can spot a toupée. You can tell them a mile off.' That assumption is correct but it only tells half the story because you only spot the bad ones. You only spot the poorly fitted and mismatched colour-faded ones.

My first introduction to the secret underworld of this vanity aid was when a customer arrived to have his regular haircut and toupée service; yes, that is correct - toupée service. This particular day I was brewing up in the back of the shop when I noticed a customer come through into the back, go into the boss's office and shut the door. 'Odd,' I thought; then my boss shouted over the partition for me to make another cup of tea for 'Mr Mystery Man'.

As I was making the tea I heard the conversation from the office about herpes. 'That's it,' I thought. The man has got a serious disease. I knocked on the door with a cup of tea, not daring to get too close in case this disease jumped on to me. That's when I dropped the cup. This bloke had walked in with hair and the bloody disease had stripped him of it in minutes.

'Wipe that lot up, Stephen, make another and then come in here. I want to show you the new hairpiece that I'm going to fit.'

I must fit a new battery to my hearing aid; I thought they were talking about herpes, not a hairpiece. I returned with another brew and watched with amazement and fascination at the evolution of this once bald man into a new younger man.

In the early seventies, styles were changing from the Beatle haircuts and Flower Power long hair to short haircuts and feather-cuts. It certainly wasn't trendy to have a bald head. Today anything goes; I suppose the shorter the better for the majority of men, but back in the dark ages, bald was unthinkable. To purchase a toupée helps to disguise the trick that nature has played. It eases the stress and the constant worry of being bald. It is a costly endeavour. Buying a toupée is similar to buying a suit from the gentleman's outfitters: you can buy a ready-made 'off the peg' piece or a made-to-measure piece for your individual head - but of course that comes with a larger price tag.

'Stephen, a new customer is coming to be measured for a new hairpiece and I want you with me. Watch and learn.'

In walked the couple, both in their early sixties and both large. It was obvious that it was Mrs Large's idea for Mr Large to have this new look, as she did all the talking. She was the one that was paying and she was the one that woke up with him in the morning.

'But you don't wear them in bed,' said my boss.

'Can he not wear it with a hair-net?' she asked.

'It isn't usually the case,' he explained.

'Well, you'll just have to go for a wee in the dark, Jim,' she told her husband. 'I want to get used to him with it on all the time instead of him taking it off every night.'

At this point we were aware that there weren't too many brain cells between the couple. Mr Large had a large head, a two-inch band of fairly thick, light-brown hair with fine strands of grey and a very wide centre parting. Once we had ascertained what Mrs Large required of this new-man image, we politely asked her to 'go for a walk' so we could get on with the intricate and complicated job of measuring up. More to the point, we could get some peace and quiet.

The 'intricate and complicated job' consists of placing a large thick-gauge plastic sheet over the head, front edge over the forehead and the rest covering the two-inch hair band, and pulling tight and taping each end under each ear. Now you know why we sent Mrs Large for a walk. Once in place, you draw round the outline of the bald area that will be covered by the base of the toupée. Next, draw the position of the parting and the way the hair is to be rooted into the base to achieve the required style. Now for the complicated bit - cover the whole sheet with layers of clear tape. With plenty of layers of clear tape, the plastic sheet is fairly rigid, and when released from the head it gives a mould of the shape of the head. Cut round the outline of the mould, and Bob's-yer-uncle. The mould is sent away with a sample of the customer's own hair and the wig-making company makes the wig to the individual requirements. You would think that nothing could possibly go wrong, but this was no ordinary customer.

Once the plastic sheet had been taped on, Mr Large started to sweat buckets and then *bloody fainted*. We had hairdryers blowing cold air, we had fans on full, windows open to the maximum. No good. Plastic off and let the man recover. After the third attempt, we managed a template. I shudder to think what would have happened if Mrs Large had come back as Mr Large was collapsed in the chair.

As I said earlier, this was no ordinary customer and the conclusion to the saga was that when Mr Large returned a month later, he took it on himself to get a haircut before he was fitted for the toupée. He not only had a haircut, he had it all shaved off as he thought 'it would be easier for the piece to fit on'. It was like blending a toupée to a large snooker ball. After another two months waiting for the hair to grow, the piece was fitted and all parties were happy. He never did come back for a hairnet!

Another aspect of the toupée trade is the regular cleaning of the hairpiece. Depending on the client's work or his day-to-day habits, the hairpiece has to be cleaned at regular intervals. In the early days, toupées were cleaned in a flammable, toxic fluid called carbon tetrachloride. You didn't sniff the stuff or you could be away with the fairies. Modern toupées with a polyurethane base could be washed with soap and water ... with care.

Whilst my boss was cutting the client's hair and trying his best to persuade him to invest in another toupée, it was my job as the apprentice to service the hairpiece and get it back to him as quickly as possible. Outside in the shed, the old double-sided adhesive tape was cleaned off, the whole piece immersed in carbon tetrachloride, shaken vigorously, then taken outside to be shaken dry. Back inside, the piece was combed up, sprayed with a conditioner to make it shine, and the double-sided tapes that stick the piece to the head replaced, then back to the customer with this new, restyled masterpiece. That was the usual tried and tested procedure, but things did blow off course from time to time.

A client's toupée was sent out to me whilst I was working on another piece in the shed, so I thought I would clean them both together - not one of my best ideas. It transpired that one of the clients had been using a red oxide paint that didn't dissolve too well in the carbon tetrachloride, and this unfortunately spread to both pieces. This was a complex situation: firstly, I had to find out which customer was waiting, then I had to decide which toupée belonged to this customer; then I had to clean every bit that was affected by the red paint. It took ages; this was one occasion when I hoped the boss had persuaded the client to purchase a new piece.

On another occasion, a junior (not me to blame this time) washed a toupée with shampoo and water, thinking it was one of the newer pieces. It wasn't and it finished up like a Brillo Pad. That was in the morning and, unbelievably, the same afternoon the same lad cocked-up again by cleaning a newer piece in carbon tetrachloride. He decided to speed the drying process up by putting the piece in the tumble dryer that we used to dry the towels. The lad watched it tumble round and... catch fire. Not only was there smoke everywhere, the toupée now resembled a large, deceased rat. Luckily the client had left the piece to be cleaned (he had several), and was calling back the next day to pick it up. We used to have a spares box with old pieces from customers who had upgraded, or from deceased clients that didn't need them anymore. We actually found a good colour match, cleaned it up and sent it out, then waited for the sonic bang from either the customer, the boss or both. To this day I struggle to understand how we got away with it, but an unsuspecting customer was wearing somebody else's toupée and didn't notice.

I was given instructions to get all the necessary equipment, as we (the boss and I) were going out on a visit to fit a toupée. I collected the dryers, scissors, combs, double-sided tape, a gown - all that you would need to complete the job. The boss had the toupée, so off we set. I wasn't told the client's name or whereabouts. After a short journey across town, we pulled up in front of this large double-fronted mansion in its own grounds. 'Somebody's got some money,' I thought.

I was packhorse and hauled all the equipment while my boss carried the boxed toupée to the front door and rang the bell. We were invited in by this thin, bespectacled, middle-aged man. The butler said in a quiet voice, 'Mr Whoever is waiting for you in the drawing room, second door on the left.'

'Thank you kindly,' my boss replied and walked down the corridor. He knocked and entered without waiting for a reply. Mr Whoever was patiently waiting for his new toupée … laid out in a coffin. We had come to a funeral parlour. I had not been informed of this extra service we supplied.

Not only was this an extra service, it was a new and terrifying experience. I had never seen anyone dead before and, given the choice, I wasn't in a hurry to see one now. I unloaded all the paraphernalia and stayed glued to the wall furthest away from the box. There was soft music playing in the background, an occupied box in the middle of the room, a box lid leaning against the wall, and a table with a small spray of flowers on it. I was fascinated but at the same time petrified. Beads of sweat oozed from my body, and I had to talk to myself to stay calm.

My boss carried on with the job in hand, though I remember very little of what he was doing, until he said, 'Stephen have you got the nails?'

'I've brought the toupée tape.'

'No lad, the nails, the special glass nails.'

'I brought all that we usually need, no glass nails.'

I was in a panic now. I didn't want to be there and I had cocked up big style.

'Stephen, we use glass nails for the deceased so they will melt at the cremation. We'll have to come back next week and finish the job.'

We left the undertakers' as quickly as possible, to my relief, but I had this awful thought hanging over me all weekend that we had to return with the glass nails. I never mentioned this experience to anyone, hoping it would go away and I wouldn't get asked to go again.

Weeks later, whilst assisting with another made-to-measure toupée, my boss happened to mention to the client: 'You wouldn't believe it, but there are some people in this world think that there are such things as glass nails. Imagine glass nails! What would you use to knock them in, a glass hammer?' As he said this he looked straight at me and said, 'Imagine, glass nails, Stephen.'

'I'll go and put the kettle on,' said I, as I scurried out of the office. I had been stitched up once again, only this time it was a deadful - sorry - dreadful experience. The experience had introduced naive Steve to death and it had helped conquer his fears, all in the line of duty.

I never did find out if Mr Whoever paid for our services. If he did, I didn't see any of it!

'Stephen, you are not paid to think, you are paid to do the job correctly,' I was told on many occasions. I accepted it then, as a young and green apprentice, but as you grow older you start to add together the gems of information you are fed. You learn with experience what to believe; then there are the mysteries of life, the ones that make you think for hours and days, even months after the customer has left the salon. It's a bit like a puzzle that stays with you until you piece together the answers.

A customer had me scratching my head many years ago, as the elements to a puzzle just didn't add up. I never did find the answer but I'm a good guesser! I will give you the puzzle and leave you to figure out a plausible ending. Before I tell you this little anecdote, let's see if you are up to speed with these mind games.

Say 'silk' five times. Now spell 'silk'. What do cows drink?

Answer: Cows drink water. If you said 'milk,' you are not concentrating.

Try this next one without using a calculator. You are driving a bus from Preston to Blackpool. In Preston, seventeen people get on the bus. In Warton, six people get off the bus and nine people get on. In Lytham, two people get off and four get on. In St. Anne's, eleven people get off and sixteen people get on. At the Pleasure Beach, three people get off and five people get on. At Blackpool Tower, six people get off and three get on. You then drive to Blackpool Bus Station. What was the name of the bus driver?

Answer: Have you forgotten your own name? It was YOU!

You are going to have to keep up with play. Keep those little grey cells moving and think about this one.

A new customer had made an appointment to be fitted for a new toupée. He told us he lived out of the area and worked abroad. It was customary that after we had made a template, the customer would pay half the fee as a deposit and pay the rest on completion of the job. Mystery Man insisted that he pay the total bill immediately, as he had won some cash on the horses. He wouldn't leave his address or his home phone number (no mobile phones then), because he was getting a toupée to surprise his wife and family, and would contact us when he was back in the country. The hairpiece was made and delivered to us, and we waited for the customer's call for it to be fitted. We fitted the toupée, and Mystery Man was elated. He was over the moon; the man was dancing on air. Normally, when you have achieved the desired effect, it is almost certain that the customer is going to keep it on his head, waltz home and astound his amazed family. But no, this customer wanted to take it home in the box!

After a few days we usually get a call to confirm all is well, or the wife thinks it could do with a little off the front, or the family think it is great. No call. Didn't hear a word; it must have been good.

Mystery Man arrived unannounced about six months later, bald, with his toupée in a box. He told us all was well and he wanted another one. He was in a hurry, he seemed agitated and he told us he had left his kids in the car - could we take the template immediately or should he call back? He had brought the original piece with him, so while my boss was making the new template I took it to give it the once over. The piece was like a dried-up hedgehog. It had seen a considerable amount of sunshine and lost much of its colour.

Whilst I was giving this piece the kiss of life, I could see the kids in the car getting hot on this warm day so, with dad's approval, I invited them in to watch me work miracles on their dad's toupée. I was shocked by their reaction. They had never seen a toupée before; they didn't know what one was. Why did it need cleaning and did it really go on a man's head? I didn't tell them it was their daddy's.

With the kids back in the car and the toupée back in its box, I returned it to its rightful owner. Mystery Man paid in cash as before and told us he would call us when he was back in the country. Again, he wouldn't leave his phone number as he wanted to surprise his wife with his new hairpiece. He called in six weeks later. We fitted it, he was happy and he left. Never saw him again.

The jigsaw pieces didn't fit together but when I approached the boss with my reaction, he repeated, 'Stephen you are not paid to think, just do the job.'

I am a good guesser - any ideas!

I am not bald, I've got a good head of skin for my age!

"If brains were taxed, some people would be due a rebate."

Chapter 20 - Things that people say! Or mouth malfunction

It is better to stay quiet and let people assume you are stupid than to open your mouth and remove all doubt. That's a statement I was told many years ago, and how true that sentence can be. We all suffer from the odd brain and mouth malfunction, usually at very inappropriate times. We wipe away the eggy fragments from our faces, hope nobody noticed, and move on.

I do wonder why some people wait until they frequent my salon before they close the intelligence window and open the obtuse flap which feeds their mouths.

Jim was reading the newspaper whilst waiting for his haircut when in walked Ernie. Both gents were retired and had renewed their bus passes on many occasions. I made the usual comment about pensioners' discount day being yesterday and effective only with their parents in attendance; it raised the usual humorous reaction as expected, and they both continued to enjoy their natter.

I went on cutting hair, occasionally tuning into their conversation as my client was a boring sod and had little to say. It wasn't long before football was mentioned, and the good old days of watching Tom Finney were high on their agenda.

'What a player. There's nowt like 'im these days, tha knows,' said Ernie, relishing the thought.

'Aye, 'e were a good un, were Tom. Do yer remember Cunningham and Shankly?' asked Jim.

'Full backs, weren't they? Weren't they both from Scotland?'

'Aye, they were. Good uns, both on 'em,' observed Jim.

'Yer see, Ah've lost a bit of me memory. It's not what it wah.'

'Aye, we're all going same way. I struggle a bit wi' remembering meself.'

'Ah've got some tablets from that there health shop for me memory. They're supposed to be good,' said Ernie.

'I could do wi' some of them. Do they work?' asked Jim.

'I don't really know, to be honest. I keep forgetting to tek 'em,' said Ernie.

Neither of them knew there was anything amusing in what they'd said. I had a good chuckle to myself, but my client didn't even raise a smile. I said he was a boring sod.

Being asked to perform magic with haircuts is part of daily life but abnormal requests do raise a smile now and again. Old George once asked me if I would be so kind as to collect the hair in a bin bag so he could experiment with using it on his allotment to see if it would help with his growing techniques; something about making his heavy soil lighter. I swept it up and George dug it in.

The off-the-cuff comments and the one-liners are everyday humour. It is only when you ask pertinent questions that the client realises that it probably came out wrong. For your entertainment I give you mouth malfunctions of the highest order.

The most common instruction by far is 'short back and sides and **LONGER** on the top please,' to which I answer, *If you want it longer on the top you could be sat there quite a while.*

'Could you cut most of the grey out and leave the dark bits, please,' answer being, *Sorry sir, the scissors are colour blind.*

'I have got a double crown at the back. Could you cut it and leave me with just one?' *Now where else would you have a crown, and how do we lose one?*

'Could you leave the fringe? Just trim it.' *Now I can leave it or trim it, but I can't leave it AND trim it. The choice is yours!*

'Could you cut all the curls off so it will grow straight?' *How will it grow straight by cutting the curls off?*

'If I get it cut very often, it will grow quicker.' *In that case I will get mine cut every day and I should have a full head of hair by Christmas!*

'It grows far too fast. I seem to be here every three months!' *Thank you, sir. My business thrives on regular customers.*

'What style will suit my face?' *Sorry, sir, I am far too kind to give you my true feelings.*

A customer is standing outside, pushing at a locked door. The blinds are down and there are no lights on in the salon. The customer notices movement in the salon, knocks on the door and then shouts, '*Are you closed?*'

A customer pushes the locked door, then knocks on the door, then shouts through the letter box, 'Can you just do another one?' All this whilst I am standing inside the salon with my coat on, the blinds are down, and there are no lights on.

I work here sir. I don't live here!

'Is there anything to put on my hair to stop it growing so fast?' *I am here to run a business, and could you grow some for me, please?*

'Is there a shampoo to use to help it to grow thicker?' *You mean that really good stuff that I use every week?*

'Can you cut it so my ears look smaller?' *Miracles take a little longer.*

'My mate came here last week. Can you cut mine the same, please? You'll know him, we go to the same school and he's the same age as me.' *The clairvoyance studies can be found on page seventeen in the manual.*

Allotment update. George spent ages digging the hair into his soil and it didn't help, with it being a windy day: 'It looked like there were dead rats all ovver t'place.'

'It grows too bloody fast. I'm always here getting it cut. I bet you have some stuff in that bottle that makes it grow quicker!' *If I had some stuff in that bottle to make it grow quicker, do you think I would be standing behind this chair with a bald head!*

'If they knock the bus station down, will it affect you?' *There is a good chance it could do, and it could do a bit of damage when that big stick of dynamite makes a big bang!*

Young lad calls into the salon with a real cocked-up haircut. 'Who cut this for you last time, or did you hack at it yourself?' I ask.

'No I didn't do it. I don't know who cut it the last time,' he tells me. *Now did he loan his head out for the day or is somebody too embarrassed to tell?*

Allotment update. 'There's been a bloody load of birds; they've come from all ovver. They come to tek th'air fo' their nests, but then they tek me peys and they started eyting tuther lad's peys as weel.'

One of the classic statements that always makes me smile is when a client is waiting for his haircut. His pal will walk in and recognise his mate: 'All right, Billy, what are you doing here?' *Hello, the clue is in the property you have just walked into - the big red chair, mirrors, and hairdresser. Odds are he isn't waiting for a bus to Cleethorpes!*

Old Jack sits down for his haircut whilst Doris, his wife of more than forty-eight years, strolls over to tell me what he - no - what she wants his hair to look like.

'Just a nice tidy trim and not too much off the top,' she instructs me. 'He hasn't got much left on the top these days. I really want something to put on it so it doesn't blow all over the place. Any ideas? He doesn't want any hairspray and no greasy stuff 'cause it makes a mess of his pillow. He doesn't want any of that blue jelly or any red jelly. I don't want him to look daft.'

Doris wanders over to look at the products on sale and picks up a bottle of gel spray. 'Will that do the trick? Is it any good for Jack's hair, to stick it down? Do you use it?'

'What would I use gel spray for with a bald head - wallpapering?' I say.

Doris looks up and explodes into laughter. She must be close to wetting her knickers. She sits giggling through the entirety of Jack's haircut.

As Jack leaves, he says in a quiet voice, 'She'd better stop laughing when I'm watching t'snooker on telly or she'll be under t'bloody patio by teatime.'

I am minding my own business working away when in walks a young man of about nineteen years. 'Are you the boss?'

'Yes mate, can I help you?' I ask.

'Do you need any help? I can cut hair.'

'Have you any qualifications? Where did you do your training?' I ask him.

'No, I haven't done any training. I cut me dad's hair and all me mates' hair and they all say I am good at cutting hair.' *I am still working on my own!*

Being situated on a bus station, at times I am called to work at hyper-speed so that the occupant of my chair can catch his bus. That is, the bus he forgot to inform me about when he sat down; it leaves in three minutes, and there isn't another one till a week on Pancake Tuesday!

This middle-aged man was from out of the area and passing

through on his bus journey. I had been instructed to cut his hair, and when I had finished could I shampoo it 'because that was his way of completing the occasion.' No problem. I was shampooing when he sat up (water all over the place) and said, 'Have they just announced the bus to Glasgow was leaving?'

Now working on the bus station for so many years, I don't hear the tannoy and when I do I can't understand what they are talking about. To me it sounds like somebody is being sick in a bucket.

'Sorry, sir. I didn't hear any announcement,' I told him.

'I'm sure it did. I'd better check.' With that, he didn't wait for me to towel dry his hair - he just got up and ran out of the salon. With water all over the floor and all over himself, he disappeared.

Two minutes later he returned, looking like a drowned rat. 'No, it wasn't my bus. It leaves in fifteen minutes, so I'm OK for time,' he told me.

I rinsed off the remaining three bubbles of lather, blow-dried the hair into shape and completed the job. I spent ages trying to dry his shirt with the hairdryer. He left a happy man. I had to engage with the mop once again and it left me with another tale to tell.

Allotment Update. George tells me that his potatoes are through but there seems to be more mice about this year. Also a bad year for sweet peas.

A young lad of about nineteen walks into my salon and asks, 'Can you have me out in seventeen minutes?'

'What do you want doing?' I ask; with short hair he should be good to go in seventeen minutes.

'Just a quick tidy up, please.'

The lad sits down and I get to work. 'Are you catching a bus?' I enquire.

'No I'm getting married. Where is the registry office in Preston?' he asks.

'It's way down near the railway station.'

'How long will it take to get there?'

'Probably about ten minutes,' I tell him.

'Then you've got seven minutes to cut my hair,' he tells me. I now have to work at speed.

'How long have you known your little princess?' I ask.

'About four months, I suppose. Never met her folks,' he tells me. 'I'll give it a couple of years and if she isn't any good I'll get shut.'

The lad left with a good smart haircut for the pictures of his wedding. I suppose by now he must have loads of albums to look at!

Many years ago, way before I ever knew that my pipe work was going to need a plumber, I felt some tightness in my chest, so I paid a visit to the doctor, and he swiftly sent me to hospital for an ECG. They put probes all over your chest, wire you up and take a reading of your heart. 'Anxiety pains' was the result and 'continue with your lifestyle' was the answer.

I arrived into work at about 9.50am the morning after my hospital visit. Gary had opened up the salon and was busy working.

I was greeted by: 'Where the bloody hell have you been? I've been waiting since nine o'clock.' I immediately turned round, went outside, looked above the door to check I was at the right place, and re-entered *my* salon.

'Hello, Jim. I was just checking to see if this was my salon. Now, I'm sure the last time I paid the bills for the salon I owned the business, and I'm bloody sure you didn't have an appointment with me at nine o'clock.'

Jim was not too happy about my late appearance and I was not too happy about his attitude. I got ready to work and invited him onto my chair.

'Bloody ten o'clock is no good for me. It means I'll be in work late,' Jim said; he was still not a happy punter.

'I've just been to the hospital; I've just had an ECG,' I informed him.

'What is an ECG?'

'It's a scan on the heart to make sure it's all working right; it was only a check-up.'

'Bloody hell, Steve, don't snuff it. Where the hell would I get me hair cut?' Jim says with a considerable amount of concern in his voice.

Isn't it nice to be well thought of!

Allotment update. George has found not one but two nests with furry little mice, all nice and warm, in a hair-insulated des-res.

We are all guilty of opening our speech flaps to say something that we know we meant to be correct but sounds really stupid when we analyse it. I remember as a young apprentice my mother was happy with my choice of profession but could see that I was growing up and developing new ideas. She respected my views but made me aware that I also had to respect her views. As I was leaving for work one morning, she delivered one of her classic remarks: 'Long hair may be coming into fashion in Preston but don't think you can come home with really long hair here. You must look tidy for the job.'

Now how long does it take for hair to grow really long ... I was always home by 6pm.

This guy enters the salon and takes the weight off his feet by sitting on my chair. I had attended to him before, but he is one of my usual Saturday customers, as he works in the building trade, so it is strange to see him dressed clean and tidy on a week day.

'How are you doing today? It's odd to see you in here on a Tuesday,' I comment.

'I've been in hospital overnight. I had a bit of an accident yesterday on a roof,' he tells me.

'What have you been doing?'

'Just be a bit careful. I've had stitches put in just on the side of my head near my ear,' he informs me.

'How did you manage that?' asks the nosey hairdresser.

'I was up on a roof, slating, I'd gone down the ladder to fetch more tiles up, and as I put my head above the gutter a tile slid down the roof and hit me on the head.'

'You were very lucky. It could have knocked you off the ladder,' I say sympathetically.

'I'm so fed up with people telling me how lucky I was. If I'd have been lucky, the bloody tile would have missed me.'

In hindsight I suppose it was a stupid comment. He had the pain and the scar and I'm telling him he was lucky.

Allotment update. The growing season has ceased, apart from a few leeks and a handful of sprouts left to pick. Billy, George's neighbour, has found mice in his shed. Billy doesn't know where they have come from but George has a good idea!

I had just opened for the day when this young lad of about eighteen came bounding through the door. He was clean-shaven and dressed in a suit that looked as if he had borrowed it from his grandad, and it was apparent he was in a hurry. From his appearance, it looked like he had been in a fight, done ten rounds with a professional boxer and lost, fallen out of the ring, been savaged by a Rottweiler, hit with a steam roller, crawled to the bus station and then come through my door.

His words will stay with me for many a year: 'Can you help me mate? I'm in court in an hour and I don't want 'em to think I'm a bit of a roughneck. Can you make me look intelligent?'

I cut his hair and from his eyebrows up he looked moderately better than when he walked in... but not what I would call intelligent!

~

'My brother comes here and he told me you were good,' this lad of about twenty-three tells me. 'My girlfriend usually does it for me and usually cocks it up, but I've split from her now so I thought I'd try you.' Looks like I have got a major assignment, I think. All my hairdressing experience will be needed to improve the hair his girlfriend has cut. He tells me he is going out that night and he needs his hair to look right to find another woman.

A chimpanzee with a copy of 'An Idiot's Guide to Cutting Hair' would probably have done a better job than his ex-girlfriend, but I sweat buckets to change his appearance from thick to chic - (*it wasn't that good*) - more like stupid to cupid (*I'm good, but not that good*). Probably geek to sheik, but in reality lad-with-bad-haircut to lad-that-looked-better-after-some-professional-labour. He is delighted with my efforts.

'That's bloody good, I really like that. You're better than the girlfriend,' he says.

I take comfort from his every word. 'Thanks,' I say.

'I've just started working at the local electric supermarket. If you need anything, just come in and ask for Terry. If they ask, tell them you're me *grandad*!'

'Thanks for that, but could I be your young Uncle Steve?' I ask, not wanting to be too pushy. Is that what they call a back-handed compliment?

Allotment: final findings. George studied the growing season with a new additive in his soil. Results for the season … little change. He did recognise that his radishes did slightly better when he used grey or blonde hair in the soil and asked if I could separate the lighter hair for next year's growing season… I declined the request.

With his increased family of mice and birds, I think he was christened Mickey Birdman. He was hoping that the twenty years it would take for the hair to rot would pass quickly!

I had done Brian's hair for many years, probably since he was at school when his dad brought him, so I knew the family quite well. A pleasant, likable lad who always had a smile and was full of life - only today he wasn't too happy. No smile, and he looked like he had lost the sausage out of his hotdog and the ketchup had dribbled down his leg.

'All right, Brian? How are things?' I asked, knowing there was something not right.

'I have just had a big shock,' he told me. Knowing the lad as I did, I knew it couldn't be good news.

'Do you want to talk about it?' I asked.

He sat in front of my mirror and looked lost. I stayed quiet and got on with the job in hand.

'Am I pissed off?' he said.

Now, I didn't know if that was a statement of fact, or if he was asking me a question.

'I don't really know, Brian. Are you pissed off?'

'Too bloody right I'm pissed off. You know I told you me and Sarah are going on holiday to Florida this summer?'

'Yes, that's right. You're going to visit Mickey and his friends,' I said, trying to cheer him up.

'Well, it's all off. We aren't going now. I've had to cancel the trip.'

'Have you split up? What went wrong?' I asked.

'She's only gone and got herself pregnant,' he told me.

'Was it anything to do with you?' I asked sarcastically.

'Was it hell? She should have been more responsible.'

Evening paper headlines: *Immaculate Conception Arrives in Preston!*

More complaint letters:

Will you please send someone to fix my broken path. My wife tripped and fell, and she is now pregnant.

This is to let you know our lavatory is blocked and we cannot get BBC 2.

Since the arrangements with your salesman I am having a baby and I would like to change it for a tumble-dryer.

Can you move the meter so it won't cause an obstruction to my back passage?

"If we all threw our problems in a pile and saw everyone else's, we'd grab ours back."

Chapter 21 - From the heart

When I started in this amphitheatre of fun all those years ago, I am sure I never gave a thought to growing old. Enjoy what you have got instead of moaning about what you haven't got - live for the moment. As I grew older, I aimed at learning the skills of life: marriage, being a good parent, and making sure we had enough money for the daily necessities. I suppose this is normal for most people, just striving to conquer the next problem and live life the way we want, or the way twists of fate take us.

As a lad in my twenties, I was a good target for many of my clients that worked in insurance and pensions and, I have to admit, I had many complimentary meals and free lunches. As a young lad, these companies all tried to impress me with their statistics and figures. The information about pensions confused me; I just happened to find the top pension companies by chance. But I was never too concerned about growing old. 'When it comes along I'll deal with it.' There was never any doubt in my mind that I would reach retirement or old age; it was just the passing of time, the continuity of life… or so I thought.

Although I was relatively young when my parents died, I accepted that life is a like a roll of toilet paper. We use it and we abuse it; if we are careful and look after our toilet roll, it will last longer. The same goes for life; we never know when it will end - thankfully, as we don't really want to know. Each sheet on the roll is another chapter. I have tried, and still do try, to enjoy my toilet roll of life. I really had to think hard to flush that one out!

Up to the age of thirty I could eat anything at any time of the day, sleep anywhere, didn't have any medical ailments, and could spot a bad toupée from one hundred metres. How times have changed! Older people tell you that you will start slowing down, things drop off and need replacing, you'll need artificial aids - you don't believe them but it is so true.

Eating is definitely a puzzle to me. As you grow older you don't eat as much because your body doesn't need it, but even when you eat less you put on weight. The rear end that used to have a precision timing motion now seems to work an overtime shift at any time of the day. The eyesight degenerates slowly and you compensate by holding the book further away from your face until your arms appear to have shrunk. You take an eye test to confirm the inevitable and you succumb to glasses.

My hair was slowly taking its leave a few years before I reached thirty, but to be honest it never was a big issue. My dad and my brother were bald in their early twenties, so I did well to reach thirty. Over the years I have been asked many times if it bothered me to lose my hair as I worked in the hairdressing profession, to which I always came up with the same response: priorities. Hair is superficial; so long as my heart and liver keep going, then I'm happy. I would hate to have snuffed it and be laid out in a box with people looking at me, saying how good I looked with a full head of hair. How good I looked... I was dead!

The first reality check for me came when I read in the newspaper that somebody from my school had died. It didn't feel right. He was in my class at school and his toilet roll had come to its end; he had arrived at his cardboard inner tube and he was my age. Life suddenly became precious, my responsibilities became my priority. I had a wife and family and they needed me to be there for them. I remember thinking that I had to make a will. Whether I thought making a will would keep me safe, stop me from getting knocked off my bike or getting heart disease, I don't know - but Jean and I each made one.

At the age of fifty-three I was in fine working order, or so I thought. I played golf on a regular basis; I was chairman of a football league, refereeing each week; I enjoyed walking and frequented the Lake District summits at regular intervals; I rode to work on my bike. Working for more than forty years in close proximity to the general public, who walk around with a bewildering selection of illnesses and diseases, I must have been extremely fortunate to escape with the odd cold and a case of measles. I always kept myself fit, so it came as an earth-shattering moment when I was told by a cardiologist that I needed a heart bypass. An angiogram (an X-ray picture of the blood vessels in the heart) showed narrowing of some arteries. The problematic position of these narrowed arteries was sufficiently serious that a stent (a contraption to open up the artery to allow the blood to flow) was not a solution, so I needed a heart bypass.

I was in shock for two days after the news. It felt like I was in a bubble, cut off from the outside world. Jean shed many tears; both Nicola and Emma were very concerned, but all my family gave me tremendous support. I surmised, however, that with a huge scar down the middle of my chest, nude modelling was not looking good as a career option in my retirement.

The operation was scheduled for the main heart hospital in the North of England at Blackpool, but in the event I was asked if I could go to a private hospital on the outskirts of Manchester, thirty miles away.

At the age of fifty-four, I had never been a patient in hospital and I didn't know what my reaction would be to walking through the doors. Six days later, I walked out of that hospital after a triple heart bypass with so many emotions (if they'd have put the price of bread up a penny I would have been in floods of tears) and, to my surprise and relief, with very little pain.

Surgeons are well-paid by any standards and you don't see many top doctors picketing the hospital for more money, but when you think that top footballers get paid £60,000+ a week for playing a game they love when these surgeons are giving life to real people, I do wonder if somebody has got the arithmetic wrong! Sorry - just thinking out loud.

Weeks before I was due to have the operation, I had a website designed so my customers and acquaintances, the people who wondered why the barber's wasn't open and the nosey people could find out if I was still alive and when - or if - I would be returning to play with my scissors.

The week before I went into hospital, I sat down, wrote a letter and placed it in my salon window to tell people why my salon was closed. That letter was terribly hard to write, and I am not ashamed to admit I wept as I wrote it.

27th June 2008

After thirty-one years of working on the bus station, next week will be the first time that Toptrend Hairdressing will close for a short while due to illness.

I say illness but really it is an operation that the medical people say I need; that is their job and I cut hair. I look as fit as I usually do, and most of the time I feel fit, but I suppose if the boss of the body say bits need plumbing then I have to do as I am told. It came as a big shock to me and no doubt it will be a shock to many of my friends and clients.

The business will close on Saturday 5th July.

Due to the nature of the operation, as yet I cannot say how long I will be off work but medics expect me to be up and 'RUNNING' after about a month.

On my return I have to follow a strict regime of recovery, so at first my working week will be considerably shorter and I will be operating an appointment system until I am back to full strength. Only then will I be able to supply a full service.

In the meantime, a few of my colleagues will be working here to help the continuity of the business. My colleagues' limited hours will be posted on the website whenever they can spare their own free time.

The website will be updated on a regular basis to keep you informed of my progress and when I will be taking appointments. Feel free to e-mail me or send text messages on the number provided; I will endeavour to reply ASAP.

I earnestly apologise for this interruption in my business but after thirty-one-plus years of uninterrupted business, sometimes something has to give.

The thought of this operation does not excite me one bit but the thought of working and looking after my friends and clients gives me confidence that I will return in the not too distant future.

Steve

I went into hospital on the Sunday afternoon and left my nerves at the front door. I was introduced to the anaesthetist and the surgeon who was going to perform the operation the following day. Nice guys, and if there is anybody I really want to like it is nice guys that are batting on my side. Late on Sunday night I lay quietly on my bed and contemplated my fate. It all seemed surreal, as if I was reading a book and wondering what would happen in the next chapter. A vein was to be used from my right leg, and I can remember apologising to my leg for disrupting it - but then I thanked the leg for helping with my plumbing problem and probably saving my life.

I left hospital the following Saturday afternoon and that felt strange, as Saturday is a busy day in hairdressing and not working didn't feel right. On the Sunday, six days after my triple heart bypass, Jean drove me to the salon; I wanted to be there. It is part of my life. After only five minutes I was whisked away back home to rest.

After four weeks of watching daytime television, I was restless. Remarkably, I returned to work and did four customers in two hours. I had the Rottweiler (sorry) - the wife with me at all times, and she monitored my every move. From that day I knew I was on my way back and slowly built up my strength. Six weeks later, I was allowed to drive and after eight weeks I was back to captain the ship once again. Remarkable really!

Over those two months in 2008, I was overwhelmed by the number of get well cards, e-mails and thoughtful messages I received from friends, colleagues and clients. If I didn't thank you then, I thank you now for your support in my hour of need. Whilst on the subject of support, I have to mention three people who I will always be indebted to: two are colleagues of mine that have worked in this profession longer than me, old stagers really, Dave and Ken. These two lads opened my salon on their own days off, two full days a week, until I was able to return to work, thereby keeping my business ticking over. Now, not to put too fine a point on the matter, these lads paid me the takings so that they could keep a competitor's salon open whilst he recovered. That is special; thank you, Dave Hill and Kenyon Yates. The other person I must thank is my wife, Jean, who did everything but breathe for me. She didn't mother me, she smothered me, and after a month I had to stop milking the situation; love you, thanks Miss Piggy!

Today it is January 6th 2010. We've had a very enjoyable Christmas in the Molloy household, the business was busy as expected over the Christmas period, although it suffered like many others due to such awful wintry conditions. Bitter cold winds, icy roads and an unusually large helping of snow definitely deterred people from leaving their warm homes and offices in the cause of vanity.

It is very rare for the city of Preston to be covered under a white blanket and transformed into a realistic backdrop for a new version of Disney's *Cinderella*, with our iconic bus station playing the part of Cinderella's Castle. But today, despite such dreadful snow and icy conditions, the pantomime season continues. The whole country is witnessing conditions that are more welcome in skiing resorts on the Continent.

Preston had six to ten inches of snow yesterday, minus 4°C last night, minus 7°C expected tonight, with the same conditions forecast for the next ten days.

The media are telling us to stay at home unless our journey is vital and the buses have stopped running in Preston, which is disastrous news when I work on a bus station. I have stayed at home. *Today I have not opened Toptrend Hairdressing!*

But why do I feel guilty? Why do I feel I am letting people down? My customers who arrived yesterday won't be bothered, my customers due in tomorrow won't be bothered providing I arrive tomorrow, but the customer or customers that turn up at my door today will be upset that I'm not there to provide a service. I feel guilty because I'm a hairdresser and I serve the public. This sentiment isn't just me being soft in the head; ask other hairdressers and they will tell you the same. It goes with the job.

A hairdresser knows many people through his job, and they are constantly reminded of them every day of the year. For example, you see something on TV and it prompts you to think of that person that you attended to last week; somebody asks if you know a plumber and instantly you think of the lad with the mop of curly hair - you don't know their name but you're reminded of one of your customers; on holiday, you go away to leave the job behind but there are always reminders of customers.

Call it soft, pathetic, or sad, or you could call it thoughtful, caring or sentimental, but either way it goes with the job, a job that is so special it is like being part of a large family. After forty-odd years, I feel like an elder member of that family and appreciate how lucky I am and how lucky I have been!

Dave calls for his mate Tommy on the way to the pub. Little girl opens the door and Dave asks, 'Is your daddy ready?'
Little girl starts crying and runs into the house.
Tommy's eldest son comes to the door and Dave asks, 'Is your dad ready to go darting?' **The lad looked very upset turns round and goes into the house.**
Tommy's brother comes to the door and Dave asks 'Hiya Johnny, what's up? Is Tommy not playing out tonight?'
'Hiya Dave, we have had some bad news today. Tommy went down to the allotment to pull some carrots for tea; he collapsed and died there on the spot.'
'Bloody hell, Johnny, what did you do?'
'It was hard to accept, but it was bloody lucky we had a big tin of peas in.'

"Being over the hill is better than being under it."

Chapter 22 - The aged gentlemen

Throughout this book there are stories about aged gentlemen. This chapter is dedicated to those old lads; they make me realise that one day in the not too distant future, I will be joining their ranks. A free bus pass, a Christmas fuel bonus, 10% discount on Wednesdays at DIY stores... I will be sent out shopping and, because of my age, I'll have a legitimate excuse for forgetting where I put my bus pass and shopping list.

The aged gentlemen have seen it, done it, experienced harder times and in many cases remember the detail of those times, even though they cannot for the life of them remember what they had for their dinner last night.

I suppose when a seventy-four-year-old man says he's on his way to work any curious person, never mind a nosey barber, would want to know his occupation.

I had cut Norman's hair for many a year but had no idea he was still working.

'Good morning Norman, and what are you up to today?' I ask.

'I've just been shopping and later on I'm going to work,' he informs me with a wry smile.

'Work? I didn't know you were still working.'

'Just up to Christmas. It gets me out of the house. That's why I've been shopping.'

'Where've you been, Norman?' I ask.

'I've just been to the sports shop in the precinct.'

I'm intrigued. 'What have you been to the sports shop for, Norman? Doing a bit of Christmas shopping?'

'No, I needed some shin pads,' he says.

'Who are they for, Norman? Have you got grandchildren?'

'They're for me, although the lad in the shop was a little shocked when I asked him if I could try them on.'

'What on earth do you want with a pair of shin pads?' I ask.

'They're for my new job. I start this afternoon. I play Father Christmas for the local charity hospice. I did it last year but my shins finished up black and blue. Those little children can swing their feet all they want - I'm ready for them this year.'

Sadly, Norman's second time as Father Christmas was his last but, to this day, I remember that smug smile as he announced, 'I'm ready for them this year.'

It's a sad fact that when you've been looking after the hair of regular clients for many years, it suddenly dawns on you that you miss people: the old man with the glass eye has gone AWOL; the nice man that always talked about cricket and how he would change the game if he was playing today. One only assumes that they have passed through the clouds of time.

Only last week a little old lady arrived at my door. She stood outside as though she was waiting for somebody. Eventually she came inside and asked for me by name. We had never met. She had come to tell me her husband had died and to thank me for all I had done for him over the years. I expressed my condolences and thanked her for calling. It was only after she left that I realised how hard that must have been for her and how much I had been part of that man's life. I cannot express how much I appreciated that gesture. It made me realise how special my job is.

A retired gentleman enters my salon with his wife. A virgin client, so as usual I welcome them to my emporium. As I am cutting his hair, I notice there is a small bald spot on the left side of his head: a birth mark. Experience tells me it isn't a scar, it isn't a mark from stitches many years ago and it isn't a minor area of alopecia.

I explain to the old lad that I will keep the birthmark covered with the longer top hair, to which he replies, 'Aye lad, Ahd appreciate it if tha could. I've had it quite a bit, that mark, tha knows!' He then turns round in the chair and speaks to his wife. 'Mary, can you remember how long I've had this birth mark?'

Mary looks up from her magazine. 'By 'eck Jim, you've had that a long time. You had it when I first met you, and that's over forty-six years ago.'

I don't make any comment - just smile and wonder if Jim's birthmark arrived when he was born, or on a later bus!

'Next please,' I announce as I wait for an elderly gentleman to take off his coat and occupy my chair. He explains quietly that he just wants a nice tidy trim, then he sits back and seems to go into a trance.

I try my usual 'lift the spirits' conversation. 'How are you doing on this fine sunny day? Nice and warm, that sunshine.'

'Yes it is,' is his reply. His voice is soft and gentle.

I try again. 'Are you doing the shopping today? Has she sent you with a list? All blokes need a list; they must think we're stupid. On my list it usually says 'don't forget to take your list with you', I quip.

'The lady that usually sends me with my list died at the weekend. I'm having my hair cut for the funeral on Friday.'

In an instant I changed the everyday stupid head for the concerned serious head. 'Sorry to hear that, sir. Was it expected?' I ask.

'Not at all. We'd just bought a new static caravan in the Lake District. We'd been married over forty years.'

In the next twenty-odd minutes, this stranger offloaded many private family tales, thoughts and feelings that he admitted he wouldn't tell his own family. I'd known this seventy-two-year-old gentleman for seconds, but he felt comfortable enough to reveal his feelings to me. I felt humbled but happy that I could help him at this sad time. I asked him to promise me that each day he would have at least one proper meal. He promised he would try.

When he left, he paid for his haircut and said, 'Today won't change anything in my life but you've done so much for me. I must thank you so much for your services.'

He shook my hand and, as he turned to leave, I noticed a tiny tear roll down the side of his cheek. As I watched him leave the salon I realised my own eyes were a little damp, so I sloped off to put the kettle on.

I tell this tale because it is everyday life in a tiny hairdresser's - not for any bonus points or to enlarge my ego, just to relate the satisfaction I get from doing my job.

There is an old lad who has been a regular customer for many years. He will never call in if there is anybody waiting; he always calls in after lunch because it takes him till midday to sober up from the night before (his words, not mine). His wife went on holiday and didn't come home and, to my knowledge, he has been drawing his pension for well over fifteen years. A private person, he says very little. He told me once he doesn't like waste so he doesn't waste words in trivial conversation, and he doesn't waste time as he doesn't know what time he has left.

These are the instructions for his haircut he gives me every time I cut his hair: 'I want it short and I want it quick. If I don't survive this ordeal, my money is in the top inside pocket of my coat!'

That's it. He doesn't speak again until he says 'thanks' and leaves the salon.

Not too many months ago I was busy working when I noticed an old couple outside my salon. They walked up and down, looking like spies working for the KGB. After minutes of inspecting the price list and minutes of watching to see if I really could cut hair, they ventured inside.

'Would it be possible for you to cut my husband's hair, please?' the lady enquired.

'Certainly. If he'd just like to take a seat, I'll be with him shortly,' I told her.

I finished the young lad on my chair and then asked the old gentleman to take my big chair. Too late. He was up and in my chair before I could blink. If he'd been any quicker, he would have sat on the previous customer's knee.

'He would like a nice trim, please - not too short. He noticed you through the window and said he would like his hair cut like yours!'

Now, readers who know me will be shocked to know that there is *one* person happy to walk round with a haircut like mine. I couldn't remember the last time anybody acknowledged that I even had hair, let alone wanted to have a similar haircut.

I spent the next fifteen minutes trimming the old lad's hair and having a pleasant conversation with them both. I could tell he was happy as he kept smiling at himself in the mirror and telling me he would be coming again for his haircut next time.

Haircut over and his wife had paid. The old lad walked over to the mirror and had one last look; he smiled and then said to me, 'That's just what I wanted. It is just like yours. We could be mistaken for *twins* now, me and you!' he said.

His wife smiled and said, 'You daft bugger, the barber isn't eighty-three yet!'

I really do need to change my hairstyle! I was going to grow a ponytail but you know what's under a ponytail?

An ar**-hole! (That's a very old barber's joke).

Old Brian had been calling in for his haircut on a regular basis for a couple of years. I knew little about his lifestyle, except that his main pastime since he retired was having a flutter on the horses. His highlight of the year was the Cheltenham Festival, a major event for the top horses and riders held around March. He didn't just talk about his winnings and his losses - the racing festival was his life. He never went to the meeting but he watched every scrap of televised material.

It is a four-day meeting. As he arrives in my salon on the last day, I quip, 'Hello Brian, is it that big week in your life again?'

'It sure is, and what a week I've had. I've made some serious money this week,' he tells me. He explains to me how lucky he has been, then asks, 'Steve, could you do me a big favour?'

'No, Brian I haven't any money to blow on gee-gees,' I tell him.

'Could I leave some cash with you so that I'm not walking about with it and I'm not tempted to spend it?'

'No problem. When will you be collecting it? After 5pm?' I say.

'Some time later on,' he tells me, and gives me an envelope. Old Brian goes out looking tidy, and also looking for a long-odds winner.

An hour or so later, in he walks. 'I'll go and fetch your package,' I say.

'No, don't need it. Can you put this with it?' He hands me another envelope and leaves the salon.

I didn't see Brian till the day after when he came to collect his two packages; he thanked me and went on his way. Weeks later, when he called in for his haircut, I asked him about his fortunes with the horses.

'Did bloody well on the Cheltenham Festival, you know. Thanks for looking after me money.'

'So how much did you win over the week?'

'Don't really know. In that first packet there was more than £6,000 but I don't know how much was in the second packet - probably another £2,000.'

He left more than £8,000 with me overnight, then walked out with the cash on his person - and to look at him, you would have thought he bought his clothes from the local jumble sale.

Brian died a few years later, coincidentally during the big racing festival in March. Now what odds would he have got for that?

'Can I just have a trim please, lad,' the old man says to me in a strong Welsh accent.

'With that accent I can tell you're a stranger to our shores,' I say, knowing I hadn't attended to this aged gent before. Dragging a suitcase gives the game away that he lives further afield than Morecambe.

'That's correct, lad. I'm just passing through on my way to visit my daughter in Cumbria. I usually visit once every couple of months,' he tells me.

'So what part of Wales?' I ask.

'A small village near Merthyr Tydfil. Southern Wales, where we play rugby.'

Now there are two things I know about Wales: number one is it rains a lot, and number two is the way Welsh people pronounce the word 'rugby'; they don't say the word, they sing it, and it sounds brilliant. If I'd been born in Wales and the game hadn't been so rough, I'd have played rugby!

'Isn't that near to that little village of Aberfan?' I ask. As a kid of about eleven, I saw the black-and-white television pictures of this tiny village where a school was swept away by a mudslide due to heavy rain. Many children lost their lives.

'That's the very same, lad. I was working in the pits nearby and we were called to help at the site. I was one of the first workers on site that morning. It was a national disaster. There were kids…' He stops talking. He is lost in thought. I notice his chin quiver and a tear slowly roll down his cheek.

'Do you go to watch the rugby?' I ask, diverting the conversation to a lighter topic. Taffy soon returns to planet earth. 'That's right, lad. I watch the rugby now. I used to play but the buggers got too fast for me!'

The old man's hair was tidy and he was soon on his way to Cumbria. I felt a touch guilty for broaching the subject that brought back such vivid and painful memories for him, memories from more than forty years ago that still inhabit his thoughts today.

An elderly couple had been dating for some time. Finally they decided it was time for marriage. Before the wedding, they went out to dinner and had a long conversation about how their marriage might work. They discussed finances, living arrangements, and so on.

Finally the old gentleman decided it was time to broach the subject of their physical relationship. 'How do you feel about sex?' he asked.

'Well,' she says, responding very carefully, 'I'd have to say I would like it infrequently.'

The old gentleman sat quietly for a moment. Then, over his glasses, he looked her in the eye casually and asked, 'Was that one word or two?'

"If at first you don't succeed, destroy all evidence that you tried!"

Chapter 23 - My faux pas

"I said "MUFC"!!"

These stories of people saying, admitting to, or just doing stupid things don't stop with my customers. For more than forty years, the bloke behind the chair has been busy making his own chapter in this book. I have to admit to numerous acts of thoughtlessness, and to making senseless comments. I fall into the same pool of absurdity as many of my customers.

I was told many years ago by my elders that you don't make comments about anything you don't know about. If asked for an opinion, then be honest but polite. I have tried to follow those words of wisdom. On a few occasions, however, the eggy stuff had

257

to be removed from my smiley little face with a large hanky.

This young lady had brought her son, David, in for his haircut and we had the usual chatter about how he was doing at school, holidays and her shopping habits. She was quite happy showing me what she had bought and asked my opinion about her purchases. I noticed that she must have either enrolled at her local 'wear what you eat class' or she was pregnant. I suspected the latter.

She must have put on quite a bit of weight as I, like 98% of men, don't usually notice things like that. We men notice the price of beer and we need to know the latest football gossip, but increases in weight don't fall into the 'urgent and extremely important' in-tray.

I racked my brains and convinced myself that the last time I had spoken to her she had told me that another little David might soon be on the cards.

'So how far have you to go?' I asked.

'Not so far,' she informed me. She hadn't understood my question, or maybe she was keeping it from David, I thought. I tried again in cryptic language.

'Not all that far to go?' I asked.

'No, we're on the bus. It won't take long,' she told me, still not cottoning on.

In hindsight, I should have stopped there but 'Bulldozer Bill' had to continue to make himself understood. 'So have you got a date yet?' I asked.

'Date for what? You didn't think I was pregnant, did you? I'm not pregnant; I've just pigged out on my holidays and put on loads of weight,' she said indignantly.

With egg splattered all over my face, I finished David's haircut, and went to hide.

On a similar occasion, I had a little lad of about seven-years-old in for his haircut. He asked for his hair to be cut bald on the back and sides and very short on the top. I told him that most schools didn't allow very short haircuts like the one he wanted, but I would cut it as short as possible. Just then an elderly lady walked in and acknowledged the little lad.

'He's going to cut it short but not too short,' the youngster informed the lady.

I explained to the lady that schools are very particular about very short haircuts, then I said to the youngster, 'We don't want you to get into trouble at school and we don't want your gran to get into trouble with your mum when you go home.'

'That is my mum,' the lad told me quietly. Then he turned to his mum and said, 'Muuuum, barber thought you were me gran.'

Strangely enough, I didn't see that little lad for his haircut again!

Preston Guild Hall has been the location for many televised events in the sporting calendar. My salon is all of one hundred metres from the venue and over the years I have attended to many people who have performed or been involved in the organisation of events there. On this occasion, bowling was being televised from the Guild Hall and, unbeknown to me, certain players had called in for their haircuts. As it is a minor sport, I knew little of the bowling fraternity. I wasn't aware of the players that had been in... until I noticed them on the telly that evening.

'Yes sir, is it just a trim?' I ask.

This fairly rounded lad of about thirty with a strong Scottish accent answers, 'Yes, please, same again if you can remember.' I vaguely remember seeing the lad before but can't put a name to his face, only I can recall something about a postman...

'Do you watch the bowling on the telly?' he asks.

'Just now and again,' I reply, trying to figure out where I know this man from.

'I'm one of the players in the tournament across the way,' he tells me. 'I won it last year and you cut my hair, so this year I'm trying to do everything the same. Superstition, I suppose.'

I realise where I've seen him before - he is the 'Bowling Postman'. We spend the duration of the haircut going through his previous year's success. He informs me he is due to play his next round the following day.

The following day at about 4.30, I was surveying the sights of the bus station when I recognised the young player walking past the salon. I opened the door to speak to the lad. 'All the best in your next match. With that haircut you can't fail,' I said.

His smile had disappeared. 'I've just been beaten. I'm on my way home,' he told me.

Being one of the favourites to win a national tournament and losing is one big disappointment, but to be told you can't fail to win with a new haircut - it was *definitely* the wrong time. That was probably the nearest I came to a Glasgow kiss.

It was early November and the snooker lads were in town for the annual snooker tournament. It was played over two weeks but only the last eight days were televised. The players often ambled past the salon from the hotel to the venue to either practise or play their matches. As the days went by, the players got fewer as they were knocked out and went home. It was only in the latter stages of the tournament that the surviving players called in to the salon for a wash and blow-dry before they performed on television.

'Next, please,' I say.

A large gentleman fills my chair. 'Just a wash and blow-dry, please,' he says.

I shampoo his hair and, whilst I am blow-drying it, he tells me he is up for the snooker.

'Do you follow the snooker?' I ask.

'I travel quite a bit with the game - as far as Thailand and Australia.'

What a life, just watching snooker and seeing the world. Nice for some!

'Do you play?' he asks me.

'Very occasionally. The balls are too big and the pockets aren't big enough.' I continue: 'So you must be the man that knows who's going to win the tournament this year.'

'Me, I hope,' he says, not sounding too cocky. 'I've a good draw this year but it all depends on the run of the balls and the luck on the night.'

The sports-loving hairdresser with the hairdryer hadn't a clue his customer was a player. Result: he lost in the next round and didn't need my services with the hairdryer until the following year.

With the amount of sport, especially football, on television these days, even for a sportaholic like me it can become a little too much. I suppose it won't be long before we will be able to watch ten games on one screen at the same time in 'Dolby Sound' and in HD, whilst wearing our 3D super-focus television glasses. Rewind to the years before satellite TV, when the only live football occurred every year, mid-May on a Saturday afternoon: the FA Cup Final from Wembley.

This major sporting occasion was broadcast at a time when all good hairdressers were working. This was the day when all the tennis-loving, horse-loving, ping-pong-loving, anti-football customers converged on hairdressers to get away from watching football on the TV, with no queuing for a haircut. Every year I used to borrow the mother-in-law's small black and white fourteen-inch portable TV and spend ages balancing a poxy cheap aerial to get a sub-standard picture. At least I was in on the act. I watched the FA Cup Final live, even if it was snippets from behind somebody's big head. Watch a bit, then when nothing was happening, work at the other side of the client's head until a roar went up, and then back to the other side. Haircuts took longer on Cup Final day.

A week after this big soccer day, this young lad arrives for his haircut and specifically asks for me. He sits down in my chair, looks in the mirror and smiles at me. I smile back and ask him how he would like his hair cut. He doesn't say a word but looks at his hair in the mirror and smiles again.

'Yes, sir. Is there a problem? How would you like it cutting?'

'I would like it short on this side so that it matches the other side, please,' he instructs me.

I stand behind the chair and look at his haircut. One side has been cut above his ear and the other side is covering his ear. I am just about to ask who the hell cut his hair the last time when I realise I had cut it the previous week whilst watching the FA Cup Final.

I think quickly on my feet. 'Did you ask for it shorter on one side?' I ask.

'No, it was you spending too much time watching the football on the right-hand-side.'

'Weren't you watching the football as well?'

'Don't watch football. I play tennis,' he tells me.

'So if I cocked up, how come you left the salon with one side longer than the other? Didn't you notice the difference?' I ask.

'Didn't you?'

'No, I couldn't have done. I was too busy watching the Cup Final.'

Result: my team won and that same customer still comes for his haircut ... but not on Cup Final day.

It is common knowledge that as we get older certain bodily functions work as they should do but not as quickly or as efficiently as they used to. For example, breaking wind. When I was a kid I thought it was funny to 'let one go'! You had it, you wanted rid of it and you weren't bothered who knew about it. As one gets older, one has to master the art of releasing it without being recognised as the culprit. To let one go, you either have to be on your own and release it with unrelenting pleasure or you have to release it in silence with at least two other people in the vicinity, so that each one is not totally certain who was responsible. If we fast-forward in time to the next level of rear aromas, it becomes a bit more of a dilemma.

Now I am not saying I have reached that age, or am speaking from experience, but it can become a frightful decision. Do I squeeze the bum cheeks and hope nothing slips through, do I try to withstand the pressure that is building within and hold on till the appropriate time, or do I release with it and hope that it is just wind and not a pant-filler?

With that said, I have to admit my salon door has been open to the public many times when really I should have been somewhere more appropriate. 'Huggies' and 'Tena' have gone a long way to help, when working a one-man business. Another secret I have to admit to is the disposal of the one that escaped. If one of the little blighters just so happens to slip through when I'm on my own with a customer, it's easy to spot the culprit. The sure-fire quick eraser is deployed: whilst engaging the customer in conversation, preferably asking him questions so as to take his mind off the aroma, the hairdryer is switched to maximum power and I pretend to blow the hairs away from the client's nose and face whilst quickly blowing the air away from the posterior.

I find that this method always works, but it is very important that there are not too many bottom burps and not too many questions, or the customer will leave the salon thinking his hairdresser is a nosey, noisy and smelly person.

Another function that we take for granted is that we tend to hear something and instantly the brain relates what we heard to a picture. More often than not, the brain gets it right; on rare occasions, we tend to sail in the wrong direction.

'Yes sir, and how would you like your hair cutting?' I ask a regular client who is in a happy mood.

'Just a trim please. I've just finished work for two whole weeks and I'm going for a pint to celebrate,' he tells me.

'So have you any plans for the holidays? Are you going away?'

'Paignton.'

I am well aware of the delights of Paignton in Devon, as I had been there on holiday with my family the previous year.

'You'll like that. It's a wonderful place. There are loads of places to visit, it has a good beach and, providing the weather is good, you can't go wrong.' For the next five minutes I enthuse about the delights of this south coast town.

The lad, having arrived in a bubbly mood, has gone somewhat quiet. He seems deflated. His spark has been extinguished. He's just finished work for a fortnight and he appears to have lost the will to live.

'It should be great to get away. Have you been before? Do you not want to go? What's wrong?' I ask him, now aware that I haven't sold Paington's delights too well.

The lad doesn't speak. He just exposes his hand from under the gown and slowly makes what appears to be a paintbrush stroke.

'What's that? What are you doing?' I ask, wondering what the hand motion means.

'Painting, I'm bloody painting. I've got two bloody weeks of painting. I used to go to Paignton as a kid every bloody year, hated it, but I would rather go to Paignton that paint the outside of me bloody house.'

Now you have to admit, the words do sound the same!

It is Saturday afternoon, the salon is surprisingly quiet and the door is opened by a young lady of about twenty years.

'Yes, can I help you?' I ask.

'Is it possible for a young lad to get his haircut today, please?'

Many hairdressers have a policy to work on adults on Saturdays because of their customers' working commitments, but providing I am not too busy, I accommodate kids.

I decide to give the lad a trim. 'I can do him now providing he'll sit still,' I inform her. Kids usually get fed up waiting for long periods of time, so that by the time they get to their haircut they are as high as kites, fidgety and quickly upset.

I notice a slight smile as she says, 'I'll go and get him. He's just outside.'

I collect the child's seat from the rear of the salon and place it on my big chair, dig out the blue fishy gown and prepare myself for what could be a difficult operation. I wait and wonder if she has taken him to the toilet. After a few minutes the young lady walks in with... her boyfriend.

It transpired that she told him he was having his hair cut, although he didn't want it doing. She said she would pay for the cut, and then said she had made an appointment so that he couldn't back out or she would lose her money.

I was tempted to sit him on the child's seat and make him wear the fishy gown. I ask how old the child is before I commit to cutting their hair now.

Over many years of doing this job, a job that looks easy until you have a go and decide differently, certain little details become second nature. It's like during the day, you don't think, 'I'll put my shoes on,' you just do it; everyday tasks are done instinctively and you don't even know you have done them.

I have a habit of cutting the hair at the back of the head and when I am satisfied with my work, walking back a pace from the chair to check and admire the finished effect.

'What yer bloody looking at?' asks the old lad as I check my work.

'I'm standing back to see if you look good enough to meet your admirers,' I quip.

'Bloody painters do that when they are painting a picture,' he tells me. 'You're like a bloody artist wi' a pair of scissors.'

'Yes sir, an artist stands back to check and admire his work. He applies paint to achieve his goal and I take off hair to achieve my picture,' I tell him, with tongue firmly in cheek.

'Well, can you tell Picasso to be quick. Me bus leaves in ten minutes!'

Are my talents wasted?

When you watch cowboy films the goodies always tend to blow their smoke off their guns when they have shot the baddies. Well, another foible of mine is to blow the hair off my clippers at very regular intervals - a habit I have had for many years and still maintain to this day.

I was working on this young lad and I remember quite vividly that we were talking about the local football team. We were having the usual debate about team selection when the door flew open with what seemed a hell of a bang.

'What did you do, then?' this man was virtually shouting at me from the doorway.

I was stunned. 'Sorry sir? What is the problem?' I asked in a shocked but aggressive manner.

'What did you just do?' The man was irate. I was lost for words; I didn't understand his question, as I was working happily in my own salon not bothering anybody.

Now when you are 101% positive that you are 'squeaky clean' and you are being accused of something you have supposedly done, even I become a little bemused. Professional but bemused!

'I haven't a clue what you are perturbed about and I would ask you to explain, please.' This man was in his early forties. I honestly think that the puzzled looks on my client's face and mine made him realise he had just lit the wrong end of the firework and had two seconds before it went off in his hand.

'Sorry for bothering you. I thought you made a gesture to me as I was passing.' He left quickly with a very embarrassed expression on his face.

I was blowing the hair off my clippers and I presume the vain gentleman thought I was blowing a kiss to him. How sweet!

It is mid-morning on a Saturday, the very early birds have flown (the ones that pitch their tent outside the door so that they can be first in the queue) and I am getting ready for a coffee. As I sweep up, the door is opened by a young African man. He speaks in broken English that I struggle to understand.

'Hello, are you the owner?' he asks.

'Yes sir, can I help you?' I reply, hoping I can make him understand.

'Are you Kenyan?' he asks me.

Now whether it was the time of the day, the brain reacting too quickly, or it could have been that this guy was probably from Kenya and my brain mixed the signals up; I can't honestly say. I answered: 'Sorry sir, did you ask if I am Kenyan? Do I look Kenyan?' I wasn't upset, I was shocked, and I didn't look anything like Kenyan.

'Hello, are you Kenyan?' he asks again. 'Are you Kenyan?'

Now I have been called some things in my time as a referee, and my voice has been mistaken many times for George Formby's, but Kenyan - sorry, not guilty.

'Sorry sir. I am not Kenyan.' As I try to make myself understood again I suddenly realise where this man is coming from. A colleague of mine who had spent some time working in my salon whilst I was off work was now working part-time as a hairdressing tutor at a local college. It transpired that this gentleman had been taught by my colleague and was looking for him. My colleague's name? KENYON.

A case of brain working too quickly or brain switched off.

It was Saturday the 13th February, and I was just about to close after a hectic day. As I cleaned up, I found a carrier bag had been left by a customer sometime during the day. As I inspected the lost property, I realised that tomorrow was Valentine's Day, the day for love and the giving of all sorts of soppy merchandise to your loved one. Inside the carrier bag was a big bunch of flowers, a card with mushy words, and a red teddy bear with a big red heart attached.

I cleaned up, switched the lights off, then realised nobody had returned to collect their gifts of love. I thought: 'Somebody is going to be upset,' then had this pathetic thought that brownie points might be coming my way in the morning. By the time I returned to work on Tuesday, the special day would be over, the flowers would be dead and the teddy and card would have lost their significance.

Sunday morning and Jean was lost for words. Her gasp had been flabbered and I was one hell of a good guy, even though she had her doubts about her unexpected presents. In all our years of marriage, many Valentine's Days had come and gone without it making any mark on our calendar. Then suddenly Mr Smoothy showed a more caring side to his character. My lady was elated, my girls were shocked, and I had pulled the unthinkable off.

A month later, Jean was in the salon on a Saturday afternoon, helping clean up. This young lad of about fifteen-years-old called in for a haircut. Just as he was leaving and about to pay, he mentioned that he had lost a bag with some stuff for his girlfriend for Valentine's Day. I tried to speak quietly, hoping my lady with elephant ears working in the back would not hear, and told him that I felt sorry for him and he could have his haircut for nothing so he could buy her more flowers and goodies.

It didn't work; to this day I am still in arrears with my brownie points. If he had come in any other day than Saturday, I would have got away with it. When my girls found out about dad's misguided present, I was in the dog house! Every year I am still reminded of the teddy and flowers. My loving gesture was definitely not appreciated!

Having once been a boy scout all those years ago, I still aim to do my best on most days of the week. With more than thirty-six years working on a bus station, I try to be friendly, knowledgeable and helpful. Now when I say knowledgeable, I still do not know which bus goes from where and at what time, or which colour bus goes to Blackpool, and I don't know if the big bus that goes to Scotland has a toilet on board. I work *on* a bus station, my business is sign-written TOPTREND HAIRDRESSING and I have never driven a bus or worn a bus inspector's uniform. If I had a pound for every time I was asked for bus information, I would have retired at puberty.

This lady opens my door and asks if it is possible for me to cut her boy's hair. After a positive response, she struggles to bring her belongings into my salon. She has a push-chair laden with about seven shopping bags, and wedged within is a little lad with long hair and another little lad carrying another two shopping bags. This lady looks knackered, her patience is way passed fraying at the edges - it is threadbare She is in quite a pickle, and to help her day move to dizzy heights, as she wheels the push-chair into the salon the front wheel falls off. Now I don't know how many straws a camel has, as I have never seen many camels with straws, but there were too many on this lady's camel. Enter super-hero!

I invite her to sit down and calm down. I assure her I will try to fix her push-chair's wheel. She tells me it isn't the first time it has collapsed but with a good belt with a hammer, it will go back into place and it will be good enough to get her home.

I find the 'if all else fails' toolkit and assess the situation. I am down on all fours, she is down on all fours; she is holding the wheel and I am tapping it to persuade it to locate the vacant hole in the push-chair.

'You'll need to hit it harder than that to make it stick,' she tells me. I try putting more power into making this damn wheel fit. 'Hit it harder,' she yells, as I give it a real hairdresser's clout.

'F*!^%/g hell,' she yells. 'You've just hit me f*!^%\g finger.'

There is blood everywhere. I empty the first aid kit of plasters and try calming this crying lady down. After about ten minutes, result. I have calmed the lady, I have fixed the push-chair and am well on the way to cutting junior's hair. I am thinking to myself that things have eventually turned out for the best, when the lady's phone starts to ring.

'Hello, is that you, Dave? Yes, I'm in the hairdresser's on the bus station getting Johnny's hair cut. You know that front wheel on his push-chair, the one that keeps coming off? Well, you didn't do it as good this time 'cause it's just fallen off in the hairdresser's.'

As I listen to this one-sided conversation, I smugly expect the lady to inform her partner that this super hero of a hairdresser has fixed it for her, until,

'Yeh, I'd done all the shopping with the kids and called into the barber's for Johnny's haircut. This barber chap put the wheel back on. Yeah, I might be home a bit late, though. When he put the wheel on, he hit me finger with the hammer and I think it may be broken. I'll have to go to the hospital on me way home.'

I have to say that even with all my DIY experience and helpful intentions, sometimes my talents go to waste. I can't give you a conclusion to this tale. Her partner must have accepted her version of events, since my windows stayed intact and little Johnny or his mum didn't call again to use my wealth of experience in fixing push-chairs.

I'm also good with sticky-backed plastic!

This chapter is pay-back time. For all the stupid statements and daft tales that have been told in this book about the public, I can equal the best. Out of all my faux pas, this one holds the candle for sheer, unadulterated stupidity. To this day, I smile when I think of what I did in a quite ordinary situation. I have gone on about what other people do, how people's brains congeal or even solidify, but this day I must have enrolled into the college for Dumbos.

An elderly gentleman enters my salon and I welcome him. He takes his coat off and sits down on my big chair.

'And how are you today?' I ask. The well-dressed gentleman

smiles but doesn't speak. I then notice that under his chin is what appears to be a small white button in the vicinity of his windpipe.

He hands me a note which reads: *I have just come out of hospital, having had an operation on my throat. Sorry I can't talk. Please may I have a tidy trim?*

I read the note, smile at this old lad and put my thumb up, indicating that I will look after him. He smiles back. I cut his hair in silence. The haircut doesn't take long, as he has little hair to cut, but my services will make him feel better.

Once finished, I take his piece of paper and write: *Is that OK for you? It looks better and it will make you feel tidy.*

I hand the paper back to the old lad; he reads it, smiles, and then writes: *Yes thank you. I did say I can't talk but I can still hear.*

It is cringe time.

I take the paper off him again and actually write: *Yes of course, that will be £7 please.*

This graduate of common sense and master of dealing with the public actually writes it down, after the old man has told me he could still hear me speak. He smiles again. I apologise to him. As he leaves, he smiles and gives me a big wink.

It probably made his day; it made me feel I had entered the realms of stupidity.

My neighbour knocked on my door at 2.37am this morning; can you believe that, 2.37am!
Luckily for him I was still up playing my bag-pipes!

"Ham and eggs: a day's work for a hen, a lifetime of commitment for a pig"

Chapter 24 A day in the life

A day in the life of a gentleman's hairdresser: no appointment system and no agenda for the day. Each day is a blank canvas. Here I open my box of colours to paint a picture of a fictitious day with genuine tales I have encountered along the way.

Beep, beep, beep - the eyes flicker, an outstretched arm reaches out to turn off that annoying noise, and the cogs very slowly start to turn. What day is it? It's Wednesday. It's a work day. What will today bring? It is the middle of the month and people have spent up; and I can hear rain, so that will keep customers indoors. The schools are on holiday so I could be busy with kids, and Ramadan is due to end soon, so that could make quite a difference.

Beep, beep, beep - that bloody noise; it's that time of the day. I regularly wake up grumpy but I leave her in bed and I hit the ground running. One hour later I arrive at Preston Bus Station, not knowing what will occur in the next eight hours.

I collect the newspapers and turn the corner to find three customers guarding my door like sentries at Buckingham Palace: two pensioners and an anxious young lad on his way to work. I assess the situation and ask both old lads if the young one could go first, as he needs to get to work. One old lad is out for the day; he has escaped the wrath of his wife and is quite happy to allow the lad to go first. The second pensioner has other ideas; he wouldn't let a ten-ton truck pass him. He is ex-army and still adopts a sergeant-major's attitude. There is more chance of me growing a fringe than this bossy ex-serviceman letting the young worker warm the chair.

Three customers later, nobody waiting. I sweep up and wonder who, or what, my next predicament could be. I don't have to wait long, as the next challenge comes in the form of a young lady in her early twenties with bright, dyed red hair. She asks the question of the day: 'Excuse me, do you do women?'

Being the perfect gentleman, I reject any thoughts of the obvious answer and decline her request for me to cut her hair. After she has vacated the premises I use the air freshener to eradicate the smell of a brewery.

It is time for coffee and, as I pick up the newspaper, in walk mum and son. Mum tells me little Thomas is three years old; she assures me that he usually sits still and loves having his hair cut. He sits high up on the children's chair wearing the fishy gown and watches very intently. My clippers remove the fine blond hair as the chin starts to tremble and the tears start to well up in the eyes. My reassuring tones help so much that he breaks into floods of tears. Plan B is instantly adopted and the scissors take the place of the noisy clippers; these are greeted with screams as he jumps up and down hysterically on the chair. I am halfway round his head and we take a time-out. I suggest an adjournment for ten minutes, but to no avail. Mum and son are both upset and mum puts Thomas's baseball cap on him and takes him for a walk with half a haircut.

By now the waiting chairs are all but fully occupied. Now why is it that when mum, son and hairdresser are having a hard time, everybody thinks it's very amusing?

Back to the bread and butter of the job and, as one pensioner leaves, another one keeps the chair warm. I guess I will finish that cold coffee soon.

A man in his early fifties tells me that he has just bought a funeral plan, explains to me its benefits and asks me if I require one. He could get the guy to call round to see me. Now either I wasn't looking too healthy or he must have been on a 2-for-1 deal. I decline his offer.

As the funeral director's best friend leaves the salon, the phone rings. 'Good morning, Toptrend Hairdressing,' I answer.

'Hello, I'm just ringing for my dad,' this middle-aged lady says. 'My dad came in for his haircut this morning, an oldish man with grey hair and ... well...' She hesitates. 'Well, he's lost his false teeth and he thinks he might have left them in your shop.'

'Was he in for his haircut early this morning?' I ask.

'Yes, that's right. Have you found any false teeth today?'

As usual, I see the comical side of the story and my mind is full of stupid one-liners, but then I realise this lady is upset and embarrassed. I struggle to keep my composure as she explains that she can't tell what her dad is saying without his teeth.

'I have to say I haven't looked for any teeth today, so it's a safe bet I haven't found any, but if you give me your number I will look around and call you back,' I explain.

Luckily nobody has jumped onto my chair so I have a quick look and turn the chair around to discover a hanky under the footrest. The hanky is held together with a red elastic band and it is obvious it contains a set of false teeth.

I have to say I am not too squeamish, but hypodermic needles and false teeth are relatively high on my list of 'rather-not-see' articles. I tentatively pick up this hanky and its contents from the floor, deposit them into a carrier bag and hide them in the back of the salon. I ring a very relieved lady and she thanks me for my trouble.

The old gentleman (the bossy ex-sergeant major), whose teeth sat in my salon overnight, called to collect them the day after. It appeared that whilst I was in the back making a brew, he took his bus pass out of his pocket and, unbeknown to him, his hanky containing his teeth fell out.

A young lad of about twelve, accompanied by his mum, is next. As I cut his hair, I ask him: 'Is there no school today?'

She informs me, 'He wanted his hair cut and a new game for his computer, so I kept him off school'.

It wouldn't have happen in my school-days! Now I'm really sounding like my dad.

While I am cutting this young lad's hair, a middle-aged man walks in. I notice he has left his wife outside the salon, talking on her phone. After a while his wife starts frantically waving to attract her husband's attention. He goes outside to find out where the fire is, rushes back inside the salon, grabs his coat and says, 'I have to go now. She needs me, I'll see you tomorrow, Steve.' He disappears faster than a jockey late for his mount in the 2.30 at Aintree.

Sure enough, he did come back the next day and, like all nosey hairdressers, I enquired as to the reason for his hasty departure. It turned out his wife had been to check her lottery ticket and was told she needed to ring the lottery company. She rang, to be told she had won a substantial amount of money. She had to ring another number with the ticket number. At this stage of the proceedings, she lost her nerve and started waving for her husband's help. He left the salon and they tried to compose themselves as they travelled back home on the bus, before ringing and finding out they had won in excess of £130,000.

Eventually the salon is empty and I am left with my own company. I sweep up and my thoughts drift towards lunch, whether to eat early or later. The decision is made for me, as a young lad in his early twenties enters the salon, taking away all thoughts of my butties.

He is a regular customer but one I haven't seen for a while, as he has been working with the armed services in Iraq. When I start the haircut, I notice a tiny dint in the top of his head. He assures me it is not sore but it was when it happened. In the war zone where he was working, it was common practice for haphazard shooting to occur and a stray bullet had hit him in the head. He *walked* to the hospital. He had the photos of the X-rays on his phone, which he took great delight in showing me. Amazingly, the back of the bullet (the flat end) was flush with the top of his scalp but the bullet didn't penetrate his brain. That was one lucky lad!

Next up is a young lad who is in quite a bit of pain. He struggles into the salon with one arm in a plaster cast; in his other arm he is carrying a crutch to help him walk, as his leg is also in a plaster cast. He tells me that a week ago he was on the way to the pub when he slipped and fell on his arm. It was sore but he continued to the pub. As the night wore on, the arm became more painful, so he drank more to ease the pain. On his way home, with the icy conditions, a sore arm and eleveteen pints of falling-down water inside him, he fell again. He wobbled back home to sleep it off, only to wake up during the night in mega pain. A trip in the white van with the flashing blue illuminations took him to the human repair shop and confirmed he had broken his arm in two places. In his second fall, he had broken his leg.

He tells me it was hard work getting on and off the bus to my salon, but his hair needs cutting because he is going out with his mates round the town centre pubs and, if he feels OK, they are going clubbing later that night. Is there an age at which common sense replaces immaturity?

The lunchtime two hours usually pass by with the same common denominator: to transform a client from untidy to presentable and give them enough time to eat lunch and return to their workplace.

It is fast approaching two o'clock and my thoughts return to my stomach. With the kettle switched on, and sandwich in hand, the door opens and in walks a long-haired man of pensionable age. I politely inform the old lad that I am just having a sandwich and I will be with him in five minutes. He tells me he only needs a quick short back and sides and he is catching a bus in ten minutes, and I could eat my lunch after I've cut his hair. The hair was so long it would have taken me twenty minutes to find his ears! I decline his thoughtful offer and waste a full five minutes eating my sandwich.

Selfishness is a trait we always attribute to other people!

With my lunch hour (well, all of five minutes) over, I am now ready to continue doing what I do well. I try to complete the Sudoku puzzle in the paper. I know that I still have to finish something a little more taxing than the daily puzzle, and it has just arrived through my door.

Thomas and his mum arrive for their second sitting. She tells me she has taken him for lunch but instructed him to leave his cap on. I try to continue where I left off as the tears start to run down his little face. Just before the screaming ab-dabs commence, old Bobby walks through the door for his haircut.

'Alright Steve, how are you doing?' he asks.

'I'm doing well but Thomas is having a bad time,' I tell him.

'What's a big lad like that crying for? He must be a bit soft,' Bobby says. Not one of Bobby's best lines, as Thomas's mum takes a dislike to the comment and also to Bobby.

'What do you mean he must be soft? He isn't soft. He's still a baby,' she retorts.

'Yon lad isn't a babby. He's a big lad.'

Now cutting Thomas's hair is one thing, but I'm not expecting a war of words between two adults.

'Bobby, sit down and read the paper,' I tell him. He sits down.

I notice mum is starting to cry. Strangely enough, Thomas has stopped crying and is sitting very still. Order had been restored. As I quickly finish Thomas's haircut, he shuts his eyes and instantly falls asleep. I haven't noticed his eyes shutting but soon realize what has happened as he slowly starts to fall forward. I stop him from falling off the chair and he wakes with a fright. Then he starts crying again. Eventually mum and son leave my salon. Neither Thomas's mum nor Bobby make eye contact with each other. Today they are both still customers of mine, but I suppose one day I may be called in again to referee the next round.

With my own strict rule of no alcohol during the day, I put the kettle on and try and analyse what has just happened. My thoughts are shattered as the phone rings.

'Good afternoon, Toptrend Hairdressing,' I answer.

'Hello, is that Toptrend Hairdressing?'

'Yes, that is me.'

'Is that the hairdresser's on the bus station?'

'Yes, that is me,' I say knowing this person has not got through to the final stages of *Mastermind*.

'How much will it be for my haircut?' he asks.

'It all depends on what needs doing and what you want me to do.'

'I don't really know what I want; I thought you could choose for me.'

'If you don't really know what you want, how can I tell you how much it will cost?' I say.

He then comes up with a line that tells me that he doesn't have all his cornflakes in one box. 'Well, what do you think will suit me?' he asks. This lad is on the other end of a phone and he asks me what hairstyle would suit him.

'Just call in to the salon when you're passing and I can give you an idea what can be done and how much it would cost,' I tell him.

'Thank you, good bye.'

The 'Fun House' continues to operate as Colin enters the salon. Now Colin says he gets his hair cut every five weeks and he swears blind that nobody but me cuts his hair, as he doesn't trust anybody else. He tells me the same yarn every visit but, as expected, when I check the hair it looks like scissors have attacked it when nobody was watching. He assures me he hasn't done it himself.

'It must grow like that,' he tells me.

'Colin, hair grows at an approximate rate of six inches a year. The average male has 150,000 hairs on his head, with each hair having a life expectancy of up to three years. During those three years, another hair pushes the old hair out to continue the hair life-cycle. If you times 150,000 hairs by six inches, the scalp is capable of growing about fourteen miles of hair a year. It is nature's way for a person to lose about a hundred hairs a day. I reckon in your case, certain parts of your hair must go on holiday for a few months at a time, as it seems strange that it was like this the last time you turned up for your haircut. It was cut to a uniform length when you left here and it's all uneven again,' I explain.

There are many people like Colin who will try to deceive you. It is easier than telling the truth and makes them feel they have hoodwinked the barber. Colin must have degrees for deception, as it didn't end there. When I finish his haircut and he tells me the usual tripe about how he'll see me in five weeks, he ups the stakes:

'Oh Steve, I forgot to go to the bank before I came in. I was in a rush. I don't suppose I could pay you with this, could I?' Colin produces a lottery ticket out of his wallet. 'There's a tenner on it. I won it on last Saturday's draw. You can keep the change.'

'Sorry, Colin. The last time I gambled I finished up with the wife. I don't take luncheon vouchers, savings stamps, credit cards, bus tickets or lottery tickets.'

'No problem. I'll just go and cash it and I'll be back in two minutes.'

Within minutes Colin arrives back and I get paid. I have no doubt it was a genuine ticket, but can you imagine taking twenty-odd lottery tickets to the bank?

There is a lull in the proceedings so I start to sweep the floor. The phone rings; it is Jean, my matrimonial supervisor, reminding me that I have to call at 'old Billy's' on the way home. Old Billy has been a customer of mine for many years and recently he rang to ask me to call round to his house to cut his hair, as he was off his legs. I've arranged to call tonight on my way home.

I notice a young lad of about twenty walking up and down outside the salon with a certain amount of hesitancy. After what appears to be a little persuasion from his girlfriend, he enters. He is wearing shorts and a football shirt, as it is a warm summer's day, together with a large scarf tied round his head like a bandana and a baseball cap on the top of his bandana.

'Yes sir, can I help you?' I ask.

'I really hope so. I've made a bit of a mess with my hair. I say *I* have; well, really it was both of us.' He points to his girlfriend. She looks quite sheepish as he starts to explain,

'We were bleaching my hair blond and it went wrong.'

'If you let me have a look I'll be able to see if we can improve the situation,' I say.

'It's a bit embarrassing. I can't ask you to close up but could you shut the blinds?' he asks.

'Sorry, not possible, but you can sit behind the screen if that helps,' I suggest, wondering what the hell I'm going to witness.

He is happy to sit out of sight from the passing flow of people and he slowly removes his headgear. As he reveals the results of their skills as hairdressers, one phrase springs to mind: *Coco the Clown*. I smile but keep my '*don't let them see I'm killing myself laughing inside*' professional hairdresser's head on, even though it is bloody funny. The hair has been bleached so much that there is more life in a cemetery. You could lose this lad in a field full of sunflowers, it is so yellow.

I comb through the hair and it starts breaking off. After a lengthy discussion it is agreed that I cut it short but leave it as long as possible. I cut it; he keeps his eyes shut for the duration of the haircut and his girlfriend cries all the way through. This nosey hairdresser is totally bewildered as to how they could have obtained such a result.

'This wasn't our first time. We'd done it before and most times it turned out OK. The last time it didn't take so good and it wasn't as light as I wanted it, so this time I wanted it a lot lighter. The instructions said that I could leave it on for a maximum of forty-five minutes. When she'd finished putting the stuff on my head, we sat down to watch the football with the proviso that at half-time we'd rinse the stuff off. We hadn't accounted for a player breaking his leg, and also there was a delay when the floodlights went off during the game. The stuff had been on my head for well over an hour when we realised.'

'Did you not feel it burning your scalp? Wasn't uncomfortable?' I ask.

'Didn't notice. Only noticed when she started to wash it off. There were handfuls of hair coming out.'

I can't really say whether there is a satisfactory ending to this tale, as his girlfriend walked out of my salon still crying and he maintained he must still wear his bandana under his baseball cap. It probably wasn't one of the best days of his life but it gave me material for another half page of my book.

By now it is that time of the day all workers look forward to - yes, even self-employed business owners who deal with the public. It is home time. I close the blinds and cash up, sweep and clean up, making sure everything is in place for start of play tomorrow. I switch the lights out, and I'm just locking the door when...

'Are they closed?' a man with a briefcase asks me. I am locking the door with my keys and he asks 'Are *they* closed?' Who the hell are they - more to the point, who the hell am I? The cleaner or the door locker?

'Yes, sir, I am. I will be open at 9am tomorrow,' I inform him.

'Don't suppose you could do another one. I need a haircut for Friday.' (It is Wednesday.) 'I have to attend my works gala dinner and I'm extremely busy, I won't have any more time to get it cut,' he tells me.

Everybody has their own choices to make in life, and a man that has to attend such an important occasion in *two days' time* and realises that he needs a haircut at 5pm falls into the unlucky category!

'Sorry, sir,' I tell him politely.

As promised, on my way home I make my way to old Billy's to cut his hair. He lives on the seventh floor in a tidy block of flats. I understand why he can't get about, as the lift isn't working, so I hike up the stairs to Billy's pad. I knock; no answer. I knock, and again no answer. After my fourth attempt, the elderly man from across the corridor opens his door and asks me who I'm looking for.

'I'm here to cut Billy's hair; I'm told he's off his legs. Can he get to the door to open it?' I ask.

'Aye lad. He con get tut dower all reet; in fact there's nowt wrong wi' his legs. Yer won't catch him in at this time on a Wednesday neet. He goes to his dancing class wi' his lady friend.'

'Thanks. Can you tell him Steve has been to cut his hair and ask him to call in to the shop for his P45?'

Needless to say, I don't see Billy again. He must have rung MUGS WANTED in the yellow pages!

I arrive home half an hour earlier than expected, so our evening meal isn't ready. Just as Jean and I sit down to eat, both our girls, Nicola and Emma, arrive with their husbands Colin and Steve, and grandchildren Victoria, Callum and Phoebe. Any time is a good time to see my family, whether it is a surprise visit or an organised family get-together. They are occasions in life that you don't really appreciate until you reach your maturing years.

A fitting end to another day in ~~paradise~~ business.

'So, while the lads are here, you might as well cut their hair,' my ever-thoughtful wife suggests.

I must need the practice!

So I said to the gym instructor, 'Can you teach me to do the splits?'
He said, 'How flexible are you?'
I said, 'I can't make Tuesdays.'

"God must love stupid people. He made so many!"

Chapter 25 - Stupid tales of excellence

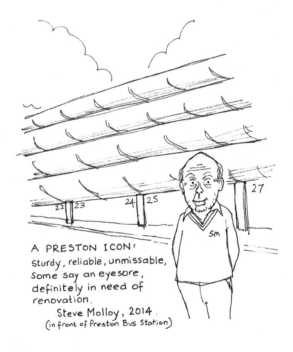

A PRESTON ICON:
Sturdy, reliable, unmissable,
Some say an eyesore,
definitely in need of
renovation.
      Steve Molloy, 2014.
   (in front of Preston Bus Station)

Styles come and go, and it is that principle that stops this job from stagnating. In 2013, it is trendy to be bald. The shorter the better, for all ages, in all walks of life; even the toupée wearer has had a bad case of alopecia overnight and lifted the lid.

With hair cut to about one inch long, the hairdresser can create a style to suit all parties; we can spike the hair, wave it, part it, slick it back or brush it forward. With hair going still shorter, most of the male population look like they've been conscripted into the armed forces or fallen out of prison. Very short hair is easy to look after and keep clean; it needs little attention and can be cut by anybody that owns a pair of clippers (or so people think, with some disastrous results).

It is mid-week and the kids are at school. It is warm for an early summer's day. In walks a very embarrassed lady with her son wearing his woolly hat.

'Excuse me, could you help me with his hair? Go on, Jimmy, tek yer hat off,' the lady says, instructing the lad of about twelve years to reveal all. 'He wanted his hair cut last night 'cause they towd him at school it needed cutting, but he only towd me at 11 o'clock. I'd had a few cans of beer by then and, well, I couldn't really see reet,' she says, laughing and making no apology.

The hair is a total disaster. 'How long was it before you started cutting?' I ask.

'About six inches long all over, probably a bit longer. I started cutting it wiv me kitchen scissors but I was meking a mess wi' them so I started wiv the clippers we have for our Bobby - he's our dog. I use 'em to cut round his bum when it gets a bit crusty. Well, as I was doing one side near his ear, the buggers went bang and they blew up.'

If I'd have given my granddaughter a pair of scissors, blindfolded her and let her loose on this lad's hair, she couldn't have done any worse. There are pieces of hair four inches long, there are stubbly patches a quarter-inch in length, and scissor lines all over. On the side where the clippers packed up, there is a large patch of stubble from his temple to behind his left ear. I don't know about a few cans

- there must have been a brewery working overtime to catch up.

Whilst his mother sits and laughs, the young lad is motionless; his face is drained of colour, and he is close to tears. My only option is to cut the hair as short all over as the shortest length. Fifteen minutes later, it is mission accomplished,

'That looks a bit better than my effort,' says the lady. 'How much do I owe you?'

'That's £8.50, please,' I say.

'How much? £8.50? I'm not paying that. I did most of the work myself.'

'It's because you did most of the work that it costs £8.50,' I explain.

'C'mon, Jimmy, we're not coming here again.'

The mother isn't happy, the lad is upset with his new, almost bald head, and I have had the pleasure of cutting the lad's hair after the dog's bum clippers blew up.

How good is my job?

Hair has been relatively short for some time now but it was probably in the early nineties that hairstyles went shorter and shorter. With the majority of the male population walking round with a haircut that resembled either a tennis or a billiard ball, the identity crisis began. Solving crime became a nightmare: 'And what did the burglar look like?'

'He had a bald head, your honour'! Well that narrows it down a bit, doesn't it?

The short hair revolution didn't just roll into people's lives; it overhauled their lives. It was trendy to see your ears; you were with it to be without it; bald was beautiful, toupée salesmen were redundant; alopecia sufferers could walk anywhere without people staring, and, as in the fifties and sixties men, were conscious of their hair (or head), and how it looked. Many men from two to seventy-two had little or no hair.

It wasn't long before a change had to start. The change started with Afro-Caribbean culture, drawing patterns and design work on younger heads. It gave personality and it gave individuality. Tram lines, borders, stars and stripes, any design was distinctive; it gave the person a new image. It said, 'Look at me, I've been personalized.'

The fashion soon took off and soon we were personalizing our own customers, mainly youngsters, a few in their twenties. But when grandad wanted a tramline to match his son and his two grandchildren, we knew we were a major cast member in this passing circus and we had to work quickly before the men in white coats called to collect the old man.

To cut hair to about one-eighth of an inch, or three millimetres, and then draw an image on the scalp is no mean feat. You have one go at it, and you have no eraser to correct any slip-ups. It is time-consuming, and it can be intricate and tricky, but - boy - did we have fun with those designs.

Schoolchildren were the usual candidates because they would have a small emblem or a trade mark like a 'NIKE' tick cut into the back of their head at the start of the school holidays. Then it would grow out by the time they returned to school … in theory.

Billy was sent home from school, not to return until 'the inconceivable mess on Billy's head has disappeared' was what the note (from Billy's school) said. I read it when his mum brought him back to have his head shaved. The problem was that when I had cut the small tick design in the back of Billy's head it measured about one and a half inches in circumference. His mum's effort a week later was supposed to follow my line, only her mess measured three inches by four inches and looked nothing like the original. She told me she had used the razor that she shaved her legs with, and when it didn't look right, she kept making it bigger.

I had one lad who rang up to ask if I could inscribe a football team's name on his head. I said I could, providing it wasn't Stenhousemuir… He wanted West Ham United. After a lengthy discussion I persuaded him to settle for the team's emblem, which consisted of two crossed hammers. It worked; it took me ages, and the lad was overjoyed. *I do the job; I don't have to like it*!

There were all sorts of wacky designs. I would inscribe a lad's name into the back of his head, or even girls' names. PNE was a favourite, and a five-pointed star was always a difficult one, but I never did anything offensive.

Two things I always insisted on if the customer was of school age: I asked them if their parents approved, and then they had to draw or write the design on paper. That gave me the spelling of the design and I had them draw it in their own handwriting, in case mum or dad came back to complain about my artistic talents.

Words of three, four and five letters could look good. They were about big enough for the target area at the centre of the head. Anything with more letters, and the design would be too small and indistinct to stand out. The trick to scribing a name was to take the centre letter, if possible, and work outwards to help with the spacing… If only I had explained this trick to Gary.

A lad of about eighteen sits on Gary's chair and asks, 'Can yer put me one of them designs in t'back o'me 'ead, mate?'

'Yes, sure. What do you want me to write?'

'Can yer write me 'skunk'?'

Gary has his usual silly smirk on his face while he gets the lad to write down the design for his new hair style. He writes down SKUNK in big letters. Gary doesn't comment but gets to work, cutting all the hair short before he starts his artistic masterpiece.

He is at it ages and, by the expression on his face, I can tell the operation is not going to plan. The smile has gone and he is constantly asking the lad to keep his head still. Finally the clippers fall silent and the smile returns; Gary shows the lad the back in the mirror and he is pleased.

Gary says, 'You were bloody lucky there, you know, mate. With you moving your head all over the place you nearly finished up with SKULL. I nearly ran out of head.' Big heads for big words!

A lad in his early twenties calls in to ask if I can write something on the back of his head and how much would it cost. I assure the lad I can write small words and the cost depends on how long it takes to achieve the finished effect. He tells me he will return the following day. No show, but he comes back the next week and asks the same questions, only this time he tells me he wants JESUS written on the back of his head. He will definitely be in tomorrow. At this point in the proceedings, I realise I'm not dealing with a member of the Einstein family. It appears he likes to visit my salon, threatens to get his head personalized, and then loses his nerve. I ask him: if he does eventually decide to have Jesus written on his head, could he bring somebody with him for some support? He arrives the day after and, as asked, he has brought his mate/carer/uncle/dad, whichever he was. It was plain to see they were both a few fries short of a Happy Meal.

The lad sits down on my big chair, with his mate hovering close by. He tells me there could be a change of heart at the last minute.

'I don't know whether to have Jesus or God written. What do you think?' he asks me.

'It's your call, but once we start I can't change it,' I tell him.

After a lengthy debate with Uncle Fester, they decide on Jesus. I cut the lad's hair short then start on the lettering. I have just started on the round at the bottom of the centre S when he decides he wants God. He is positive it has to be God. I can salvage the original S to an O and we are going for it. I complete the O, which is about one and a half inches in diameter, when all of a sudden the lad shouts 'STOP!' He is shaking; he looks as if he is going to have a fit.

I stand back in shock and silence the clippers. 'What's the problem?' I ask.

The lad sits there in a daze, struggling for words, then eventually says, 'I've had a thought. If you write GOD on my head, when you show me the back with the mirror it will say 'DOG' and I don't want DOG on my head.'

It took me five minutes to explain and then write it on paper to show him in the mirror that it didn't look like DOG.

And it came to pass that two disciples left my salon, happy to continue on another pilgrimage and - unbeknown to themselves - to spread their own words of insanity.

It had been snowing all night and the city had been brought to a standstill. In Preston it is very rare to have a mountain of snow dumped on us but we must have thrown a double six that night. I had no chance of driving to work so I walked there and arrived twenty minutes late.

'I've been waiting ages for you. Where have you been? I'm bloody frozen,' a very disgruntled old lad tells me.

'You would have been colder if I hadn't come at all.'

'No, not really. I only live across road.' He lives about a hundred yards from the salon door and he's telling me off for being late.

Just then the phone rings. 'Hello, Toptrend Hairdressing,' I answer.

'Hello. Is that the bus station,' this old lady asks.

'Yes, it is. I work on the bus station.'

'Could you tell me when the Plungington bus is coming?' she asks.

'I'm sorry, but this is the hairdresser's on the bus station.'

'Well, do you know when the Plungington bus is coming?'

'Sorry, but with the heavy snow overnight, the buses are going to be late today.'

'Can you see any buses leaving the bus station?' the lady asks.

'Yes I can, although there aren't many moving because of the snow.'

'Is the one you can see a Plungington bus?'

'The inspector's office will be able to tell you when the bus will be with you.'

'Where's that?'

'Here on the bus station.'

'Can you go and ask when the Plungington bus is coming?'

'Sorry, but I have a hairdressing business to run.'

'Do you know the number of the inspector's office?'

'Sorry, I don't. But it will be in the phone book,' I tell her.

'OK.'

No thank you or anything. As she is putting down the phone, I hear her say to her husband, 'He was a f*****g waste of time.'

A lad comes home from school and excitedly tells his dad that he has a part in the school play and he is playing a man who has been married for twenty-five years.

The dad says, 'Never mind, son, maybe next year you'll get a speaking part.'

"It's true that money can't buy happiness, but is does buy nice places to be miserable in!"

Chapter 26 - Odds & sods

"There you go sir:
a fiver's worth"

This book has been a project of mine for many years. I had planned to publish it on the 9th September 2009 to mark my forty years associated with this job. I am, however, way behind, which is due to my inability to understand that there are only 168 hours in a week, and every day I open the door for business there is another tale to tell. This chapter is about the everyday tales that have pressed my chuckle button, and made me puzzle at the outcome of some strange situations.

This guy in his early forties had been working hard at making his new wife pregnant. It was a standing joke about him being tired and having to 'produce the goods' (his words, not mine). Conception was achieved and baby Jonathan was born. For Christmas he bought his son a Scalextric car racing set and a Hornby OO train set and track. Dad's reasoning behind these big boys' toys was that he had always wanted them as a kid and never got them. Now he could afford them he could justify buying them, as they were for his son… who was twenty-seven days old!

Monty (a regular customer) and his wife had been invited by their friends, Dave and Sue from Southampton, to celebrate the New Year with their friends, Bert and Dotty, who lived in France. They were Americans who had emigrated to Provence in France (are you following the plot so far?). The American people (Bert and Dotty) were holding a New Year's party and the story goes that the Englanders were told it would be fancy dress.

The four of them travelled to France and stayed in a hotel about ten miles away from the Americans' residence. On the 31st of December, they all went by taxi dressed up as the Four Musketeers, ready to meet new people and enjoy a fun-filled evening. The guy that opened the door was dressed in a white tuxedo; Monty commented on how much he resembled James Bond… wrong! The evening was a celebration for the local mayor of the town and the instruction for the invited guests was DRESS FANCY, an American term for 'dress posh'. Imagine being in a foreign country, not speaking the language, everybody dressed up for a formal occasion, and you and three other English 'turkeys' are dressed like clowns, waiting not just for midnight but for the taxi to return at 3am. Monty assured me they really enjoyed the bizarre experience, although he didn't expect to be invited back the following year.

This next tale was not only traumatic for the lad in question but it could serve as a lesson to all those who don't know... I didn't know, and probably you don't either.

Warren was a car-salesman with his own little business selling older used cars. This particular day he was attending to a lad who had just bought a car. He was finishing the paperwork, when a young couple arrived and asked if they could take one of the cars on his forecourt for a test drive. He asked the couple to leave their car and car keys for their own newer car, and he let them take his car for a short drive to see if the girlfriend could handle it.

Less then twenty minutes later, the couple arrived back with the news that it wasn't what they wanted; the girlfriend didn't like the colour!

Ten days later, a summons arrived in the post stating that this car was clocked by a speed camera. Was Warren the driver? Warren was horrified, as he had nine penalty points on his licence and couldn't afford another three. He had no recollection of the couple who had given him this despicable present. The outcome was that Warren lost his licence and his business.

A car salesman with no licence is comparable to a blind optician. Every time Warren called for his haircut, he would tell me how many days and months were left before he could claim back his beloved driving licence.

The sting was waiting in the tail! When he applied for new

insurance, the quotes were through the roof... he had allowed somebody to drive his car whom he not only did not know personally but didn't even know their name.

That was a public service information notice sponsored by TOPTREND HAIRDRESSING!

Over the years, I have met many people with terrifying jobs: lads that work up electricity pylons to maintain and restore power to our homes, with 275,000 volts passing inches above their heads; a lad that worked welding on the seabed and lived in a pressurised submarine for weeks at a time; a test pilot that worked for the aircraft industry. The ultimate must be Dave - a bomb disposal technician in the army.

Dave calls in for his haircut and tells me he has just returned from active service abroad; he tells me he has two weeks off to enjoy life at home with his family, then it's back to the front line. He tells me that lads walk in front of him with probes to find sunken bombs and, when they find a bomb, it is his job to disarm it. He is dressed with all the appropriate gear and he wears a large 'nappy' to protect his best bits. As he tells me his daily routine, I find myself sweating with anxiety and realise the dedication these lads have for Queen and Country. He couldn't wait to get back to work!

Now, on the subject of danger and facing pain, I speak from firsthand knowledge. I know a little about suffering, as Hairdresser's Nipple can cause excruciating pain. There has even been a report in the *British Medical Journal* about this sensitive condition. Short, stubbly, prickly hairs fly all over the place and have a nasty habit of penetrating clothing.

I remember being in Manchester Airport, waiting to fly away on holiday, when I felt a severe pain under one of my toes. We found a quiet seating area, Jean bought some tweezers and a magnifying glass at the chemist's, and fished and prodded until I was able to walk without pain. The pain is like a needle being pushed into the skin. It will irritate for days before it goes septic, and eventually abscesses can occur. Get one in the nipple and - we are talking pain. Blond hairs are the sharpest and hardest to find.

It's about 10.30am. The early-bird customers have flown and we have just had the morning brew. That scratch I felt earlier has now turned into a painful thorny nipple. I go into the back of the shop, pull up my jumper and shirt to investigate with a magnifying glass; it's as much use as an ashtray on a motorbike because I can't get my head low enough to see through the glass to find the hair.

'I'll have a look and see if I can find it,' Gary says.

Dilemma of the day: do I let Gung-Ho Gary near my nipple with a pair of tweezers?

'I think I can see it,' he tells me.

'Owwwwwww,' I screech.

'No, that wasn't it,' he tells me. He prods and pokes about, looking for this miniscule hair that is giving me agony. He is about an inch away from my nipple, looking through a magnifying glass when …
a customer walks in.

'Won't be long, sir. I'm just looking at Steve's nipple for a hair,' Gary tells a familiar face. Just glad it was a regular customer and glad he didn't try to suck it out!

'I'm getting married in October to Laura and me and t'lads are 'aving a bloody good piss-up fo' me stag do, Steve,' Ken tells me. 'There's loads of us going t'Benidorm in September, der yer fancy comin' wiv us, Steve?'

Now what he would drink on the bus to the airport would see

me on planet Zog for a month. When it comes to drinking, I am D-minus, I am bantam-weight and I'm out of my depth in a car-park puddle. I make my apologies for my absence from the Benidorm Police Cell Inspection Outing due to my liver. I want to keep it!

'Laura hasn't to know. It's a secret. All the lads are keeping shtumm. If yer see Laura, promise not to tell her about me stag do. She'll kill me if she finds out.'

I promise.

Over the next couple of months he explains the lengths he is going to hide all evidence of the excursion. When he goes to visit his mother, he takes a shirt or a pair of pants with him so he can pack his case there.

'So when will she know you're going to Benidorm?' I ask.

'I'm going to ring her from t'airport just before we board the plane. It'll be too late to stop me going then,' he tells me. He adds that he will be in for his haircut on Thursday, as they are going Friday teatime.

No sign of him Thursday or even Friday, but he arrives for his haircut the following Tuesday. 'You shouldn't be here today. I expected you last Thursday. What happened?' I ask.

'She found out and she stopped me going. She found me passport in me pocket and found me ticket inside. She went mental; she threatened to call the wedding off if I went.'

'So what did you do?' I ask.

'I went down to the pub on Friday teatime and waved the lads off. They all went on my stag do without me! They came back yesterday and they all said they'd had a brilliant time. She had me decorating at home all weekend.' I used to play this game as a kid; we called it Call My Bluff.

~

The public throws up some extraordinary situations that you couldn't make up. The next three tales rank high on my 'Thank You God for Making Steve Molloy a Hairdresser' list. All are told as they happened on the day, and I can recall them as if they happened yesterday. I assure you the last tale will take some beating.

It is Saturday afternoon and my salon is as it should be - fairly busy, radio on in the background, a regular customer moaning about the class of newspapers and dated magazines provided (all in good fun), a little lad giving his dad some earache about wanting to open the box containing his model plane Airfix kit, his dad telling him there were too many bits and he would lose some and ... he did open the box and... he did lose some of the bits. But apart from that, the day was ticking along nicely.

The door opened and in walked a newbie, a young lad of about twenty-three. I assumed I hadn't cut his hair before. He stood at the door until everybody moved along the waiting chairs, and then sat down. It must have taken about forty-five minutes from the lad walking in to me shouting 'next please'.

'Yes sir, would you like to sit yourself down in my large chair?' I ask politely, wanting to make the lad feel welcome.

'No, I don't want a haircut. I just want to buy a comb,' he tells me.

'You've waited all that time to buy a comb?' I ask. 'There you are, sir. You can have that for being patient.' I give him the comb for free.

'Thank you so much' he says and leaves the salon.

The following Saturday the lad reappears. 'You haven't lost your comb,' I ask, as I recognise the 'longest comb waiter in history' from the previous week.

'No, I want a haircut this week,' he tells me.

The lad climbs into my chair and I make a start on his haircut.

'Have you more time on your hands this week? You seemed in a hurry last week.'

'No, I have to admit I was sounding you out,' he tells me. 'From a very early age I've travelled all over this country and abroad with my family. My dad was in the army and we were on the move many times over the years. The downside to moving is meeting and losing good friends, and dodgy haircuts. New town, new hairdresser - or butcher, as the case may be. As I grew up and it wasn't necessary for my mother to tag along to the hairdresser's, I had to find my own. I devised a trick to see if the haircuts were any good. I would walk into a hairdresser's or barber's, sit down and watch what was being turned out. If they were awful haircuts, I would buy a comb and leave. It was better than getting my hair cocked up and then having to wait two months to find another hairdresser.'

'So I passed the test last week, did I?' I ask.

'You'll know if you see me in six weeks' time,' he tells me with a smile.

I have done Jeremy's hair for well over five years now. He has moved several times but makes a visit to Preston when he is in the area. *Was it the haircut or the free comb?*

This particular Wednesday was like any other Wednesday, or so I thought: people ambling past my salon doing their own thing in their own little world, a fraction of the male community wanting to offload some of their hair onto my floor and pay me for the privilege. We'd been fairly busy in the morning but as usual the two o'clock slump had arrived. I remember I was reading the paper when, all of a sudden, the door swung open and then shut. I glanced up to see what was happening, when the door opened again. Standing in the doorway was a huge man - so huge that at his first attempt he managed to push the door but didn't get through. He wasn't huge tall but huge sideways, with a large everything!

I welcomed the man and helped him off with his coat, as he said he was hot. He was hot - and sweaty. I turned the chair round so that it was easier for him to position his large posterior. The gown I usually used was too small, so I found the larger one and we were up and running. He told me that he had always had this size problem but as he got older he found it harder to get the weight off because, he told me, he had an overactive knife and fork (his words not mine). He explained that carrying that amount of weight had its problems - and it wasn't long before it wasn't just his problem.

One good haircut later and he tried to get out of the chair... he was stuck. This all-singing, all-dancing Belmont Chair that weighs in the region of 62.5 kg was welded to him; he was wedged in in no uncertain manner. He tried to stand up and the chair went with him. Question was, how could I help? What do I pull? Did I put my hands under his bum and try and lift? He was more than twenty stone, probably nearer twenty-five. He tried to struggle free but to no avail, then started to sweat even more - and he was getting agitated.

I talked quietly to calm the situation, asked him to stop panicking and just rest for a while, mainly to give me some thinking time. I have massive glass windows and at this point nobody called in to see if they could help; to my knowledge nobody even noticed. We had a five-minute rest and then tried again, but no bum was going to shuffle that day. My options were the security people on the bus station or the fire brigade.

'All right, Steve, how are you doing?' Dave, a regular of my salon and a regular at the local gym, called in for his haircut.

'I've been looking for you,' I said, somewhat relieved. 'Give me a hand with this man.'

The man lifted himself up a fraction, just enough for us to push the children's board under his bum, and after the count of three we all heaved. It was like a cork out of a bottle, only there wasn't a pop - just elation. To be fair, the man took it in his stride with little embarrassment. He thanked me and my co-ejector, paid and left the building. I haven't seen him again to this day. That particular ordinary Wednesday turned out to be a memorable Wednesday.

I suppose this is the one for me that says 'Steve Molloy, you have made it, you have served the public well for more than forty years and you think you have seen and heard it all; well, Steve, this one is for you.'

If I picked this book up in the dentist's waiting room, flicked through the pages and stumbled on this tale, I wouldn't believe it. Was the writer/hairdresser on magic mushrooms or drunk? Not so!

It is a week before Christmas, about 4.45pm. I have had a busy day and I am ready to leave this glorious bus station for a cup of tea and a date with Coronation Street. I am just finishing my last customer when the door opens.

'Excuse me, would it be possible for you to cut my hair now?' says this young man of about twenty-one years.

'I'm just about to close, sir but, if you're desperate, I can do it now. You're my last one today,' I tell him.

'How much will it be, please?'

'For your haircut it will be £8.50, sir,' I tell him. The lad is standing in the doorway with the door wide open.

'I've just been at the staff Christmas party and I don't know if I've got that much on me.' To be fair, you could tell he'd had a drink but he wasn't drunk. He had a count-up, trawling through all his pockets. 'No, sorry, mate. I've only got £5.'

'OK, then. You leave it till tomorrow until you've got enough. See yer,' I tell him.

He closes the door, goes outside and rifles through his pants pockets once again. Then he's back.

'Excuse me, mate. I can't find any more money. I must have spent more than I thought. What can you do for a fiver?'

'You can hang your coat up for a fiver,' I say, with a stupid grin.

'No, be *serious*. What can you do *for a fiver? Can you start and stop when me fiver's up?*'

'Just shut the door behind you. You're letting the cold air in.'

The lad turns round and leaves the salon. I remember asking my customer on my chair if that really happened. He confirmed what I thought had happened, left - and the Christmas Party Pumpkin arrived back for another inquisition on what he could get for a fiver.

'Would it be possible if you cut the top for a fiver and leave the back and sides, or do the back and sides and leave the top, whichever is cheaper?'

'Just shut the door behind you,' I said in my ever-so-pleasant-but-knackered-from-the-neck-down tone of voice.

'Does that mean no?' he asked. He turned and left the building, looking for another hairdresser to relieve him of his last fiver.

SUCCESS:
At age four success is .... not piddling in your pants.
At age twelve success is .... having friends.
At age seventeen success is .... having a driver's licence.
At age thirty-five success is .... having money.
At age fifty success is .... having money.
At age seventy success is .... having a driver's licence.
At age seventy-five success is .... having friends.
At age eighty success is .... not piddling in your pants.

"If at first you don't succeed, skydiving is not for you!"

Chapter 27 - Closing time

This is the one I have been looking for, the final chapter.

It must be nearly 5pm, closing time. Pull down the shutters and cash up the till; it is home time. Make sure the sink is shining and the floor is hairless, the magazines are tidy and the cups are washed. It all has to be ready for the next day's customers. I am in charge of the inside of this building and if it isn't right, it is down to me. The outside is out of my control; it is a bus station, when all is said and done.

Toptrend Hairdressing has been part of this bus station for more than thirty-six years. When we arrived, it was a gamble to run a hairdresser's here. Would it work? It worked. Over the years I've been asked many times if I would have liked a salon in the city centre, or in the leafy lanes on the outskirts of the city, or a chic salon in a department store, or a larger salon with a lot of staff. I am a big believer in the time-served saying, 'If it works then don't fix it.' I never look back and wish I'd have done this or bought that. I did what I have done for the right reasons at the time. This controversial bus station is not the most illustrious or distinguished building in the area but it does a job and serves the people well; it did work, it still works - don't destroy it, nurture it. The bus station has many a tale to tell; this book is full of them, and here are a few more before

I switch the lights out.

Like it or loathe it, the building is iconic. Its design is unique and one of the unfortunate statistics that relate to it is that it's probably the most popular building in the area for suicides. Many years ago, there were numerous people who wanted to spend their last moments hanging over the edge of the parapet above my salon. One particular Friday, we had a full salon mid-afternoon when the blue-light brigade stormed the bus station. There were sirens from fire engines and ambulances, and total commotion ensued. Word got out that there was somebody hanging over the side of the top deck of the bus station and one by one the salon slowly emptied until there was nobody left. Gary was itching to have a nosy and was just about to go and have a look when a bloke walked in and told him it was not worth going to see; the man had jumped and they had covered him up.

For weeks after a suicide we got the usual comments: 'Was that one of your customers that jumped? He saw what a mess you'd made of his hair and he wouldn't dare go home looking like that!'

Saturday afternoon, mid-summer, and it was very warm, verging on humidly hot. The bus station was fairly quiet because people were enjoying the sunshine outside, and the salon door was wedged open.

We had enjoyed a busy morning and now we were quiet. Gary and I were glad of the respite and found it pleasant to sit outside the salon and people-watch. A young man of about twenty-three was waiting for his bus and leaning on the window of my salon, minding his own business, listening to his iPod.

A bus had just arrived that he assumed was his, so he started to walk towards it. He found it wasn't his bus, so he back-tracked to his leaning position against the window. Within minutes another bus arrived; the lad took two strides forward, only to find again that it wasn't his bus. Without turning, he stepped back two paces and leaned back on what he thought was the window - only he had miscalculated and fell arse-first through the open door and sat on the salon floor with a thud.

The lad's face was a picture. He shot up, red-faced and upset, with his own dignity dented, only to be faced with two hairdressers trying their upmost to stifle the giggling so as not to make him too upset. Didn't work ... he was bloody livid!

Dislikes

Throughout this book I have tried to show you how much I enjoy my work dealing with the public, from youngsters with their innocence, purity and simplicity, a world of answers waiting for them to find the questions, right through to the elderly who have seen changes through the years, with endless stories to tell about their own experiences. I have to say, I chose the right career.

That said, although there aren't that many moans, like all jobs it isn't always perfect. Life doesn't work like that but you have to make it the best you can. Many of my dislikes will be true of any job in which one has to deal with the public at close quarters: body odour, bad breath and rude-mannered people. The one that all hairdressers will agree on is when you cut somebody's fringe and you are working at close quarters to their face, and the client will almost certainly blow the hair into your face. You can understand children doing that, but come on, people - what if hairdressers blew it back into *your* face?

There is another awkward situation to which I have never found a suitable response. (I know the answer. It's just that I have never had the balls to administer the appropriate command: 'Speak when you're spoken to!').

I am working on this regular customer and we are having our usual conversation about football when in walks Jim.

'Morning, Steve. It's bloody cold out there.'

Morning, Jim. Yes, it is,' I say. I continue talking to my customer.

'Says it could get colder tonight,' Jim says.

'Yes,' I say, whilst keeping up my football conversation.

'Have you been busy, Steve?' Jim asks.

I am now in the middle of a three-way conversation about football and how busy my business has been. I think, 'If I don't answer Jim, he might shut up,' but he doesn't.

'Is it quiet at the moment?' Jim asks.

I don't answer but keep on discussing football.

Jim asks, 'Do you like football, Steve?'

'Jim, there's some newspapers there,' I say, trying to shut him up.

The door opens and: 'Morning Steve, it's freezing out there. Are you're busy?' Dave asks.

I don't answer.

Contrary to all that has been said about men only being able to do one thing at a time, I have mastered the art of cutting hair and talking, but three- and four-way conversations are prohibited. When a person puts his bum in my big red chair, he is my main priority. That's the way it is… it's the way I was taught.

Regrets

As I said earlier, I am not one for looking back and wishing things were different; I'm happy with the way my life and career have turned out. But, like everybody who has breathed the air on this earth, I have sat and thought, 'What if? If only… I could have if I'd… Why didn't I?' I don't say I'm disappointed but there are things about which I wonder, 'What would have been the outcome if...?'

I was trained by two people who had wonderful pedigrees when it came to hairdressing competitions. Both my bosses won competitions in this country and abroad, and I still wonder today why I didn't enter any. To satisfy a panel of judges instead of the public, and to compete against your fellow workers in your trade, must be quite a buzz; but unfortunately my buzz was concentrating on my business in the buzz station.

Just after I got married, I started to referee local soccer matches on a Sunday morning. It was a case of my wife giving me earache to help her clean up the house or go and referee a footie match. These days, I would rather listen to my wife give me earache than have twenty-two players abuse me. In my first couple of seasons I was appointed to many cup finals and awarded a handful of trophies. On a few occasions I was told I could make the grade in higher leagues provided I refereed every Saturday. A hairdresser playing sport on a Saturday? Unthinkable! Saturday is the 'bread and butter day'; if you break your leg on Friday night you limp into work on Saturday. You can rest your leg for twenty minutes at lunch time. I trained to be a hairdresser and from day one I knew what was expected of me. It has served me well, but would I have given that penalty at Old Trafford for Man Utd to beat Chelsea? I will never know.

This next story I tell in strictest confidence; keep it to yourself as I have done for well over twenty years. Only two people know about this situation and if you ever meet my wife, don't tell her; even she isn't privy to it. You will soon see why!

It was just after 5pm and the 'Le-Mans' start to get out of the salon was in full swing. Gaz was always first out, closely followed by Guy.

As I was getting ready to leave, I spotted a young lady outside the salon with two small children; the same lady that had been in hours earlier for her children's haircuts. The two lads and their dad were regular customers and I had known the family for quite some time. She waved to me, so I went to the door to see if there was a problem. She asked to speak to me and walked into the salon, leaving the two children outside by the door. My first thought was that the haircuts weren't right ... not so. She asked me if I could help with a delicate situation!

She explained that it was her husband's birthday the following week and, as a surprise, she had an idea, and would I help? My mind was racing. I was thinking, draw a design on his head? Draw a design on her head? Go round to their house and shave all his hair off? Surprise him at the pub in front of his mates by cutting all his hair off? What else could I do to be of assistance?

She appeared quite nervous and embarrassed as she asked me if I could cut and shave a heart into her pubic hair!!!

Time stood still. Why was I sweating? Why was water dripping off my nose and my legs wobbling? I stuttered over my words and I think I had a silly smile on my face, or was that fear? Why me? She told me that she didn't know anybody that could do it. She had known me for years as a nice man, her husband knew me; she didn't want to ring up because she knew I wouldn't have taken it seriously (*too bloody right I wouldn't*). She had planned it all out and she could call at the salon at night or I could go to her house when the coast was clear, or she could call at my house, or she could use her mate's house, whichever suited me... She would call back in two days to give me some time to think about whether I would do it.

I didn't tell anybody about her proposition. If I told the lads at work, do you think I would have been doing it on my own? If I told the wife, do you think I would have been fit enough to stand and walk, let alone use a razor? I thought about it for two days and two sleepless nights. If I did it … her husband was a big bloke. When I told Jean, would I be castigated or castrated? If I didn't do it, would I think 'if only' for years to come? And which lucky bastard would get the job that I turned down?

She called in after work two days later. I made sure the lads had gone home early and I had visited the toilet once again, the very same toilet that had been a great part of my life for the last two days. As she walked into the salon, I felt sick. It felt like I was taking part in a very sordid affair. She looked embarrassed and we both started to talk at the same time. We stopped talking, and then I let her speak. Nervously, she told me her husband had thought of the same idea as she had, and she was sorry for wasting my time but he had already done it for her. The nerves, the anxiety, the relief were obvious on both our faces and we started to laugh. I lost three customers, as I never saw the family again but … I saved on toilet rolls!

A genuine tale… Would I have? Don't ask 'cause I won't tell you the answer!

Disappointments

By dealing with the public, you soon learn their mannerisms. How people sit and wait: they fidget, they daydream, they want to talk to anybody that will listen, and they clean their nails or try peeling a long nail down to size. There are people who love to admire themselves in the mirror and people who won't look at their own face in the mirror. One customer needs to hold a towel whilst having his haircut, one tells the same joke every haircut, and many have to constantly yarn throughout their haircut. I am sure I could recognise 70% of my regular customers by voice alone.

That said, when you don't see certain customers you miss them after a while; you have formed a bond that is sometimes better than a friendship. You might not miss them for weeks, even months, then something triggers the memory - probably a little like a distant relative passing away. It is sad to hear of customers that have left our planet but I don't get upset - and I don't lose sleep over a regular customer going to another hairdresser; that is life. I am the hub of this big wheel where all my customers require my services when necessary. If for whatever reason they decide to go to another hairdresser, I find it disappointing that the same once-regular customer won't recognise me when walking down the street. He will walk on the other side of the street rather than acknowledge me. To my knowledge I haven't murdered anyone, appeared on *Crimewatch* or had a criminal record, but on a few occasions it felt as if I had.

I can say I have no criminal record, as I have been checked. Probably one of the most disappointing chapters in my career came not many years ago, just after my date with the saw on my chest. I had recovered well and was back at work, doing what I do best, but I needed a challenge, a new direction. My life revolved around my family, closely followed by my business and its customers. I wasn't in a position to let that drift but I wanted to be of service, to contribute something with my many years of experience in dealing with the public.

My family were happy to give me any support I needed, although Jean was a little apprehensive so soon after a heart by-pass. I researched ideas, and becoming a Samaritan was high on the list, when a regular customer asked me if I would consider being a magistrate. He had been a magistrate for years and was soon to retire. 'A clean-living person with no criminal record, a football referee for more than thirty years and someone who's dealt with the public for more than forty years is the model person for the job.'(*His words not mine.*)

I researched all there was to know about becoming a magistrate. I attended court as an observer on many occasions and, after much thought, I applied. A magistrate has to meet six criteria: being of good character; understanding and communication; social awareness; maturity and sound temperament; sound judgement; and commitment and reliability. I thought I fitted those criteria.

I attended two interviews only to receive a letter telling me I had ticked five of the boxes but I had not been successful on SOCIAL AWARENESS. Forty years of dealing with the public and I wasn't aware of today's society. I would rather have been sent a letter stating, 'Sorry, not suitable due to contracting Mad Cow Disease.'

(*Due to the nature of the judiciary I feel this book is not the right place to air my views regarding my dealings connected with this matter. If you are interested or would like my completed story, please ask!*)

The whole chapter left me numb; not because I had been knocked back, as I am a big lad with long pants and I can accept rejection. It was the manner and the way the situation was dealt with. I lost respect for a judicial system I thought was fair. Life isn't fair... so, get used to it!

～

My future

This book is scheduled be published just after I have celebrated a birthday containing a zero. Hopefully there will be plenty of life left in the hands to work a pair of scissors, and my legs will be able to walk around my ever-faithful chair, although a pair of windows (glasses) may need to be installed in the not too distant future. Probably because of my operation, and due to the uncertainty about the fate of the bus station, 'When will you be retiring?' has become a regular question. Retire?

I looked up the word *retire* in my dictionary and it mentioned such words as *leave and part company*, which are all alien to me, although the word above was *retard*, which is probably more apt to yours truly.

Providing my health is good, then I won't stop doing what I enjoy. My bizarre plan will probably kick in when eight hours on my feet feels like an eternity. When I get to a certain age, I propose to work four days and listen to what my sweet little wife instructs me to do on the other three days. After a time, I will hopefully restrict my working hours to three days; I intend to operate an appointment system. I will be cutting the hair of the people I want to attend to. No rude people, no smelly people, no drunks, no arrogant and offensive people. I will be able to spend time with whoever I want: the genuine people; the nice people who have been part of my life for many years; the pleasant, likable people; the lads that laugh at my jokes. I will be able to spend my working day chatting to people who are special to me. *Good plan if it works.*

A few years ago a client I had looked after for well over thirty years died. Similar age and outlook to myself - we were good companions with comparable interests in sport. He had spent time at my home and knew all my family. I received a call from his wife to tell me that he had died and would I attend the funeral, and could I meet with her at her home?

I called to meet his wife, whom I had never met, and was asked if I would read a eulogy at the funeral, as the family would be too upset to contemplate such a task. I agreed, and the following Friday Jean and I sat amongst the congregation to honour a good mate.

At the appropriate nod from the priest, I walked forward to address a sea of sad faces. His wife had written the speech and I was asked to add the amusing one-liners. The proceedings lasted about six minutes and, as I left the lectern, I received a standing ovation. I tell this story because she had asked me, his barber to read a eulogy. Outside my family life, I think it was probably one of the most poignant and proud moments in a lifetime associated with my job.

Which gets me to thinking, if I can stand up at a funeral and be part of a situation that helps others, as well as make people smile in our everyday lives, then once this book is in print I may spread the gospel of hairdressing stupidity at local venues to whoever would want to listen; the tales that weren't suitable for this book, the tales that finished on the cutting room floor due to space and my desire to keep my salon windows intact.

That's it, it must be five o'clock somewhere, and it is closing time. I had better switch the lights off and lock the door before I get the 'FAQ': 'Can you do another one, or can you do one more pleeeeeeeeeeeeeeeeeease!'

The best one I had was, 'Can you do me, please. I have to go to a funeral.' When I asked if the funeral was the following morning he told me he didn't know exactly when it was, as his uncle hadn't died yet, *but it wouldn't be long!*

I said that about finishing this book... well it is now!

Little Michael finds a sandwich with two wires sticking out of it. He phones the police and says 'I've just found a sandwich dat looks like a bomb.'
The operator asks, 'Is it tickin?'
Little Michael says, 'No I fink it's beef.'

Epilogue

I intend to live forever; so far so good!

No doubt you will have noticed that there are no stories about politics and few about religion. This is because the first instruction I received in this profession was: 'Never talk politics or religion.' It was quite a challenge when a general election arrived, but my usual tactic of agreeing with the customer was the way I found to keep my clientele.

Now religion can be another cowboy!

I am not a religious person although occasionally I attend church. I don't hold any racist views, and enjoy listening to other people's views about their own religion. Jean and I have been invited to an Indian wedding; I own a copy of the Koran, given to me by a customer, and admire the lengths people go to follow their beliefs. Years ago, I was asked if I could cut a young Asian baby's hair. I agreed, not realising the baby was five days old with a mop of black hair. The father wanted me to cut it all off so he could send the hair back to his parents in India. Mum held baby, dad held baby's head, uncle was catching every strand of hair and I was the one at the back with the clippers, frightened of hurting baby.

I'm not big on confrontations and controversy and, in these final few pages, I'm not going to start now. The few downs and many ups in my lifetime, and the many good and bad, happy and sad tales I have been party to, have made me see life from different angles. If all those years ago I'd decided to be a joiner when leaving school, then wood would have been my world. I chose hairdressing, and people have been my life. Writing this book has made me think outside of the box. With that said, I am turning the lights out on this book with my own take on life.

The game of life
We are all given a route, a path, a journey, which in my instruction manual is called a destiny. This is given to all players at the start of the game. Nobody knows how long their destiny is. You can endeavour to make it longer and you can cheat and go to bed early, but no player knows when their game will finish.

The winner
Sorry, there are no winners! To be picked to play is a privilege, so try to enjoy the good bits, tolerate the ordinary bits and endure the bad bits.

The aim of the game
The rules are really simple: you roll the dice of life when it is your turn and try to keep within the lines of your destiny. One other thing, and this is where it becomes a bit tricky: you're not on your own. You have a helper or helpers; the tricky bit is, you can't see them and you can't hear them speak to you. Well, I say it's a helper. It's usually some person or persons that may have been related to you, who has played the game of life and finished their destiny. The big thing is, they have a dice as well, relating to family history,

and occasionally they may pop up and change the course of your destiny. Usually they try to keep you within your destiny BUT they have no control of their dice. Whoopsies do occur from time to time and you have to deal with them.

In the game of life you will be given options on every throw of the dice. The more effort and concentration you apply to the game, the more you will enjoy it.

You can only move forward, you cannot travel back. If you cock-up, you can try and remedy the cock-up by throwing a six.

Caution: if you get bored and want to go to bed without finishing the game, there are penalties. Most important: if you stop someone else finishing their game, there are severe penalties.

The circle of life
When your destiny comes to an end, then this is the amazing twist: you become a helper and are given a dice to throw for somebody else. When their destiny is ended and you have helped them along their way, it is your turn again and you start the game of life once more, but this time you are someone completely different. The adjudicator of the game of life is the big boss man; he invented the game and he owns the rights to decide who plays, where you start your game, what colour, what gender you are. He tracks your previous game on his big computer and sends you somewhere on the planet to start again as a different person in different circumstances. There are more than six billion people on our globe so the odds of you bumping into anybody you know are slim; although sometimes when you think 'I've been here before' or somebody looks familiar… you never know!

Nobody knows how the adjudicator's computer works, but one would hope that the people who were bad last time around will make a better attempt in their next incarnation. Most importantly, whilst we are playing our game of life we don't know how long our game is going to last. We don't know where we will be next time round, but if we do good now, then hopefully the adjudicator's computer may look favourably on us.

In reality we probably live, procreate, snuff it and give somebody else a chance. Many people tell us how good it will be 'on the other side', but there aren't many people rushing to get there. This is my take on life. Don't knock it, as nobody has come back to tell us how good it really is 'on the other side'.

This book has been part of me for more than nine years. I started it for two reasons. When you deal with the public, you are told so many tales, you learn so much about people and not to document my life experiences would have been such a waste. Secondly, many thought I couldn't write a book or wouldn't finish it. I had my doubts at times, but continued to fight this bloody keyboard till I arrived at my last chapter. I have thoroughly enjoyed the experience, as no fabrication was needed; the public were the cast in the daily pantomime of life.

I planned the structure of the book based on various stages of my life, and then I fitted all the tales around my own. Once the chapters were in some sort of order I just wrote the tales in no real sequence; as a new tale came to light, I would write it up and drop it into the appropriate chapter. The final chapter was started on the 22 April 2012 so that I could complete this book and it was as up to date as possible.

I thank all the people who have encouraged me to write it and I thank the people that kept asking for the book. That really gave me the inspiration to complete it. I humbly apologise for its late arrival.

I only told people I was writing the book after I had been writing for over five years. When people knew about it that was my incentive to complete it. I wrote about the early years a long time ago. It's quite amazing to sit down and focus on one's youth and it's surprising how much you start to remember. In our younger years, we just took life in our stride; we took it for granted.

Thank you for reading *Tales From Behind the Chair*. I hope it gave you an insight to my (*he only cuts hair*) job. Dealing with the public all my working life was definitely worth my while. I hope reading this book was worth your while.

My next venture into the literary world is hopefully to produce a book of coincidences, and you the public can help me. Everybody at some time of life is faced with coincidences: your aunty marries a grocer from Melbourne, Australia, and his next-door neighbour Down Under is my landlord's father! The lady who married us at the registry office last week was in Hong Kong Airport when we flew to New Zealand. My first wife got married to my new wife's uncle in Peru! You know the script and, when you think about it, you must hear about similar stories every day. Please e-mail your facts and stories to steve@stevetoptrend.co.uk and, if there is enough material to produce a book, I have another project.

Life isn't tied with a bow, but it's still a gift.

Lightning Source UK Ltd.
Milton Keynes UK
UKOW04f0612151117
312724UK00001B/65/P